THE STRUGGLE FOR ARAB INDEPENDENCE

THE STRUGGLE FOR ARAB INDEPENDENCE

Western Diplomacy and the Rise and Fall of Faiṣal's Kingdom in Syria

by

ZEINE N. ZEINE

American University of Beirut

CARAVAN BOOKS

Delmar, New York

The Struggle for Arab Independence

First Edition 1960

Second Edition 1977

Published by Caravan Books,

P. O. Box 344, Delmar, New York 12054

Printed in Lebanon

Library of Congress Cataloging in Publication Data

Zeine, Zeine N.

The Struggle for Arab Independence

Includes bibliographical references.

1. Syria — History — 20th century.
2. Great Britain — Foreign relations — Near East.
3. Near East — Foreign relations — Great Britain.
4. France — Foreign relations — Near East.
5. Near East — History — 20th century.

I. Title.

DS 98. Z4 1977 956. 91'04 77-5149

ISBN 088206-002-3

CONTENTS

		Page
Preface		vii
Chapter		
I	Introduction: The Secret Agreements	1
II	The Allies in Syria and the Lebanon — 1918	25
III	Faiṣal, Great Britain and France	45
IV	The Peace Conference of Paris, 1919	62
V	The Conflict between Lloyd George and Clemenceau	80
VI	The Settlement of the "Syrian Question" — 1919	99
VII	Faiṣal proclaimed King of "United Kingdom of Syria"	118
VIII	Syria falls under French Mandate	138
IX	The End of Faiṣal's Government in Syria	153
X	An Interpretation of the Allied "Promises"	172
XI	International Relations and the Old Diplomacy	191
Appendices		
A	Translation of a letter from Sir H. McMahon, His Majesty's High Commissioner at Cairo, to the Sherīf of Mecca	209
B	Translation of a letter from the Sherīf of Mecca to Sir H. McMahon, His Majesty's High Commissioner at Cairo	212
C	Memorandum by the Emīr Faiṣal submitted to the Peace Conference	216
D	"Territorial Claims of the Government of the Hedjaz", presented to the Peace Conference by the Emīr Faiṣal	219

E Extract from an "Outline of Tentative Report and Recommendations Prepared by the Intelligence Section, in Accordance with Instructions, for the President and the Plenipotentiaries, February 21, 1919" 220

F Statement made by President Howard S. Bliss of the Syrian Protestant College, Beirut, Syria, before the Paris Conference (The 'Big Ten') on Thursday afternoon, February 13th at the Quai d'Orsay, Paris 222

G Aide-Mémoire in Regard to the Occupation of Syria, Palestine and Mesopotamia Pending the Decision in Regard to Mandates 226

H Letter from President Clemenceau to the Maronite Patriarch 228

I The Program of the Syrian Congress [Extracts from the King-Crane Report] 230

Bibliography

I Books and Official Publications 235

II Documents 246

A. Published 246

B. Unpublished 247

III Periodicals 249

Index 251

Illustrations, following page 98

Plates, following page 226

PREFACE

The Struggle for Arab Independence deals primarily with the policies of Great Britain and France and with the struggle of Arab nationalist leaders, particularly the Emīr Faiṣal, against those policies during and immediately after the First World War. These policies determined the fate of the whole of the Near East for more than a quarter of a century after the war.

This work is about an admittedly controversial period in the modern diplomatic history of the Middle East. Passions and prejudices, hidden motives and influences underlie the facts, confusing and puzzling the student of history. Many points of view have been expressed by commentators during the last fifty years, apportioning blame indiscriminately and condemning one side or the other for its mistakes or for Machiavellian power-politics.

All the principal actors in the history of those days appear to have been sincerely convinced of the righteousness of their cause. But a careful examination of the facts reveals that they were misled by ignorance, misguided by enthusiasm, and blinded by national interest and the lust for prestige and power. Before reaching this conclusion, it is necessary to examine primary sources which have hitherto remained unavailable or which have been neglected, and to reexamine secondary works accordingly. In this study both European and Arabic sources, written and oral, have been consulted in an effort to construct a plain factual account of the main events of this period.

Primary sources include documents in private collections as well as in government archives. They contain illuminating information on the situation in Syria and the Lebanon and on the Syrian and Lebanese attitudes towards the Allies.

Official diplomatic documents are necessary for the writing of political history. However, the task of obtaining access to them is difficult and complex. First, there is the difficulty of tracking down scattered and fragmentary facts and records from sources hundreds of miles apart. In this case, the sources are in such widely separated cities as Baghdad and Washington. During the course of my research it has been necessary to travel to various Arab countries of the Middle East, then to Istanbul, Paris, and London, in search of facts and documents. Secondly, some governments are still reluctant to open all their archives to historians, although the situation has greatly improved in recent years. Thirdly, official documents published by government agencies generally contain only "selected materials" and may mislead the "innocent" student of history unaware of the complicated government machinery which informs such publications. As Professor Harold Temperley has pointed out, "on whatever scale such documents are published, they must always be a selection from a great mass of unpublished material." Consequently, they always contain certain lacunæ which cannot be filled and which are the "missing links" without which the writing of diplomatic history will always remain incomplete and can never become definitive and final. I have tried to compensate for these lacunæ partly by a study of the memoirs, autobiographies, and biographies of some of the principal figures involved in this story, such as King Faiṣal, Lord Grey, Lloyd George, Lord Curzon, Lord Allenby, Georges Clemenceau, and King ʻAbdullah, and partly by information obtained in interviews with a number of their contemporaries — Britons, Arabs, Frenchmen, and Turks — who had intimate knowledge of many of the principal events of those years. The weakness of these oral sources is that they involve the memory of the individual concerned and are conditioned by personal impressions nearly forty years old. Yet a considerable amount of most enlightening information was obtained during those interviews.

In addition to these sources, I have made use of numerous "chapters" on this period included in various histories of the Middle East, as well as a few surveys and general works, and a large number of articles in newspapers and periodicals. They contain informative and interesting material, especially in the shape of current views, often presented as apologia for or denunciations of one side or the other.

The present work may lay claim to some originality by its use of

Oriental and European sources, both written and oral, not used before, and by its attempt to see the dynamics of the various events through cause and effect relationships. But if it has any merit, I cherish the hope that it will be found in the nonpartisan and unbiased account and interpretation of the events of those turbulent and passion-filled years.

It would be impossible to record here the names of all the eminent persons, some of whom are no longer living, who shared their reminiscences with me and provided invaluable material necessary to explain and to understand the major decisions and actions taken in the course of those years. Unfortunately, certain important contributions must remain anonymous. But I am most grateful to all of them and would like to make grateful acknowledgment to the following, in particular: Lord Hankey, Lord Vansittart, Lord Samuel, Sir Ronald Storrs, Sir Kinahan Cornwallis, Sir Ronald Wingate, Professors Arnold Tonybee, Rohan Butler, and Louis Massignon. Sir Ronald Wingate very kindly allowed me to have access to some of the private papers of his father, General Sir Reginald Wingate. Among the prominent figures in the Middle East with whom I was very fortunate to have interviews were King ʻAbdullah of the Hashemite Kingdom of Jordan, and his brother the Emīr Zaid; Nūrī Pasha al-Saʻīd; the Emīr ʻAdil Arslān; ʻAlī Jawdat al-Ayyūbī; Sāṭiʻ al-Ḥuṣrī; Fāris al-Khūrī; Tawfīq al-Nāṭūr; Saʻīd Ḥaidar; Shaikh ʻAbdu'l Qādir al-Maghribī; Najīb al-Armanāzī; and General ʻAlī Fuat Cebesoy. Although I am deeply indebted to all of them, I would like to make it clear that they have no part in the opinions and judgments which I have formed and express herein.

Among those who were especially helpful in various ways, I would like to express my obligation and gratitude to Mr. John Nevins who made it possible for me to obtain certain documents from the United States National Archives; Dr. Harry N. Howard who read the entire manuscript of the first edition; Father Mikhā'il al-Rajjī, the Librarian of the Private Archives at the Maronite Patriarchate in Lebanon; Ṭāriq al-ʻAskarī for allowing me read the original unpublished manuscript of the memoirs of his father, General Jaʻfar Pasha al-ʻAskarī; Mrs. Byron Smith and Mrs. Leslie W. Leavitt who permitted me to study and use the personal papers of their father, Dr. Howard S. Bliss, President of the Syrian Protestant College (now the American University of Beirut); Mr. Rāmiz Sarkīs, the owner and editor of *Lisān-al-Ḥāl* who put at my disposal all the back numbers of this newspaper; and Mr. William Birbāri who sent me a copy of the minutes of the seventeenth meeting of the Syrian Moderate Party, held in Cairo, on 21 June 1919.

I am also particularly indebted to Professor Bernard Lewis and to the late Mr. Harold Bowen of the School of Oriental and African Studies, University of London, for their inestimable advice and guidance. Mr. Harold Bowen read the original manuscript of this work and made many valuable suggestions during its preparation.

Lastly, it remains for me to express my deep thanks to Mr. C.H. Fone, Deputy Librarian of the British Foreign Office Archives, to the staffs of the British Museum Library in London, the Bibliothèque Nationale in Paris, the National Archives of the Department of State, United States of America, the Royal Institute of International Affairs, Chatham House, London, the School of Oriental and African Studies, and the American University of Beirut, for their kind assistance and cooperation. Also, I would like to acknowledge the great help and support I originally received from the Arab Studies Program, and the late Professor Nabih A. Faris, at the American University of Beirut.

ZEINE N. ZEINE

Beirut
January 1977

CHAPTER ONE

THE SECRET AGREEMENTS

"... *Penelope used to weave by day and unweave during the secret watches. But the Supreme Council after the Armistice, like the Allied Governments during the War, generally weave their Oriental policies in darkness and mystery....*"

Arnold J. TOYNBEE in *A History of the Conference of Paris*, Vol. 6

FOR MORE than four hundred years, until 1918, all the independent Arab countries in the Near East today were possessions of the Ottoman Empire. On 5 November 1914, the Ottoman Empire entered the war on the side of Germany against the Allies. British policy towards the Arab Near East was thus determined by the fact that it occupied an area of strategic importance to the prosecution of the war. As the Arabs had already shown various degrees of dissatisfaction towards Ottoman rule,[1] it was natural and logical that the British should "attack the Turkish Empire through its Arab subjects."[2] "As a feature of the general strategy of the War," wrote Lloyd George, "the elimination of Turkey from the ranks of our enemies would have given us that access to Russia and Roumania which was so disastrously lacking, and without which they were driven out of the war. . . . The course of the war would have been altered and shortened. . . . The Turkish Empire lay across the track by land or water to our great possessions in the East. . . . It was vital for our communications, as it was essential for our prestige in the East, that once the Turks declared war against us, we should defeat and discredit them without loss of time. The importance of a speedy victory over the Turks for the security of the British Empire was undeniable."[3] Lloyd George wrote in his war memoirs: "Our agents among them (the Arabs), who included men long skilled

1. See Zeine, *Emergence of Arab Nationalism*, chaps. 3, 4.
2. Temperley, *History of the Peace Conference of Paris*, 6: 178.
3. Lloyd George, *War Memoirs*, 4: 1802-1803.

in the arts of Oriental diplomacy, encouraged this attitude of rebellion, and promised them arms and ammunition. . . ."[4] The British Government was particularly aware of the dissatisfactions of the Sharīf Ḥusain, Emīr of Mecca and Guardian of the twin Holy Cities in the Hejaz. For years he had tried to overthrow the personal autocracy of the Sultan and had strived "by intrigue and diplomacy to gain as much independence as possible."[5]

Nearly seven months before the outbreak of the war, Britain had actually been approached for help but at that time the help had naturally been declined as she could "never entertain the idea of supplying arms to be used against a Friendly Power." The approach had come from the Emīr 'Abdullah, second son of the Sharīf Ḥusain of Mecca and "M.P. for the Hejaz" both to Lord Kitchener and to (Sir) Ronald Storrs to whom he had "unlocked his heart during his visit to Cairo."[6] Now, however, the situation had radically changed. In the first place, the Turkish government was making every effort to win over the principal Arab shaikhs of the Arabian peninsula to its side, or at least to assure their neutrality, in case Turkey entered the war. Secondly, the Turkish govern-

4. Ibid., p. 1810.

5. Wingate, *Wingate of the Sudan*, p. 179. For a brief background history of Sharīf Ḥusain and of the Hashemite family, see Alec Kirkbride, *An Awakening*, app. 1, *The Hashemite Family*, pp. 123-24.

6. "In April 1914 occurred a visit to Cairo the ultimate impact of which upon the War and the destinies of the Near and Middle East is not even yet fully calculable. The Amir Abdallah, second son of Husain, Grand Sharif of Mecca, arrived from Constantinople as the guest of the Khedive and was received by Lord Kitchener .... Meanwhile, we were advised from Constantinople that such audiences were displeasing to the Sublime Porte, always suspicious of Arab intrigue in the Hejaz and in Syria .... Travelling by a series of delicately inclined planes .... I found myself... being categorically asked whether Great Britain would present the Grand Sharif with a dozen, or half a dozen machine guns... 'for defense'... against attack from the Turks. I needed no special instructions to inform him that we could never entertain the idea of supplying arms to be used against a Friendly Power. Abdallah can have expected no other reply, and we parted on the best of terms." Storrs, *Orientations*, pp. 122-123.

Storrs quotes a private letter from Lord Kitchener to Sir W. Tyrrell, sent from the British Agency, Cairo, on 26 April 1914, and containing the following excerpt:

"Sharif Abdallah .... He sent for Storrs who under my instructions told him the Arabs of the Hejaz could expect no encouragement from us and that our only interest in Arabia was the safety and comfort of Indian pilgrims...."

ment was putting much pressure on Sharīf Ḥusain of Mecca to make him take a definite stand in support of Constantinople, by increasing the size of its military garrisons in Mecca and Medina, and by appealing to Pan-Islamic solidarity. Thirdly, the attitude of the Sharīf seemed uncertain to the British authorities involved in Arab affairs. Hence the following two historic telegrams from Lord Kitchener,[7] now Secretary of State for War, which were the official starting point of the British invitation to the Arabs of the Hejaz to revolt and of the first famous secret agreement between the two parties,[8]

> 24 September 1914. To Mr. Cheetham [H.M.'s Representative in Cairo]. Following from Lord Kitchener. Intelligence report

7. It appears that Lord Kitchener had already, in 1912 and 1913, considered the possibility of a breaking-up of the Ottoman Empire. He became strongly imbued with the idea that "southern Syria up to Haifa and Acre and down to the Gulf of 'Akaba would be on political and strategic grounds, an indispensable asset to the British Empire." Lord Kitchener's views on this matter were further confirmed by the result of the military survey of the Sinai Peninsula which was instigated by himself and carried out in 1913. Great Britain, *Report of a Committee set up to consider Certain Correspondence between Sir Henry McMahon (His Majesty's High Commissioner in Egypt) and the Sharif of Mecca in 1915 and 1916* (Cmd. 5974), p.12.

8. "At the same time Storrs and Gilbert Clayton of the Military Intelligence approached 'Azīz al-Miṣrī and others concerning the possibility of starting an Arab revolt." Kirk, *A Short History of the Middle East*, p. 125.

'Azīz 'Alī al-Miṣrī was an Arabic-speaking army officer of Circassian origin, born in Egypt and educated in Istanbul. Although "equally loyal to Egypt and to the Ottoman Caliphate," he became closely associated with the Arab nationalist movement during the First World War. While serving in the Ottoman army, he had founded sometime towards the end of 1913 and the beginning of 1914, the secret society of *al-'Ahd* (the Covenant) composed originally of army officers, both Arabs and Turks. He had been arrested and condemned to death by the Turkish government, probably because of the personal jealousy and animosity on the part of Enver Pasha. He was reprieved and released by the intervention of the British Ambassador in Constantinople, Sir Louis Mallet. He had sailed for Egypt in April 1914 where he was now living. See Muḥammad Ṭāhir al-'Umarī, *Ta'rīkh Muqaddarāt al-'Irāq al-Siyāsiyyah*, [1]: pp. 367-379, Antonius, *The Arab Awakening*, pp. 118-121, and Gooch and Temperley, *British Documents on the Origins of the War, 1898-1914*, vol. 10, Part 2, pp. 833-838. For a critical study of al-Miṣrī's career, see Mājid Khaddūrī, " 'Azīz 'Alī al-Miṣrī and the Arab Nationalist Movement" in Albert Hourani, ed., *St. Anthony's Papers*, Nº 4: *Middle Eastern Affairs* (Oxford University Press, 1965), pp. 140-163.

'Azīz 'Alī al-Miṣrī became Chief of Staff and Field-Marshal of the Egyptian Army before the Second World War. He died in Cairo, on 16 June 1965, at the age of 87. See the obituary notice which appeared in *The Times* (London) of 17 June 1965, p. 14.

> 6th September statement regarding attitude of Sherif of Mecca. Tell Storrs to send secret and carefully chosen messenger from me to Sherif Abdullah to ascertain 'whether should present armed German influence in Constantinople coerce Khalif against his will, and Sublime Porte to acts of aggression and war against Great Britain, he and his father and Arabs of the Hejaz would be with us or against us." [9]

On 31 October Mr. Cheetham sent a telegram to the Foreign Office, saying in part:

> Messenger has returned from Mecca with letter from Shereef Abdalla. Communication is guarded, but friendly and favourable. Desires 'closer union' with Great Britain, but expects and 'is awaiting written promise that Great Britain will abstain from internal intervention in Arabia and guarantee Emir against foreign and Ottoman aggression'. . . .
>
> Reply is being prepared subject to your approval disclaiming all intention of internal intervention and guaranteeing, against external aggression only, independence of Shereefate. . . .[10]

The above-mentioned telegram was received in London at 1:45 p.m. At 6:35 p.m. on that same day, Lord Kitchener's reply was sent to Mr. Cheetham in a cipher telegram, the second since 24 September. Lord Kitchener's message read as follows:

> Lord Kitchener's salaam to the Shereef Abdalla. Germany has bought the Turkish Government with gold, notwithstanding that England, France and Russia guaranteed integrity of Ottoman Empire if Turkey remained neutral in the War. Turkish Government have against will of Sultan committed acts of aggression by invading the frontiers of Egypt with bands of Turkish soldiers. If Arab nation assists England in this war that has been forced upon us by Turkey, England will guarantee that no internal intervention takes place in Arabia and will give the Arabs every assistance against external foreign aggression.

At the end of this telegram a tempting and coveted prize was dangled before the eyes of the Sharīf in the following words:

> It may be that an Arab of the true race will assume the

9. Great Britain. F.O. 371/2139. Cipher telegram to Mr. Cheetham (Cairo), Nº 219 (secret).

10. Ibid., Telegram Nº 233.

> Caliphate at Mecca or Medina and so good may come by the help of God out of all evil which is now occurring.[11]

It is most important to note that the "invitation to revolt" was directed towards the Sharīf Ḥusain and "the Arabs of the Hejaz." In no way did Great Britain envisage, plan or support with men and arms a great Arab Revolt from one end of the Asiatic possessions of the Ottoman Empire to the other. All that Lord Kitchener wanted to ascertain in his cable of the 24 September was whether the Sharīf Ḥusain and "the Arabs of the Hejaz" would be "with us or against us" and all that he guaranteed in the name of England, in his telegram of 31 October was that "no intervention" would take place in "Arabia" and that England would give the Arabs (meaning the Arabs of the Hejaz) "every assistance against external foreign aggression."[12]

Actually, the immediate issue was the religious and moral significance of the Hejaz in the Muslim world and not so much its military and strategic importance. Great Britain's declaration of war against Turkey meant blockading the port of Jeddah and preventing her Muslim subjects from going on pilgrimage to Mecca and Medina which were then under the suzerainty of Turkey.[13] The three men "on the spot" who knew most about Arab affairs in Arabia, Egypt, and the Sudan — General Sir Reginald Wingate, Lord Kitchener, and Lord Hardinge, the Viceroy of India — were convinced that the pilgrimage should under no circumstances be stopped but it should be kept open for the Muslim subjects of the Allies. It was they, and particularly Kitchener who was now at the

11. Ibid., Telegram N° 303.

12. In his despatch from Constantinople, dated 4 September 1914, Sir Louis Mallet, the British ambassador, wrote to Sir Edward Grey:

"I agree that if Turkey allies herself with Germany and war becomes inevitable, probably one of the most effective weapons would be the support and organisation of an Arab movement either openly or indirectly; but an Arab movement vague in its objects would lead to nothing. I am of the opinion that it would require most careful organisation"....

Ibid. *The War.* Confidential. N° 1, Sir Louis Mallet to Sir Edward Grey.

13. "... We cannot afford to lose sight of the interests which Great Britain must always take in the Holy Places, owing to the annual pilgrimage which is attended by thousands of Indian Moslems and also by many Egyptians".... Lord Kitchener to Sir Edward Grey, Cairo, 4 April 1914. See Gooch and Temperley, vol. 10 Part 2, p. 830.

War Office and a member of the Cabinet, who urged the British Government to be seriously concerned with the Islamic complications of the war with Turkey. "The bulk of the Indian Army was Muslim; Egypt and its army all Muslim . . . the object of the Viceroy in India and of the British authorities in Egypt and the Sudan was to reassure their Muslim subjects."[14] It was indeed an incongruous and dangerous situation that all the Muslim subjects of Britain owed their spiritual allegiance to the enemy and their holy cities were in the possession of this enemy. "If these Holy Cities could be shown as not in the enemy's power, and if access to them could be guaranteed, a danger to the fabric of the Empire would be removed."[15]

It was with this purpose in mind that the Foreign Office started negotiating in December 1914, with the Sharīf Ḥusain through Sir Arthur Henry McMahon, who had been appointed High Commissioner in Egypt. Actually, Wingate had already been in contact with the Sharīf through 'Alī al-Mirghanī,[16] one of the most notable religious leaders of the Sudan. McMahon was now to persuade the Sharīf "by offers of assistance and guarantees of his future autonomy and independence, to throw off the Turkish supremacy and to keep open the pilgrimage for the Muslim subjects of the Allies.[17]

14. Wingate, p. 180. See also McMunn and Falls, *Military Operations*, pp. 211-12.

15. Ibid., p. 181.

16. In a private letter to Sir Edward Grey, Wingate wrote on May 1915:

"By a curious coincidence your telegram to McMahon asking if we could communicate with the Sharif of Mecca came shortly after I had had a long interview with Said Ali el-Morghani, a man of more religious influence in the Sudan than any one else . . . ."

The Wingate Papers. See also Philby, *Arabia*, p. 239, and Antonius, p. 144.

17. Wingate, p. 181.

"Sherif Hussein, while vacillating in policy and desirous of keeping a foot in either camp as long as possible, enjoyed the great prestige due to his family and his office. The Sherifate of Mecca had endured a thousand years, and, though Hussein's branch of the clan had ruled less than a hundred, yet he was of the Quraish or tribe of the Prophet, having thus the qualification anciently laid down for the holder of the Khalifate. At the outbreak of war, he was a man of sixty, learned in Arab literature, popular with the townsmen of Mecca and Medina and the Bedouin of their neighbourhood, ambitious but cautious." McMunn and Falls, p. 210.

As a result, a protracted exchange of letters took place between the High Commissioner and the Sharīf from 14 July 1915 to 30 January 1916 known as the McMahon-Sharīf Ḥusain Correspondence.

The story of this secret Correspondence has not yet been fully told. McMahon's letters were translated into Arabic at the British Residency in Cairo, and sent to the Sharīf Ḥusain by a special secret messenger. The Sharīf's letters to McMahon were all in Arabic and were translated into English when they arrived in Cairo. Of the ten letters which constitute the Correspondence between the Sharīf and McMahon, each wrote five. In 1939, Arab Delegations from Egypt, Iraq, Palestine, Sa'udi Arabia, and Yemen met in London at the invitation of the British Government, to discuss the Palestine Question. From 7 February to 17 March 1939 fourteen meetings known as the Conferences on Palestine were held at St. James's Palace between the United Kingdom and the Arab Delegations. During the third meeting, held on 11 February, the publication of the McMahon Correspondence was considered, and at the fifth meeting, on Tuesday, 14 February, copies of the English translation of this Correspondence were handed to the delegates. Mr. Malcolm MacDonald, Secretary of State for the Colonies, who was present, added: "A Question would be put in the House

On 14 September 1914, the British Resident in the Persian Gulf submitted to the Government of India drafts of two "notices" containing assurances concerning the freedom of the Arab "Gulf Chiefs" and the security of the Holy Places. (Great Britain. F.O. Political Intelligence Department. B. 301. Special 8 [secret.]. *Memorandum on British Commitments [during the War] to the Gulf Chiefs*). The first "notice" read:

"Your relations with Great Britain are of long standing, and I take the opportunity of assuring you that in this struggle we shall do our utmost to preserve for you your liberty and religion. No act of ours shall threaten either of these, which are dearer to humanity than life itself."

The second stated:

"From the High British Government.

"War has broken out between Great Britain and Turkey, but it is notified for the public information of all the Moslems that, as long as the Indian pilgrims proceeding to Mecca and Medina are not seriously interfered with, no hostile action will be taken by the British or Indian Government, or by their ships or soldiers, against the port of Jeddah or the Holy Places."

The Government of India approved the above-mentioned drafts with the addition of the words "or the Holy Places in Mesopotamia" after the words "Mecca and Medina," in the second draft; and these two documents were finally delivered "to the local residents at the courts of the various Chiefs."

of Commons this afternoon, and after 4 p.m. the fact that the correspondence had been circulated and was going to be published would no longer be a secret."[18] It was also decided at this meeting to distribute to the Delegations copies "of such Arabic texts (of this Correspondence) as might be available in the archives of the Foreign Office." Accordingly, the next day, 15 February, photostatic copies of the Arabic text of seven letters (Nos. 2, 4, 5, 6, 7, 9, and 10) were circulated to the Delegates. Letters Nos. 1 and 3 (from the Sharīf Ḥusain to Sir Henry McMahon) and 8 (from Sir Henry McMahon to the Sharīf Ḥusain) were "not to be found in the Foreign Office archives." A brief introduction to these letters, signed by H.F. Downie, Secretary, ends with the following two sentences: "The documents circulated cannot necessarily be regarded as exact copies of the original documents. They are copies of the documents in the Foreign office archives which were sent to London from Cairo, but whether the letters from the Sherif of Mecca are in all cases the original letters is not certain, nor is it certain whether the letters from Sir Henry McMahon correspond exactly with the letters actually despatched to the Sherif." These extraordinary words of caution throw much doubt and uncertainty on the authenticity of those documents and make it extremely difficult, if not impossible, to discover the truth of actually what the British Government wrote to Sharīf Ḥusain through Sir Henry McMahon. Precision and lucidity have rarely been the characteristics of the language of diplomacy.[19]

It is to be noted that all the ten letters published in English, in Cmd. 5957 of 1939, are headed "*Translation* of a letter from. . ." (either Sir Henry McMahon or the Sharīf of Mecca). In other words, the *original* English texts of the five letters which emanated from the Foreign Office in London and were afterwards issued from the British Residency in Cairo in Arabic, in the name of McMahon, have *not* been published; what has been published is an English translation based on the Arabic version made for the Sharīf Ḥusain

18. *Conferences on Palestine, 1939. United Kingdom-Arab meetings.* [P.C. (A) (P) 3.]

19. The result of this decision was the publication, by the British Government, of Cmd. 5957 (Miscellaneous No. 3, 1939) entitled *Correspondence between Sir Henry McMahon, His Majesty's High Commissioner at Cairo and The Sherif Hussein of Mecca, July 1915-March 1916.*

and on the original drafts in English of those letters. The letters of the Sharīf were, of course, in Arabic but none of them bears any signature.[20]

As the Sharīf Ḥusain in his letters of 14 July and 9 September 1915 insisted on the question of boundaries for the independent "lands of the Arabs" (*bilād al-'Arab*), McMahon replied on 26 October 1915 that "Great Britain is prepared to recognise and support the independence of the Arabs in all the regions within the limits demanded by the Sherif of Mecca" subject to certain modifications. These modifications were: (a) the exclusion of "the two districts of Mersina and Alexandretta and portions of Syria lying to the west of the districts of Damascus, Homs, Hama, and Aleppo (which) cannot be said to be purely Arab," and (b) that of certain regions lying within those frontiers in which Great Britain was not free to act "without detriment to the interests of her ally France."[21] The Sharīf, in his letter of 5 November 1915, accepted the modification relating to "the vilayets of Mersina and Adana," but refused to consider the "two vilayets of Aleppo and Beirut and their seacoasts" as anything but "purely Arab vilayets." On 19 December 1915, Sir Henry McMahon in a further letter to the Sharīf pointed out that the question of the two vilayets of Aleppo and Beirut required careful consideration because "the interests of our ally, France, are involved in them both." The Sharīf's reply on 1 January

20. The author has had the good fortune of seeing and studying the photostat copies of the Arabic text of seven of the above-mentioned letters which at one time belonged to one of the Delegations present at the Conferences on Palestine. A copy of letter No. 4, dated "26.10.15" ("October 24, 1915" in Cmd. 5957) and of letter No. 9, dated "February 18, 1916;" will be found in Appendices A and B not only because of their importance as original documents but also to give the Arabic-speaking reader an idea about the Arabic style of those letters. The official English translation of those two letters will also be found in those Appendices.

For the Arabic texts of letters Nos. 2, 4, 6 and 10, see also Ḥāfiz Wahbah, *Jazīrat al-'Arab fi'l-Qarn al-'Ishrīn* [The Arabian Peninsula in the 20th century], pp. 178-186.

Muḥammad Jamīl Beyhum wrote in his book *Al-'Ahd al-mukhaḍram fī Sūriyya wa Lubnān* (pp. 144-145) that when he went to Cyprus in 1929 to visit the exiled King Ḥusain, the latter showed him all the letters which were exchanged between him and Sir Henry McMahon during the war. These letters were packed in "white cotton bags."

21. For the text of this letter see Appendix A.

1916 was to the effect that he would for the time being avoid anything which might possibly injure the alliance of Great Britain and France but that "at the first opportunity after this war is finished, we shall ask you (what we avert our eyes from today) for what we now leave to France in Beirut and its coasts." He also added that "the citizens of Beirut will decidedly never accept such a dismemberment" and that "it is impossible to allow any derogation that gives France, or any other Power, a span of land in those regions." Nothing more was said about Syria and the Lebanon in the correspondence which followed during the next two months. The Sharīf had understood from McMahon's letter of 26 October 1915 that at least a part of Syria, comprising Damascus, Homs, Hama, and Aleppo, was included within the regions in which Great Britain was prepared to recognize and support the independence of the Arabs. The Sharīf of Mecca in his ambition of rebuilding an Arab Empire with himself as King and Caliph had, in his letter of 14 July 1915 to Sir Henry McMahon, asked for the independence of "the whole of the Arab nation" inhabiting Syria, Mesopotamia, and Arabia proper.[22] He had even given Great Britain an "ultimatum" of "thirty days" to answer "positively or negatively," and "if this period should lapse before they ('the Arab nation') receive an answer, they reserve to themselves complete freedom of action."[23] The British Government in their Correspondence with the Sharīf had unfortunately conveyed to him the notion that they were dealing with him as the representative of all the Arabs and thus confirmed him in the dangerous illusions which he cherished.[24]

22. John Presland, *Deedes Bey: A Study of Sir Wyndham Deedes, 1883-1923* (London, 1924), pp. 244-245. See also al-Raiḥānī, *Mulūk al-'Arab* [The Kings of the Arabs], vol. 1, pp. 66-67.

23. With regards to the "limitless ambition" of the Sharīf Ḥussain, see 'Abdu'l Raḥman Shahbandar, "Faiṣal Ibn al-Ḥusain" in *Al-Muqtaṭaf*, vol. 83, Part 3 (Cairo, 1933), p. 258.

24. It is believed that with regards to the question of boundaries of an independent Arab Kingdom, the Sharīf Ḥusain was guided by the Damascus Protocol. In this connection, George Antonius wrote: "Faisal was back in Damascus on the 23rd of May (1915), and found that his colleagues in *al-Fatāt* and *al-'Ahd* had concerted a plan of action in his absence. They had drawn up a protocol defining the conditions on which the Arab leaders would be prepared to co-operate with Great Britain against Turkey, and their plan was that Faisal should take it to Mecca and ask his father to find out whether it was acceptable

This was due perhaps partly to the confusion and muddle of the "experts" on Arab affairs at the Arab Bureau in Cairo — some of the prominent among whom were archæologists and travelers, romanticists and idealists, all inexperienced in the art of politics — partly to a "combination of ignorance and misapplied fervour" and partly still because the British Government could not take the Sharīf seriously and therefore sought merely to appease him. "With the party of the Shereef," wrote Sir Windham Deedes in February 1916, "we really are negotiating on the lines of a spiritual and temporal Arab Kingdom. That, at all events, is what the Shereef wants. Personally, and I think it is the view of most of us... this is not a practical one. For it will never be possible to get all the Arabs of Syria, Iraq, Yemen and the others to acknowledge one temporal chief. . . . The Shereef of Mecca's influence is accepted over a certain part of the countries named but not over others. . . ." [25]

to the British Government as a basis for concerted action. The protocol is important enough to be quoted in full:

'The recognition by Great Britain of the independence of the Arab countries lying within the following frontiers:

North: The line Mersin-Adana to parallel 37° N. and thence along the line Birejik-Urfa-Mardin-Midiat-Jazirat (Ibn 'Umar)-Amadia to the Persian frontier;

East: The Persian frontier down to the Persian Gulf;

South: The Indian Ocean (with the exclusion of Aden, whose status was to be maintained);

West: The Red Sea and the Mediterranean Sea back to Mersin.

'The abolition of all exceptional privileges granted to foreigners under the Capitulations.

'The conclusion of a defensive alliance between Great Britain and the future independent Arab state.

'The grant of economic preference to Great Britain.' [1]"

("1. The text as given above is my translation of the Arabic version lent to me by the late King Faiṣal.") Antonius, pp. 157-158. See also King Abdullah's *Mudhakkarātī* [My Memoirs], pp. 102-103, 241-242; Kirk, pp. 125-126, and Presland, pp. 245-246.

25. The maze of Arabian politics included "assurances," "agreements" and treaties with other Arab rulers in the Arabian Peninsula, besides Sharīf Ḥusain. "On the 3rd November, 1914, Shaykh Mubarak of Kuwayt received from the British Government — on the condition, which he promptly fulfilled, that he should cooperate in the capture of Basrah — an assurance that Kuwayt should be recognized as an independent principality under British protection. The independence of the Idrīsī Sayyid of Sabyā (in the 'Asīr), 'within his own domain,' was guaranteed by Great Britain in a treaty signed on the 30th April,

Meanwhile, the French Government, according to Lloyd George, was informed of the tenor of the negotiations with the Sharīf Ḥusain. On 23 November 1915, Sir Arthur Nicolson, Permanent Under-Secretary of State for Foreign Affairs, pointed out to M. Georges-Picot the British Government's attitude towards the Arabs and their dealings with the Sharīf. On 21 December "M. Picot informed Sir Arthur Nicolson that, after great difficulties, he had obtained permission from his Government to agree to the towns of Aleppo, Hama, Homs, and Damascus being included in the Arab dominions to be administered by the Arabs under French influence."[26] With due regard to the traditional interests of France in Syria, "the British Government were anxious not to offend French susceptibilities in their dealings with the Arabs."[27] But Lloyd George admitted that the French suspected "ulterior designs" in those negotiations. It was now time for the Allies to think of protecting their own interests in Turkey and to settle the Eastern Question by an agreed partitioning of the Ottoman Empire. Indeed, this process had already begun. After much hesitation, Great Britain and France had reached a secret agreement with Russia in March 1915 conceding her demand that in the event of Allied victory Constantinople and the Straits should be annexed by the

and ratified on the 6th November, 1915. The independence of Ibn Sa'ūd, 'in the territories of his countries,' was recognized by Great Britain in a treaty signed on the 26th December, 1915, and ratified on the 18th July, 1916." Toynbee, *Survey of International Affairs 1925*, vol. 1, *The Islamic World*, p. 272. See also al-Raiḥānī, *Ta'rīkh Najd al-Ḥadīth wa Mulḥaqātih* [Modern History of Nejd and Dependencies], pp. 206-207. In almost every case "gifts of gold" were placed "at the service of the Arab chiefs." The subsidies which Sharīf Ḥusain received will be referred to, later (see p. 15, n. 37 below). The Wahhabī ruler, 'Abdu'l-'Azīz Ibn Sa'ūd was paid "at the more modest rate of £5,000 a month." He was still being subsidized until the end of the financial year on 3 March 1924, "and it was not until the latter date that British subsidies to Arabian princes ceased altogether." Toynbee, 1: 273.

26. *Documents on British Foreign Policy, 1919-1939*, 1st Ser., ed. vol. 4, Woodward and Butler, p. 481 (*Documents*, 1:4 in later references)

27. David Lloyd George, *The Truth About the Peace Treaties*, vol. 2, p. 1021. Raymond Poincaré recorded the following, in his diary for 26 October 1915: "Some curious pourparlers have been exchanged between Great Britain and the Cherif of Mecca; the latter has been promised the Caliphate, and he will lend the British all the help he can against Turkey...." Poincaré, *Au Service de la France*, 7: 206 and 250.

Tsar.[28] There remained now the question of what Great Britain and France would be receiving from the spoils of the war when Turkey was defeated, not only as a settlement of the Eastern Question but also to preserve the balance of power in the Mediterranean and the Middle East. Actually, at the time of the Constantinople Agreement, Russia had agreed to recognize "the rights of Great Britain and France in Asiatic Turkey" ("*la reconnaissance des droits de l'Angleterre et de la France dans la Turquie d'Asie*") and to place the Muslim Holy Places and Arabia under an independent Muslim Government.[29]

While Great Britain had not yet definitely stated her desirada in the Ottoman Empire, France had specifically asked and obtained the consent of the Tsar to annex Syria, the Gulf of Alexandretta, and Cilicia.[30] It was natural then and necessary that the agreement on Constantinople should be followed by what has come to be known as the Sykes-Picot Agreement, originally called by Viscount Grey the "Franco-British-Russian secret agreement about spheres in Asia Minor."[31] It began owing apparently to French initiative. On 23 March 1915, the French Ambassador, in Paris, M. Paul Cambon, informed Sir Edward Grey that M. Delcassé had observed that "as the question of Constantinople and the Straits, which was the chief question affecting Russia, had now been disposed of, it was rather for France and Great Britain to discuss other questions respecting Asia Minor." M. Delcassé proposed an unofficial discussion of these questions. "I agreed to this," wrote Grey, "and said that it would be better that the discussion should be between M. Cambon and myself."[32] Negotiations between the British,

28 *Documents*, 1:4, pp. 635-638. J. Polonsky, *Les Documents diplomatiques secrets russes*, p. 292; F. Seymour Cocks, *The Secret Treaties and Understandings*, pp. 15-24.

29. E. Laloy, *Les Documents secrets des Archives du Ministère des Affaires Étrangères de Russie*, pp. 107-109. The establishment of a Muslim political unit to include the Holy Places and Arabia was the British Cabinet's stipulation as recorded by Sir Edward Grey.

30. "...Le Gouvernment de la République, ayant étudié les conditions de la paix à imposer à la Turquie, désirerait annexer la Syrie avec la région du golfe d'Alexandrette et la Cilicie jusqu'à la Chaîne du Taurus." See Polonsky, p. 288 and also pp. 290-291.

31. Viscount Grey, *Twenty-Five Years*, 2: p. 236.

32. Ibid.

French, and Russian Governments, lasted over a year.[33] Finally, as a result of an exchange of letters between Sir Edward, M. Cambon, and Serge Sazanov, the Russian Minister of Foreign Affairs, a secret agreement was reached among the three Great Powers defining their own respective claims in Asiatic Turkey — "unofficially and also unjustly known as the Sykes-Picot Agreement."[34] Its terms were embodied in a letter written by Sir Edward to M. Cambon, datelined "Foreign Office, May 16, 1916."

According to the Sykes-Picot Agreement, both France and Great Britain were prepared "to recognise and protect an independent Arab State or a confederation of Arab States" in areas designated (A) and (B), under the suzerainty of an Arab chief.[35] Area (A) was to be under the wing of France, whereas Area (B) was to be under that of Great Britain. Area (A) included not only the principal towns and cities of Syria — Damascus, Homs, Hama, and Aleppo — but also Mosul, in northern Iraq. It thus comprised much of the Ottoman vilayets of "Shām" (Damascus), Aleppo, and Mosul. France also received a "Blue Area" and Great Britain a "Red Area" in which each was "allowed to establish such direct or indirect administration or control" as it desired. This "Blue Area" comprised the coast of Syria, including such towns as Alexandretta, Latakia, Tripoli, Beirut, Sidon, and Tyre and extended

33. Serge Sazanov, *Fateful Years*, pp. 259-260.

34. Arnold J. Toynbee, *The Western Question in Greece and Turkey* (London, 1922), p. 48. Toynbee adds in explanation the following footnote: "The final text of the agreement was drafted by Sir Mark Sykes and M. Georges Picot on behalf of the British and French Governments respectively, but these gentlemen only settled details of phraseology. The fundamental points in the agreement had already been worked out in conferences of leading statesmen and officials on both sides, before it was handed over to them for completion. The unofficial name, used for brevity, gives a wrong impression of the part they played and now that the agreement is discredited and Sir Mark Sykes unable to defend himself, owing to his lamentable death from influenza during the Peace Conference at Paris, it is important that no injustice should be done to his memory. The responsibility on the British side for this agreement lies with the British Government."

See also D. Lloyd George, *War Memoirs*, vol. 4, p. 1826.

35. M. Cambon wrote to Sir Edward Grey on 25 August, 1916, suggesting to substitute the word "uphold" ("*soutenir*") for the word "protect" ("*protéger*") in the phrase "protect an independent Arab State," in order to avoid in future errors of interpretation. The British Government adopted the suggestion.

over the province of the Lebanon. It also included Cilicia and a large area of central and southeastern Asia Minor. The British "Red Area" covered much of the Ottoman vilayet of Baghdad.[36] For all practical purposes. France was given in the Skyes-Picot Agreement control over the Lebanon and Syria with the exception of "southern Syria" or Palestine which was marked as the "Brown Area" where an "international administration" was to be established. Syria became thus the twice-promised land, partly promised to the Sharīf Ḥusain and entirely promised to France. But the Sharīf was not informed about the Sykes-Picot Agreement at the time it was concluded.

The final outcome of the negotiations with Sharīf Ḥusain was what has come to be known during the last sixty years as the Arab Revolt. It started on 10 June 1916 under the leadership of Sharīf Ḥusain, and with the military and financial support of Great Britain.[37]

36. See the "Map to Illustrate the Agreement of 1916" and compare with the map of the Ottoman Vilayets, in this Volume. For the official and authoritative documents of the Sykes-Picot Agreement, see *Documents*, 1:4, pp. 241-251. See also Académie Diplomatique Internationale, *Dictionnaire Diplomatique*, vol. 2 (Paris, 1933), pp. 892-3: Annex I to article on "Syrie" by François Georges-Picot; A. Pingaud, *Histoire diplomatique de la France pendant la Grande Guerre*, vol. 3, pp. 223-252; Shane Leslie, *Mark Sykes, His life and Letters*, pp. 250-258; 272-275; Laloy, pp. 158-159; *Temps*, 22 May 1919; *L'Asie Française*, August-November 1919, and *Die Welt des Islams*, vol. 8., pt. 1 (Berlin 1923), pp. 22-24.

37. On 14 December 1915, Sir Henry McMahon, at the end of his letter to Sharīf Ḥusain, wrote: As an earnest of our intentions, and in order to aid you in your efforts in our joint cause, I am sending you by your trustworthy messenger a sum of twenty thousand pounds." On 18 February 1916, the Sharīf in stating his needs of food supplies, arms and ammunition, put in the first place, "the amount of £ 50,000 in gold for the monthly pay of the troops levied and other things the necessity of which needs no explanation." He added, "We beg you to send it with all possible haste." On 10 March 1916, McMahon wrote: "... and that which you asked to be sent with all haste is being despatched with your messenger, who is also the bearer of this letter." At the end of May 1916, when Sir Ronald Storrs went to Jedda to meet Sharīf Ḥusain, he took with him £ 10,000 in gold. In a new list of requests ("*ṭalabs*") written by the Sharīf and handed to Storrs by the Emīr Sa'īd, mention was made of a total of £ 70,000 in gold. Storrs told the Emīr that "the movement once demonstrably on foot, they would find His Majesty's Government very far from niggardly in its dealings with its Allies." Storrs has written that the total cost to the British taxpayer of the Revolt in the Desert amounted to £ 11,000,000. "In addition to the initial sums I took... Ḥusain received from August 8th 1916,

On the Arab side, the principal participants were the four sons of Sharīf Ḥusain, the Emīrs 'Alī, 'Abdullah, Faiṣal, and Zaid and a large number of Arab army officers who organized and led the Bedouin tribes and Ḥejāzī forces who joined the rebellion in support of Sharīf Ḥusain. The majority of the army officers were Iraqis who had served in the Ottoman army, as the most numerous group of Arab officers serving with the Turks was of Iraqi origin.[38] They had either been captured by the British and taken to India as prisoners of war and then released to serve the Arab cause or they had voluntarily come to the British lines for the same purpose.[39] The

£125,000 a month...." It should also be remembered that the Arab Government which was established in Syria, in October 1918, under Faiṣal with British advisers, was financed by the British Government at the rate of £ 150,000 a month. In November 1919, that subsidy was reduced to £ 75,000, the French Government having agreed to pay the Emīr Faiṣal a similar subsidy.

It should be added that the French Government, too, contributed its help which, though limited, nevertheless, in the words of Sir Reginald Wingate "assisted largely in the success of the joint operations in which they took a very gallant and conspicuous part." A French Military Mission, headed by Lieutenant-Colonel Brémond and composed of notable Muslim representatives of Algeria, Tunisia, Morocco, and French West Africa, arrived at Jedda on 20 September 1916, bringing with it for the Sharīf Ḥusain a subsidy of 1,250,000 gold francs. It was followed shortly by a small contingent of French forces and a small number of French machine guns, field artillery and rifles. The Mission was warmly welcomed by Sharīf Ḥusain. See Storrs, pp. 153, 155, and 159; Cmd. 5957 of 1939: *Correspondence Between Sir Henry McMahon (His Majesty's High Commissioner at Cairo) and the Sherif Hussein of Mecca, July* 1915-*March* 1916; *Documents* 1:4, p. 509; Brémond, *Le Hedjaz dans la Guerre Mondiale*, pp. 48-53, 64-67, and 348-349, and Toynbee, *Survey of International Affairs, 1925*, vol. 1, p. 273, where the subsidy to King Ḥusain is given as £ 200,000 a month "from the time of his intervention in the war down to the 1st February, 1919." See also Howard, *The Partition of Turkey*, pp. 187-193.

38. The leading officers belonged to the secret Arab Society called *Al-'Ahd* ("The Covenant"). See above, n. 8.

39. Among these officers, the following may be mentioned: Nūrī al-Sa'īd, Ja'far al-'Askarī, 'Alī Jawdat al-Ayyūbī, Jamīl al-Madfa'ī, Mawlūd Mokhliṣ, Shākir 'Abdu'l-Wahhāb al-Shaikhalī, Ḥāmid al-Shālijī, 'Abdu'l-Laṭīf Nūrī al-Baghdādī, Ibrāhīm al-Rāwī and Muḥammad Sharīf al-Farūqī. The latter was also a member of the *Al-'Ahd*. Apparently, the nature of the information which he disclosed to the British authorities in Egypt concerning the Arab cause and the Arab nationalist aspirations, greatly impressed them. His first letter to the Sharīf Ḥusain from Cairo, dated "27 Muḥarram, 1334" (6 January 1916) reveals the fact that he discussed with those authorities the Arab claims for independence in Syria and "'the impossibility of surrendering one span of the earth of Syria'' to France. It has been suggested that Sir Mark Sykes

Emīr Faiṣal was chosen to lead the Arab forces northward from Mecca towards 'Aqaba.[40] It was also during this Revolt that a young British archæologist, Thomas Edward Lawrence, serving at the beginning of the War as Staff Captain under Sir Gilbert Clayton in the Intelligence Section in Egypt, joined the Bedouin forces under Faiṣal and acquired worldwide fame as Lawrence of Arabia.

On the Allied side, Sir Reginald Wingate "was made General Officer commanding the Hejaz . . . responsible for the strategy, even the tactics, the feeding and the supply, and the difficult and involved diplomacy of the revolt once the Sharīf had shown his hand."[41] The story of the Arab Revolt has been told numerous times elsewhere and is not our concern here.[42]

It may, however, be of interest to note that Sharīf Ḥusain's rebellion against the Sultan-Caliph came as a shock to many Muslims throughout the world, particularly the Indian Muslims.[43] The Turks actually considered the Sharīf as a "traitor" to Islam. Soon

took into consideration the opinion and suggestions of Farūqī as a basis for the Sykes-Picot Agreement which was subsequently drawn up by the Allies for the partition of the Near East. The Sharīf Ḥusain appointed al-Farūqī as his representative in Cairo. Al-Farūqī's letters to the Sharīf Ḥusain are most informative and interesting. See Nūrī al-Sa'īd, *Muḥādarāt 'an al-Ḥarakat al-'Askariyyah l'il-Jaish al-'Arabī* [Lectures on the military operations of the Arab army] pp. 18-19 and 53; al-'Umarī, vol. 1, pp. 219-234; 274-300 and vol. 2, pp. 53-151 and Cmd. 5974, pp. 23-24.

40. For an "impression" of Faiṣal, see Robert Lansing, *The Big Four,* pp. 161-167. See also al-Raiḥānī, *Faiṣāl al-Awwal* [Faisal I] pp. 24-26 and 164-167 and al-Ghuṣain, *Mudhakkarātī* [My Memoirs], pp. 245-250. In 1916, Faiṣal was thirty-three years of age.

41. Wingate, p. 175.

42. See T.E. Lawrence, *Seven Pillars of Wisdom,* chaps. 4, 5, and 6; Temperley, vol. 6, pp. 118-133; Antonious, pp. 164-183, and Appendix A, pp. 413-427; Storrs, chap. 8; Cmd. 5957 of 1939 and Cmd. 5974, also of 1939, known as *Report of a Committee set up to consider Certain Correspondence between Sir Henry McMahon (His Majesty's High Commissioner in Egypt) and the Sharif of Mecca in 1915 and* 1916, and 'Abdullah, *Mudhakkarātī,* pp. 67-167.

43. On 29 June 1916, the Viceroy of India wrote in a secret despatch to the Secretary of State for India, in London:

"Secret. Arab Revolt. It is too early to gauge the full effect of announcement, but there is no doubt that profound sensation has been caused among Mohammedans. Arab revolt under Sherif had not been foreseen and came as a bombshell..." F.O. 371/2139.

after the Arab Revolt was proclaimed, the Turkish Government appointed Sharīf 'Alī Ḥaidar as the Emīr of Mecca, to replace Sharīf Ḥusain. Sharīf 'Alī Ḥaidar was the favorite grandson of 'Abdul Muṭṭalib who belonged to the original reigning family of the Sharīfs — the Dhawī-Zaid — before they were replaced at the beginning of the nineteenth century by the House of Dhawī-'Awn to which Sharīf Ḥusain belonged.[44]

In 1923 the Caliph 'Abdul Majīd in his "Recommendation" of the Sharīf 'Alī Ḥaidar to the Muslim world wrote as follows:

> At a time when all Muslims should have worked together in unity, Shereef Hussein of the Hedjaz shocked the Islamic World by his rebellion and oppression. The late Caliph, Mohammed Rechad Khan, thereupon charged the Emir Shereef Ali Haidar with the Emirate of Holy Mecca which was rightly his inheritance.
>
> Thus, one result of the rebellion of Shereef Hussein was to return the Emirate to the Dar-el-Caliph.[45]

Sharīf 'Alī Ḥaidar reached Medina but could not get to Mecca, for the Revolt had already begun. He was recalled to Constantinople where he arrived in September 1918, having spent the winter and spring of 1917-18 in Beirut. (He, subsequently, returned to Beirut where he died in March 1935.)

It is, perhaps, idle to speculate on the matter, but had Sharīf 'Alī Ḥaidar taken the place of Sharīf Ḥusain in the Emirate of Mecca, the Arab Revolt could not have originated in Mecca and the events in the Near East might have taken a different turn.[46]

In 1915 and 1916, the Allies had been on the defensive in the Middle East, but 1917 was a year of victories, first in Mesopotamia and then in Palestine. It is significant that early during this year when for the first time the execution of the Sykes-Picot Agreement

44. For a brief history of the Sharīfs of Mecca, see D.G. Hogarth, *Arabia*, pp. 82-93.

45. Stitt, *A Prince of Arabia*, App. 5, p. 312.

46. The Turks have considered the Sharīf Ḥusain, and not the Arabs, as the instigator of the Arab Revolt. General 'Alī Fu'ād Erden has written in his memoirs, that the Ḥejaz Revolt was not an Arab Revolt but a revolt of Sharīf Ḥusain with the help of British agents who attracted the Bedouin Arabs with British gold, British wheat and rice. See Erden, *Birinci Dunya Harbinde Suriye Hatiralari* [Syrian Memories of the First World War], vol. 1 (Istanbul, 1954), p. 71.

seemed probable, Sir Mark Sykes and M. François Georges-Picot went to Egypt. E. H. Byrne in his "Report on the Desires of the Syrians" wrote that M. Georges-Picot called a meeting of all the prominent Syrians in Egypt, Muslims and Christians, and announced that he had been appointed by the French Government as the future Resident in Syria — implying in his speech that "a French Protectorate" would be established over Syria. Sykes, who seemed to be working in harmony with Georges-Picot, interviewed several of the prominent Syrians in Egypt and "practically admitted that a French occupation of Syria was contemplated" but asserted that "a certain part of Syria, (which he was not at liberty to name) would be independent." Sykes at the same time let it be known that "the rule of one of the sons of the King of Hedjaz over this independent Arab state would be favoured by the British."[47] As King Ḥusain had become apprehensive about the Sykes-Picot mission to Cairo and wanted some assurances, the Foreign Office sent Sir Mark Sykes to the Hejaz in May 1917. On 3 May Sykes saw Faiṣal and on 5 May King Ḥusain. Sykes reported the results of both interviews to be satisfactory, "inasmuch as the leaders have been brought to understand that they have to deal with an indivisible Entente; that under whatever overlord, an enlightened progressive regime must be established in Syria; and that certain districts of the latter, which present peculiar difficulties, must remain under special tutelage in any event."[48] During that same month M. Georges-Picot also had two interviews with King Ḥusain and delivered to him a message from the French Government. In answer to that message a declaration by the King was read aloud to M. Georges-Picot during the second interview, to the following effect:

> H.M. the King of the Hedjaz learned with satisfaction that the French Government approved of Arab national aspirations; and that, as he had confidence in Great Britain, he would be content if the French Government pursued the same policy towards Arab aspirations on the Moslem-Syrian littoral as the British did in Baghdad.[49]

47. U.S. Department of State, *General Records of the American Commission to Negotiate Peace, Paris, 1918-1919 Inquiry Document No. 82.*

48. *Arab Bulletin* 50 (13 May 1917): 207.

49. D. Lloyd George, *The Truth about the Peace Treaties*, vol. 2, p. 1034. See also Brémond, pp. 165-169.

For a glimpse of what the future had in store for the Arab Near East, it is important to be acquainted with a British document written in 1917, well after the promises given to the Sharīf Ḥusain in 1915 and the Sykes-Picot Agreement of 1916. This document is a "Statement on Foreign Policy made to the Imperial War Council" and communicated to the American Secretary of State. Robert Lansing, in Washington on 18 May 1917 by Mr. Arthur James Balfour, Chief of the British Special Mission, which was then visiting the United States. The policy concerning Turkey, ominous and apocalyptic, was as follows:

> The practical destruction of the Turkish Empire is undoubtedly one of the objects which we desire to attain. The Turks may well be left — I hope they will be left — in a more or less independent position in Asia Minor. If we are successful, unquestionably Turkey will be deprived of all that in the larger sense may be called Arabia; she will be deprived of the most important portions of the Valley of the Euphrates and the Tigris; she will lose Constantinople; and Syria, Armenia and the southern parts of Asia Minor will, if not annexed by the Entente Powers, probably fall more or less under their domination.[50]

In November 1917 the existence of the secret treaties became known for the first time when they were found in the archives of the Russian Foreign Office and published by orders of Leon Trotsky, Commissar for Foreign Affairs. Speaking before the Central Executive Committee of the Soviets, in Petrograd, Trotsky was reported to have said: ". . . All the secret treaties are now in my hands. These documents which are more cynical in their provisions than we supposed, will soon be published. . . . We sweep all secret treaties into the dustbin."[51] The *Manchester Guardian* was the first newspaper in Great Britain to publish (in its issues of 26 and 28 November 1917) summaries of the secret treaties relating to Constantinople and to Asiatic Turkey (the Sykes-Picot Agreement) which were

50. Needless to say that this document was a great "top secret". In the Note which accompanied it, Mr. Balfour wrote to Mr. Lansing: "The proceedings of the Imperial War Council are, of course, absolutely secret." See U.S., Department of State, *Papers Relating to the Foreign Relations of the United States: The Lansing Papers, 1914-1920*, vol. 2, p. 23.

51. The *Manchester Guardian*, Monday, 26 November 1917, p. 5, col. 6.

communicated to it telegraphically by its correspondent in Petrograd, Mr. Philips Price.[52] Embarrassing questions about these secret treaties were asked in the House of Commons on 12 December by Mr. Dillon and Mr. Hogge. In reply, Mr. Balfour, the Secretary of State for Foreign Affairs, said that "the documents in question ought not to have been published, and I do not propose to republish them", and he added: "Of course, a lot of the documents have nothing whatever to do with this country; they have got to do with the Governments of our Allies, and the notion that we should republish documents relating to our Allies, is, I should have thought, too absurd to deserve attention."[53]

Towards the end of November, Jemāl Pasha communicated the text of the Sykes-Picot Agreement to the Emīr Faiṣal in two letters which he sent by secret emissary to ʻAqaba, one to Faiṣal and the other to Jaʻfar Pasha al-ʻAskarī. He proposed at the same time a separate Turko-Arab peace.[54] King Ḥusain forwarded the above mentioned letters which he received from Faiṣal, to Sir Reginald Wingate, His Majesty's High Commissioner for Egypt. On 8 February 1918 Lt. Colonel J.R. Bassett, the Acting British Agent in Jeddah communicated to King Ḥusain on behalf of Wingate the text of a telegraphic message which the latter had received from the

52. *Izvestia* (Moscow) and *Pravda* (Moscow) published the full text of these secret documents in their issues of 23 November 1917. A copy of these papers reached the *Manchester Guardian* which on 12 December 1917, published an English translation of the Russian version of the secret treaties.

See M. Philips Price, *A History of Turkey, From Empire to Republic* (London, 1956), p. 96.

53. *Parliamentary Debates, Fifth Series, House of Commons*, vol. 100, December 1917, pp. 1152, col. 2 and 1153, col. 1.

54. Antonius, p. 257; Lawrence, pp. 555-556. On 4 December 1917, Jemāl Pasha, at a banquet in Beirut, announced the Turkish offer of peace to King Ḥusain and disclosed the Sykes-Picot Agreement. The Turks gave the widest possible publicity to this document in the Arab countries.

Lawrence wrote: "For a while the disclosure hurt us; justly, for we and the French had thought to plaster over a split in policy by a formula vague enough for each to interpret in his divergent way. Fortunately, I had early betrayed the treaty's existence to Faiṣal . . . and had convinced him that his escape was to help the British so much that after peace they would not be able, for shame, to shoot him down in its fulfilment: while, if the Arabs did as I intended, there would be no one-side talk of shooting. I begged him to trust not in our promises, like his father, but in his own strong performance." Lawrence, p. 555.

Foreign Office. The message expressed the British Government's "liveliest satisfaction" for the "loyal motives" which had prompted King Ḥusain to forward to the High Commissioner "the letter addressed by the Turkish Commander-in-Chief in Syria to his Highness the Amir Faisal and to Ja'far Pasha," continuing: "It would be superfluous to point out that the object aimed at by Turkey is to sow doubt and suspicion between the Allied Powers and those Arabs whom under Your Majesty's leadership and guidance, are striving nobly to recover their ancient freedom. . . . His Majesty's Government and their allies stand steadfastly by every cause aiming at the liberation of the oppressed nations, and they are determined to stand by the Arab peoples in their struggle for the establishment of an Arab world in which law shall replace Ottoman injustice and in which unity shall prevail over the rivalries artificially provoked by the policy of Turkish officials. His Majesty's Government reaffirm their former pledge in regard to the liberation of the Arab peoples. . . ."[55] Already on 4 January 1918, D. G. Hogarth had been instructed to deliver a message to King Ḥusain. The message began with this assertion: "The Entente Powers are determined that the Arab race shall be given full opportunity of once again forming a nation in the world. This can only be achieved by the Arabs themselves uniting, and Great Britain and her Allies will pursue a policy with this ultimate unity in view."[56] Six months later, there was one more reassuring message on Arab independence and sovereignty to a group of seven Syrians resident in Cairo who had presented a memorial anonymously to His Majesty's Government through Mr. O. Walrond of the Arab Bureau. The memorialists were members of a newly formed party of Syrian leaders in Egypt, called the Syrian Unity Party. They wanted to know whether it was the aim of the British Government that the inhabitants of the Arab countries

55. Nurī Al-Sa'īd, *Arab Independence and Unity* (Baghdad: Government Press, 1943), p. 32 (Appendix E); Antonious, pp. 431-432.

Temperley wrote that the Arab leaders were startled by the revelation of the Sykes-Picot Agreement, but "their belief in the good faith of Great Britain was strong and the discovery did not affect their loyal co-operation with their British Ally." Temperley, vol. 6, p. 137.

56. Cmd. 5974, p. 3.

should enjoy "complete independence" and whether the British Government would favor the establishment of a "decentralised Arab Government" and thus make it possible for Syria to obtain administrative autonomy within an independent Arab Kingdom.[57] In its "Declaration to the Seven," delivered to the memorialists "on about the 16th June, 1918" by Commander Hogarth and Mr. Walrond the British Government stated that it recognized "the complete and sovereign independence" of the Arabs inhabiting the "areas in Arabia which were free and independent before the outbreak of war" and the "areas emancipated from Turkish control by the action of the Arabs themselves during the present war." As to the "areas formerly under Ottoman dominion, occupied by the Allied forces during the present war," it was "the wish and desire of His Majesty's Government that the future government of these regions should be based upon the principle of the consent of the governed, and this policy has and will continue to have the support of His Majesty's Government."[58]

While the British Government was giving these assurances to King Ḥusain, the Emīr Faiṣal and his Arab forces, helped by T.E. Lawrence, had captured 'Aqaba on 6 July 1917 and were already operating south and southeast of the Dead Sea as an autonomous Arab army called the Northern Arab Army, commanded by the Emīr Faiṣal and under the control of General Allenby, the Commander-in-Chief of the Egyptian Expeditionary Force.[59] Allenby's

57. Antonius, p. 433; Amīn Sa'īd, *Al-Thawrah al-'Arabiyyah al-Kubrā* [The great Arab Revolt], vol. 2, pp. 37-40.

58. Cmd. 5964, p. 6.

59. "The capture of Aqaba," wrote Liddell Hart, "was like a sudden break in the clouds that overhung the Egyptian front in the spring and summer of 1917.... Strategically, it removed all danger of a Turkish raid through Sinai against the Suez Canal or the communications of the British army in Palestine It also opened up a new line of operation by which the Arabs could give positive assistance to a renewed British advance." Liddell Hart, "T. E. Lawrence," in *Arabia and After*, pp. 206 and 220.

'Aqaba was the last position on the Ḥejāz coast held by the Turks. According to General Wingate, his strategic plan had now been carried out by its capture. Mecca was safe, the Turkish forces in Medina had "no offensive capacity," the pilgrimage was not interrupted and "the Ḥejāz virtually independent and under Arab rule." He "had achieved what he had planned for the Arab Revolt." In August 1917, the Emīr Faiṣal with his forces and with

campaign in Palestine had also begun and Jerusalem was occupied on 9 December 1917.

The year 1918 was a year of great victories for the Allies in the Near East, culminating in the destruction of the Ottoman Empire. In one big onrushing wave, Allenby's forces swept through Syria and the Lebanon rolling before them the remnants of the Turkish Fourth Army. Damascus was occupied on 1 October and Beirut on 8 October. This military victory was the beginning of an extraordinary political muddle and confusion, and involved tangled diplomacy, between Great Britain and the Arabs on the one hand and between the Allies themselves on the other, leaving behind a legacy of suspicion and mistrust in the relations between the Arabs and the West during the last six decades.[60]

Lawrence his liaison officer were transferred from Wingate to Allenby. "This transfer," Sir Ronald Wingate has written, "did something the implications of which could not have been foreseen by the statesmen of the Allies, or by Wingate or Allenby. It moved Feiṣal and his men from the restricted and defined field of military operations for the freedom of the Hejaz, to the far wider and more complicated territory of a world war and world politics." Wingate, pp. 193-195. However, the letter of General Allenby written to "His Highness the Emir Faiṣal" and dated "4/1/18" will be read with much interest and with a little surprise. For the text of this letter, see Appendix below.

60. In a Memorandum "respecting Syria, Palestine and Mesopotamia," written on 11 August 1919, Mr. Balfour frankly stated: "This brings into clear relief what I fear is the unhappy truth, namely, that France, England, and America have got themselves into a position over the Syrian problem so inextricably confused that no really neat and satisfactory issue is now possible for any of them....

"... These documents are not consistent with each other; they represent no clear-cut policy; the policy which they confusedly adumbrate is not really the policy of the Allied and Associated Powers...." *Documents*, 1:4, pp. 342-343.

CHAPTER TWO

THE ALLIES IN SYRIA AND THE LEBANON, 1918

"*The Turkish portions of the present Ottoman Empire should be assured a secure sovereignty, but the other nationalities which are now under Turkish rule should be assured an undoubted security of life and an absolutely unmolested opportunity of autonomous development ...*"

The Twelfth of the "Fourteen Points" of President Wilson.

ON 30 SEPTEMBER 1918 four hundred years of Turkish rule came to an end in Damascus. During the afternoon the Arab flag of King Ḥusain of the Ḥejāz was hoisted over the Town Hall. This was the "Flag of Arab Liberation," black, white, and green, with a red chevron.[1] At midnight, the Desert Mounted Corps was at the gates of the city. At dawn the next day, Major A.C. Olden, in command of the 10th Light Horse Regiment which formed the

1. It has been claimed that the original flag was designed by Sir Mark Sykes: "Black fess for the Abbasids of Baghdad, white for the Omayyads of Damascus, green for the Alids of Kerbela, and red Chevron for Moudhar heredity." See Shane Leslie, *Mark Sykes: His Life and Letters*, p. 280. On the other hand, Ja'far Pasha al-'Askarī has recorded in his unpublished memoirs that sometime in 1917 when he was in Cairo, Clayton showed him a flag and told him: "This is your Arab flag with its four colours. It was designed by King Ḥusain himself." (Manuscript of Ja'far Pasha's Memoirs, "*Khawāṭir Ja'far Pasha al-'Askarī*," p. 81).

For a detailed history of the Arab flag, going back to the years 1909-11, when some members of *al-Muntadā al-Adabī* (the Arab Literary Club) in Constantinople discussed the question of a future Arab national flag, see Sulaimān Mūsā, *Al-Harakah al-'Arabiyyah* (The Arab Movement), pp. 135-40. Mūsā has also written that the Emīr Sa'īd al-Jazā'erī hoisted the Arab flag over the Town Hall in Damascus. It had been given to his younger brother Abdul Qādir by Sharīf Ḥusain in Mecca, the previous year (ibid. p. 321).

Lawrence who bitterly disliked the two Algerian brothers, admits that with their support and "with the help of their retainers the Arab flag was on the Town Hall before sunset as the last echelons of Germans and Turks defiled past. . . ." T.E. Lawrence, *Seven Pillars of Wisdom*, p. 643.

Advanced Guard of the 3rd Australian Light Horse Brigade, reached Damascus. According to the 3rd Light Horse Brigade "Report on the Occupation of Damascus on the Morning of 1st October 1918,"[2] when Major Olden arrived in front of the Town Hall, the time was between 6:30 and 7:00 a. m. He dismounted, went into the Town Hall and asked for the "Civil Governor." Emīr Sa'īd who was sitting in the Municipal Chair "arose, came forward as such and shook hands." Then, speaking through an interpreter he said: "In the name of the civil population of Damascus, I welcome the British Army." Shortly afterwards the Vanguard moved on through the city to the North East road, on its way to Ḥoms, Ḥama, and Aleppo. The question as to which troops, Arab or British, were the first to enter Damascus, has been the subject of a controversy for many years. The controversy was actually started by Lawrence as he always insisted that the Arab forces of the Emīr Faiṣal occupied Damascus before any other troops entered the city. But the Australian documents do not support Lawrence's contention.[3]

2. The author is very grateful to Mr. W.R. Lancaster, Director of the Australian War Memorial, for having sent him this Report.

3. The question as to which troops, Arab or British, were the first to enter Damascus, has been the subject of a controversy for many years. The controversy was actually started by Lawrence as he always insisted that the Arab forces of the Emīr Faiṣal occupied Damascus before any other troops entered the city. But the Australian documents do not support Lawrence's contention. In addition to consulting a member of official sources on the subject, such as Cyril Falls' *British Official History of the War, Military Operations. Egypt and Palestine*, vol. 2, H.S. Gullett's *Official History of Australia in the War of 1914-1918*, vol. 7, *Sinai and Palestine*, General Allenby's Dispatch on the Damascus-Aleppo Campaign, the author got in touch with the Department of External Affairs, Canberra, enquiring about Australian documents on this subject. The letter which he received from Mr. W.R. Lancaster, Director of the Australian War Memorial, dated 2 December 1968, leaves no doubt in his mind that Damascus surrendered to Major A.C.N. Olden of the 10th Light Horse Regiment which formed the Advanced Guard of the 3rd Australian Light Horse Brigade, commanded by Brigadier General L.G. Wilson.

The above-mentioned "Report on the Occupation of Damascus on the Morning of 1st October 1918" is part of the *War Diary*, Appendix 5 of the 3rd Light Horse Brigade. The concluding sentence of this Report reads as follows: "Up to the time (about 0700) that this Brigade completed its passage through the city: thereby closing the only remaining available exit for the enemy, no member of the Sherif's Army was visible in any part of the city within view

At this time neither Faiṣal nor Lawrence had entered the city. But Lawrence was very anxious that Damascus should be occupied by Arab forces first. If it were so, not only would Faiṣal's prestige be enhanced in Syria and throughout the Arab world as the Deliverer of the Arabs from Turkish tyranny, but the French whom Lawrence intensely disliked would be prevented from making a dash from Beirut and occupying Damascus.[4] He also remembered the British Government's Declaration to the Seven Arabs, in which His Majesty's Government had stated that with regard to "territories liberated from Turkish rule by the Arabs themselves," it recognized "the complete and sovereign independence" of the Arabs inhabiting those territories.[5] Hence, when Lawrence entered Damascus on 1 October, at about 7:30 a.m., the first thing that

of this Brigade."

In the above-mentioned letter, Mr. W.R. Lancaster wrote to the author: "It occurs to me that had Lawrence entered the city before the above events, surely he would have been at the town hall with the local officials arranging for the restoration of order in Damascus when Major Olden arrived with the 10th Light Horse. Yet neither Lawrence in his *Seven Pillars of Wisdom* nor the official report of the 3rd Light Horse Brigade mention any contact between Lawrence and Olden. Because of Lawrence's self-admitted interest in the capture of Damascus, it seems most unlikely that he would have remained in the background when the city was surrendered to Olden by the Emir with the words 'In the name of the civil population of Damascus I welcome the British Army.' It is equally unlikely that Major Olden would have overlooked a meeting with such a legendary figure as T.E. Lawrence."

The Emīr Sa'īd al-Jazā'erī's own account of the fall of Damascus agrees with the Australian documents. He wrote: "While we were in the Government Serai in Damascus preparing delegations of Muslim and Christian leaders to proceed to the Headquarters of the advancing British and Arab armies, the British Vanguard headed by the Australians' Major Arthur Olden rode up to Victoria Hotel, near the Serai . . . coming from the West. It was followed, on that same day (October 1) by the entry of Arab troops under the command of Nāṣir ben Rāḍī, coming from the South, accompanied by Colonel Lawrence and a few British officiers. They were joyfully received and welcomed by the population." See Muḥammad Jamīl Beyhum, *Al-'Ahd al-Mukhaḍram fī Sūrriyya wa Lubnān, 1918-1922*, p. 51). See also Archibald Wavell, *Allenby: A Study in Greatness*, pp. 284-285.

4. Lawrence had written on 22 March 1915: "The French insist upon Syria — which we are conceding to them.... If Idrisi is anything like as good as we hope, we can rush right up to Damascus, and biff the French out of all hope of Syria. It's a big game, and at least one worth playing... Won't the French be mad if we win though . . . ?" David Garnett, *Letters of T. E. Lawrence*, p. 87.

5. See p. 23, above.

he did was to go to the Town Hall where, after a stormy meeting, he deposed the Emīr al-Jazā'erī, the "Head of the Arab Government" which the Emīr had formed before the entry of the Allied troops in the city, and appointed Shukrī Pasha al-Ayyūbī (in the absence of 'Alī Riḍā Pasha al-Rikābī) as Military Governor of Damascus.[6] A temporary Arab Administration was set up and proceeded to establish law and order in the city, imposing among other things a curfew from sunset to sunrise to prevent the Bedouin forces in the Arab army from looting the stores and bazaars of the city.

An Arab Government was also formed in Beirut by its Mayor, 'Umar Bey al-Dā'ūq, on 1 October. On 30 September, the Turks withdrew from Beirut and on that same day, 'Umar Bey received a telegram from the Emīr Sa'īd in Damascus announcing the establishment of an Arab Hashemite Government after the withdrawal of the Turks and asking him to form an Arab administration in Beirut in the name of that government.[7] This was before the

6. For Lawrence's description of his entry into Damascus and the events which followed, see his *Secret Dispatches from Arabia*, pp. 170-171, and *Seven Pillars of Wisdom*, pp. 424-431. For a French version of the same events, see Gontaut-Biron, p. 48, and Philippe David, *Un Gouvernement Arabe à Damas*, pp. 8-11.

The true causes of Lawrence's animosity towards the Emīr Sa'īd and his brother are not yet known. It has been suggested that Lawrence suspected the Algerians of both pro-Turkish and pro-French sympathies.

In one of his confidential dispatches which appeared in the *Arab Bulletin* of 22 October 1918, Lawrence wrote: "I found at the Town Hall (in Damascus on 1 October 1918) Mohammad Sa'id and Abd el-Kadir, the Algerians, who had just assured possession of the provisional civil government, since there was no one in Damascus who could fight their Moorish bodyguard. They are both insane, and as well pro-Turkish and religious fanatics of the most unpleasant sort. In consequence, I sent for them, and before *beledíyeh* and the *shiyukh el-harrat*, announced that as Faisal's representative, I declared Shukri el-Ayubi Arab Military Governor (Ali Riza, the intended Governor, was missing), and the provisional civil administration of the Algerians dissolved. They took it rather hard, and had to be sent home . . . ."

See also Jean Pichon, *Sur la Route des Indes*, pp. 142-144 and 168-169.

7. For a photostatic copy of this telegram and of the Proclamation announcing the formation of an Arab Government in Beirut, see *Al-Ḥayāt* (Beirut), N° 1070, 5 November 1949, p. 1.

A similar telegram was sent to the Shi'a leaders and notables in Jabal 'Amel which is, today, the southern region of the Republic of Lebanon. It was signed by the Emīr Muḥammad Sa'īd al-Jazā'erī and was received by Maḥmūd Bey

deposition of the Emīr by Lawrence. We have two conflicting reports as to what happened immediately afterwards. According to one version, upon the insistent advice of Lawrence on the necessity of proclaiming an Arab Government in the name of the Emīr Faiṣal in Beirut, "the other great Syrian city," Faiṣal sent Shukrī Pasha al-Ayyūbī to Beirut to form an Arab Government in the Lebanon. The other version of the story[8] is to the effect that some notables of Beirut[9] sent a telegram to the "Arab High Command" in Damascus asking it to send a representative of the Sharīf Huṣain to organize an Arab Government in that city. Nūrī Pasha al-Sa'īd replied by telegram asking them to raise the Arab flag on all Government buildings (after describing the flag to them) and to await the arrival of an Arab force to help them in their new tasks. When Faiṣal was informed about the situation in Beirut, he agreed to send Shukrī Pasha immediately with a token force of one hundred Arab soldiers, eight light machine guns, and several of the new Ḥejāz flags. This force left Damascus on 2 October and reached Beirut on 4 October after two days of hard riding, the Germans having destroyed the railway communication between those two cities.[10]

Meanwhile, on 3 October, Faiṣal, riding a splendid Arabian horse and followed by 1,500 Arab horsemen, made a triumphant entry into Damascus, in the midst of scenes of great enthusiasm and

al-Faḍl in Nabatiyyah, the principal town in Jabal 'Amel. He assumed the reigns of the Government in Nabatiyyah and raised the Arab flag on his house. An Arab Government was also formed in Saida by Riyāḍ al-Ṣolḥ but did not last more than a week. The Arab Government in Jabal 'Amel lasted for a month, and came to an end when a French military government was established in that region towards the end of October. See Muḥammad Jābir al-Ṣafā, *Ta'rīkh Jabal 'Amel* [History of Jabal Amel], pp. 221-122.

8. This version was related to the author by Nūrī Pasha al-Sa'īd during an interview in Baghdad, in April 1955.

9. Among them, Aḥmad Mukhtār Beyhum and Salīm Ṭayyārah, according to Nūrī Pasha al-Sa'īd.

10. The new Arab Government of 'Umar Bey Dā'ūq in its official gazette, "Beirut," no. 3, of Thursday, 3 October 1918, extolled the virtues of the Arab Hashimite Government and addressing the people of Beirut said: "O inhabitants of Beirut, God has bestowed upon you the blessings of independence under the protection of the Arab Hashimite Government... a truthful, faithful, honourable and proud Government." See also Brémond, p. 307.

jubilation.[11] A day earlier, thousands of British, Australian, New Zealand, and Indian troops and cavalry, together with a contingent of French forces and Spahis, had marched in a great procession through the city on their way north in the wake of the retreating Turks. But the historic day was 3 October. To Faiṣal and to his ambitious father, King Ḥusain, the Sharīf of Mecca, Damascus seemed the goal of all national aspirations and its occupation, at least, the partial fulfilment of their dreams of independence and empire. But a great shock awaited Faiṣal, though it is not possible to establish to what extent that shock was unexpected. For on that day Sir Edmund Allenby, the Commander-in-Chief of the Egyptian Expeditionary Force, was racing up to Damascus full of concern for the tidings he had received from Syria. His main anxiety was the content of the messages which had been sent to him from G.H.Q. at Bīr Sālem, from the High Commissioner in Egypt, from the French Consul General in Cairo, from M. Georges-Picot, and especially from the War Office and the Foreign Office. It has been reported by a well informed contemporary that the tenor of all of those messages was "Choke off Faisal and Lawrence. Dam the Arab torrent. Remember the Sykes-Picot Agreement."[12]

Allenby entered Damascus also on 3 October and almost immediately sent for Faiṣal. The interview took place in the drawing room of the Victoria Hotel. It was the first time that the two men had met. Sir Archibald Wavell has remarked that they were a striking contrast — "the burly, confident Englishman, accustomed to command and to dominate by sheer force of personality, and the slight ascetic Arab with his princely bearing...."[13] The interview

11. In the meantime, 'Alī Riḍā Pasha al-Rikābī, Lawrence's choice as Governor of Damascus, had arrived from General Sir George Barrow's headquarters, where he had surrendered earlier when as Turkish Commander of Damascus "he had been dispatched to take charge of the Turk's last line of defence." He was now appointed military Governor of the city. See Liddell Hart, pp. 365-366. See also Brémond, p. 306.

12. See Beckles Willson, "Our Amazing Syrian Adventure," *The National Review*, September 1920, pp. 41-54.

13. Allenby wrote to his wife that evening: "You would like Feisal. He is a keen, slim, highly strung man. He has beautiful hands like a woman's, and his fingers are always moving nervously when he talks. But he is strong in will and straight in principle." Wavell, p. 286, n. 1.

was rather "breezy and boisterous." Lawrence was also present. Allenby pointed out that the War was not yet over. The territory which the forces under his command had occupied was "enemy territory." Britain was for the time being responsible for the administration of this territory. However, according to an agreement with the French, he had received instructions to allow the French to take over control of the "Blue" zone which represented Syria west of Damascus and Aleppo and which included the chief town of Beirut and the Lebanon. Lawrence admitted that he had in good faith sent Shukrī Pasha to take possession of Beirut on behalf of King Ḥusain of the Ḥejāz, who considered the whole of Syria as his heritage;[14] recognizing any French rights in Syria would have serious consequences. Allenby replied sharply that this was none of Lawrence's concern. He was never intended to occupy the seacoast. He could go home and explain the situation to the Foreign Office. It was the business of the Commander-in-Chief to carry out the instructions he had received and the engagements of the British Government. Turning to Faiṣal, Allenby explained that in zone "A" of that Agreement with the French, which included Damascus, Homs, Hama, and Aleppo, France was to be the protecting Power but she had pledged herself to uphold an independent Arab state. He, Allenby, however had now received a cable from the Foreign Office, recognizing the Arabs as belligerents. He was prepared to recognize an Arab administration under Faiṣal as representative of his father, King Ḥusain, in enemy territory east of the Jordan, from 'Aqaba to Ma'ān, to Damascus, inclusive. He would however appoint two liaison officers, one British and the other French, through whom he could get in touch with the British and French Governments regarding the affairs of the Arab administration. When Faiṣal protested strongly about the French having any control in Syria and about the appointment of a French liaison officer, Allenby insisted that his orders as

14. In a letter written to Professor William Yale in 1929, Lawrence denied his responsibility and asserted that "Shukri was sent to Beirut by Ali Riza Pasha," adding: "If Shukri told you I had urged him to Beirut, it was probably that he was getting frightened at the magnitude of his error, and wanted to make-believe that he had authority." David Garnett, *The Letters of T. E. Lawrence*, pp. 670-671.

Commander-in-Chief in Palestine and Syria had to be obeyed and that "Faiṣal must accept the situation till the peace settlement."[15] The interview came to an end. It has been reported that after Faiṣal had left, Lawrence told Allenby that he could not consent to work with a French Officer and asked for leave. The leave was granted and he left Damascus the next day.[16] Thus the Sykes-Picot Agreement had now surfaced and cast a long and dark shadow across the aspirations of King Ḥusain and the Arab nationalists. For nearly three days, from 1 to 3 October, its existence had been deliberately ignored. A Pandora's Box had been opened with dramatic suddenness. Its contents were to embitter Anglo-Arab-French relations for the next three decades. The inevitable collision took place between the Allies at a time when they were least prepared for it. Indeed, Lawrence himself had foreseen the "reaction" of Faiṣal; for he had written at the beginning of the War:

> Within our sight the only independent factor with acceptable groundwork and fighting adherents was a Sunni prince, like Feisal pretending to revive the glories of Ommayad or Ayubid. He might momentarily combine the inland men until success came with its need to transfer their debauched enthusiasm to the service of ordered government. Then would come reaction; but only after victory; and for victory everything material and moral might be pawned.[17]

Hence, the affairs of the Allies in the Middle East began to miscarry in the midst of their own conflicting ambitions and

15. Wavell, p. 286. See also Brian Gardner, *Allenby*, pp. 190-191, Captain Cyril Falls, *Military Operations: Egypt and Palestine*, Part 2, p. 592, and Sir Herbert Young, *The Independent Arab*, pp. 255-256.

16. "October 30th — Colonel Lawrence of Arabia called at War Office. He has been helping the Hedjaz Army and apparently was real Commander of their forces.... He was recommended to the King by General Staff for C.B. and D.S.O. Said he was an Arab soldier and didn't want decoration." Sam Fay, *The War Office at War* (London, 1917), p. 217.

On 14 October, Lawrence wrote from the Continental Hotel in Cairo to Major R.H. Scott:

"Dear Scott,

As we hoped we got to Damascus, and there I had to leave the Arabs — it is a pity to go and it would have been unwise to stay. I feel like a man who has suddenly dropped a heavy load — one's back hurts when one tries to walk straight." Garnett, p. 258.

17. T.E. Lawrence, *Seven Pillars of Wisdom*, p. 337.

clashing jealousies. Returning to the events of 3 October: that evening at the dinner table in the Hotel Victoria, Nūrī Pasha al-Sa'īd was sitting with General Clayton on his right and Captain Coulondre on his left. Coulondre was "Acting Chief Political Adviser" for the area of French influence. During he course of conversation, General Clayton asked about the Turkish armies outside Damascus. Nūrī Pasha replied that no appreciable forces remained near them, that many Turks had surrendered, and that the rest were retreating towards Ḥoms, Ḥama, and Aleppo. Clayton then inquired about the situation in Beirut and the Lebanon. Nūrī Pasha told him what steps had already been taken, that a small force of Sharifian cavalry had been despatched to Beirut. Coulondre who had naturally been listening to the conversation, left the table immediately without finishing his dinner and proceeded straight to Beirut in order to hasten, as was learned later, the landing of French troops there. Clayton seeing Coulondre leave the dinner table, turned to Nūrī Pasha and said: "We are going to face one of our knottiest problems with the French."[18] The French protested bitterly to the Foreign Office and to General Allenby. The upshot of the whole matter was that Allenby ordered an Intelligence Officer and staff to proceed to Beirut, remove Shukrī Pasha from office, haul down the Ḥejāz flags and give the necessary assurances to the French naval commander whose ships were waiting outside the harbor that he could land the French marines. Faiṣal himself was persuaded at the same time to send an order to his lieutenant in Beirut to return immediately to Damascus and thus avoid a collision with the French.

On 5 October Faiṣal established in Damascus an "Arab Military Government" for "Syria" with the knowledge and permission of General Allenby and issued his first official Proclamation addressed to the "People of Syria."[19] In that Proclamation, Faiṣal thanked all the Syrians for the kind and warm reception they had given to "our victorious troops" and for their allegiance

18. The above story was related to the author by Nūrī Pasha al-Sa'īd during an interview in Baghdad, in April 1955.

19. For the original Arabic text of that Proclamation, see Sāṭi' al-Ḥuṣrī, *Yawm Maisalūn* [The Day of Maisalūn] pp. 194-195.

to "Our Lord, the Sultan, the Prince of the Faithful, the Sharīf Ḥusain." Then he announced the establishment in Syria of an "Arab Constitutional Government... fully and absolutely independent, in the name of our Lord, Sultan Ḥusain," and extending its authority over "all Syria". 'Alī Riḍā Pasha al-Rikābī had been appointed as the Head of that Government. The rest of the Proclamation consisted of an appeal to keep law and order and obey the new Government. With a view to allaying the apprehensions of the Christian and other minorities in Syria, Faiṣal ended the announcement by emphasizing that his Government was an *Arab* Government based on justice and equality for all Arabs, who would enjoy the same rights, be they Muslim, Christian, or Jew.

Meanwhile the situation in Beirut and the Lebanon was confused and was causing great anxiety to the Christians and Muslims alike. The population had been nearly decimated by famine and starvation during the last two years of the war. One eyewitness reported that early in October he saw the most abject cases of starvation in the streets of Beirut: little children were like "sacks of frail bones and were dying in the gutters." [20] Politically there was a sharp line of demarcation between the desires of the Muslims and the Christian majority of the Maronites for the future of the Lebanon. The Lebanon of 1918, known more specifically in Arabic as "Jabal Lubnān" (literally, Mount Lebanon) was much smaller in size and population than the "Grand Liban" which the French established later and which became the Republic of Lebanon.

Up until the first half of the nineteenth century, the Arab vilayets of the Ottoman Empire had been Mosul, Baghdad, "Ḥaleb" (Aleppo), "Saida" (Sidon), and "Shām" (Damascus), with a total estimated population of 500,000 in the chief towns.[21] In Arabia, there were the vilayets of Ḥejāz and the Yemen. After the civil war of 1860 in Mount Lebanon and in Damascus, the Porte started a reorganization of its administrative units in the

20. See *The Times* (London), 1 November 1918, p. 2, col. 4.

21. Farley gives the following statistics for population: "Mosul, 65,000, Baghdad 105,000, Aleppo 100,000, Beyrouth 50,000 and Damascus 180,000." J. Lewis Farley, *The Resources of Turkey* (London, 1863), p. 5.

Arab provinces. Geographical Syria was divided into two vilayets: Aleppo and "Shām". The Vilayet of Shām no longer included the Lebanon. According to the new "Protocole" of 1861 submitted by the Ambassadors of Five Powers[22] to the Porte and accepted by the latter, Mount Lebanon was detached from Syria and formed an autonomous sanjak ruled by a Muteṣarrif.[23] The "Protocole" embodied the "Règlements Organiques" of 5 June 1861, as superseded by those of 6 September 1864 and amended by the Protocole of 28 July 1868.[24]

In 1887, because of the growing importance of Jerusalem, the Porte created a new administrative unit in the independent sanjak of Jerusalem in the south of Palestine. This sanjak was detached from the vilayet of Shām and put under the direct control of the Porte. Meanwhile the town of Beirut was expanding and its commercial prosperity increasing rapidly. Consequently the Porte decided to establish in 1888 the new Vilayet of Beirut to which the four sanjaks of Latakia, Tripoli, Acre, and Nablus were attached. Thus from 1888 onwards Syria was divided into three vilayets (Aleppo, "Shām," and Beirut) and two detached sanjaks (Lebanon and Jerusalem).

After the tragic events of 1860, the Maronites in the Lebanon never ceased to work for their complete separation from the Ottoman Empire and the establishment of Lebanon's independence under French protection. Some foreign protection was obviously necessary and it was equally obvious that in the case of the Lebanon, that protection was going to come from France, the traditional protector of the Maronites and Catholics in the Near East. In Maronite Lebanon anti-Turkish sentiment was fostered by several factors such as Western education, the political ideals of the French

22. Great Britain, Russia, France, Austria, and Prussia.

23. "Its governor was necessarily a Christian and its administrative council consisted of four Maronites, three Druses, two Greek Orthodox Christians, one Greek Catholic, one Moslem and one Metwali. The sanjak was divided into seven Kazas, of which four were Maronite, one Greek Orthodox, one Greek Catholic and one (Shūf) Moslem... The head of the police was always a Maronite. The Province enjoyed a system of taxation of its own." Great Britain, Admiralty, *A Handbook of Syria (including Palestine)*, p. 243.

24. For the full texts of the Protocols and the "Règlements Organiques," see C. Young, *Corps de Droit Ottoman* (Oxford, 1925), vol. 1, pp. 139-159.

Revolution, travel abroad, more frequent contacts with the West and the periodic return of Lebanese emigrants from the United States. But, above all, it was primarily due to the fact that the Christians were an alien island in an ocean of Turkish-Muslim sovereignty. They simply did not feel "at home" under Turkish rule and as Christians they looked upon the Christians of the West and particularly upon the French as the leading lights in the progress of Western civilization.

"While the Catholic sects as a body," wrote Captain William Yale,[25] "asked for the independence of Greater Mount Lebanon from Syria under the guidance of France, they asked also that Syria be under a French Mandate. However, they wished Mount Lebanon to be separated from Syria whether or not France should be the Mandatory Power in Syria. A party among the Greek Orthodox joined in with the Catholics in their program for a Greater Mount Lebanon." According to Captain Yale's report, "The Christians of Mount Lebanon numbered approximately before the war 345,000 and of Greater Mount Lebanon 519,000. If the total population of Syria be placed at 2,500,000, this means that over one fifth demand that Greater Mount Lebanon should be constituted as a separate state with no political relations with the interior." On the other hand, the Muslims of Beirut, Tyre, Sidon, and other parts of the Lebanon, made it clear to Captain William Yale that they opposed the separation of Mount Lebanon from Syria, endorsed Syrian Independence under the Emīr Faiṣal and were "determined that the Young Arab Government shall dominate the coast and the Lebanon." But Yale adds: "Mount Lebanon is a distinctly Christian country and it is quite natural that the Christians have no desire to fall under the Moslem domination of the interior."[26]

25. U.S., National Archives and Records Service, Record Group 256, "A Report on Syria, Palestine and Mount Lebanon for the American Commissioners prepared by Captain William Yale, Technical Advisor to the American Section of the International Commission on Mandates in Turkey, July 26, 1919." U.S., National Archives, *General Records of the American Commission to Negotiate Peace, Paris 1918-1919*, p. 12.

26. "There are at hand no accurate statistics of the population of Mount Lebanon. Approximately before the war, the population of the Province of Lebanon was 75% Christian, 21% non-Christian (Druses, Sunnites, Shiites,

With such a background to the history of the Lebanon, it was distinctly a short-sighted policy and, indeed, a blunder on the part of Faiṣal and Lawrence — encouraged by some Muslim notables of Beirut — to send an Arab force and Shukrī Pasha to establish an "Arab Hashemite Government" in Beirut and the Lebanon in the name of the King of the Ḥejāz.[27] It aroused in the French not only distrust of Faiṣal but also grave misgivings with regard to British intentions in the Lebanon. In fact, the Emīr Sa'īd al-Jazā'erī was the first to send (on 30 September) a telegram[28] to the Maronite Patriarch Eliās Buṭrus Ḥuwaiyik asking him to establish an Arab Government in Mount Lebanon.[29] The Patriarch

etc.); of the Christian population 84% was Catholics and 16% non-Catholics. In Beirut approximately 30% was non-Christian, and of the Christian population 52% were Catholics. In the Saida district 51% were non-Christians (Sunnites and Shiites), and of the Christians 75% were Catholics. In the Tyre district 46% were non-Christians and of the Christians 58% were Catholics. These figures are but approximate, but they give in a general way the relative proportion of the strength of the various sects." Ibid.

27. Al-Raiḥānī, vol. 1, p. 298.

28. The Emīr sent another telegram "to the people of Lebanon" dated 1 October 1918. It was addressed to "the village heads in the Lebanon." The following is the literal translation into English of this telegram:

"To the people of the Lebanon:

Syria announces the independence of the Arabs. She has scattered the forces of the Turks. Let all people go to Be'abda to organize an independent government. Rise to action, O Syrian youths — you are Arabs above all. Hold celebrations. Our lord, the first Sultan of the Arabs, the Emir Faiṣal, has entered Damascus with great celebrations, such as Syria has never before witnessed. The Arab army filled the plains and the mountains. Fear not. Put down all opposition. Shed blood, but with justice. Protect the lives of people of other sects for they are our brothers in nationality. Long live independence. Long live the Sultan of the Arabs. Let us know what your wishes are.

Your Wakeel el-Sultan and President of the Arab government:

The Emir Said el-Hassan el-Jazā'erī."

It is to be noted that Faiṣal had not yet entered Damascus on 1 October but the author of the above-mentioned telegram was obviously anticipating his entry and, consequently, reported it as if it had already taken place!

I am indebted, for a copy of the above-mentioned document, to Professor Leslie W. Leavitt, former President of International College, American University of Beirut.

29. For the original Arabic text of the telegram, see Ibrāhīm Ḥarfūsh, *Dalā'il al-'Ināyat al-Samadāniyyah* [Proofs of Divine Assistance], p. 583.

It must be stated in all fairness that the majority of the Druzes and the Greek orthodox had pro-British sympathies. Both France and Great Britain did not answer but waited anxiously for further developments. An almost similar telegram had been sent to 'Umar al-Dā'ūq, the Mayor of Beirut and as noted earlier, the latter formed an Arab Government in Beirut on 1 October, a day after Isma'īl Haqqī Bey, Wali of Beirut, had left the city and had handed the Government over to al-Dā'ūq.[30] Meanwhile the Muteṣarrif of the Lebanon, Mumtāz Bey, before his departure had entrusted the Government of the Mountain to Ḥabīb Fayyāḍ, the Mayor of Be'abda,

Be'abda was then the seat of the Lebanese Government. The officials of that Government elected Mālik Shehāb and 'Adil Arslān to be temporarily at the Head of a Provisional Government for the Lebanon. When the latter informed the Maronite Patriarch of the formation of such a Government, the Patriarch cabled Mālik Shehāb to carry on the Government of Lebanon "with firmness and wisdom" and to advise the people of the Mountain, through the local administrators, to refrain from communicating with anyone concerning the affairs and the future of the country until such time when it would be possible for them and the Patriarch to exchange views on those matters.[31] The Patriarch's telegram is dated 5 October 1918. By this time, Shukrī Pasha had arrived from Damascus, claiming that he had been appointed as the new "Wali of Beirut" by King Ḥusain of the Ḥejāz. Arab Ḥejāzi flags were already flying from the principal Government buildings in Beirut. After much negotiation with some Muslim notables in that city, Shukrī Pasha went to Be'abda and there in an official ceremony on 7 October appointed Ḥabīb Pasha al-Sa'd, in the name of King Ḥusain, as Head of the new Government of Lebanon which comprised the members of the previous Administrative Council who were now confirmed in office.[32] The Arab flag was

have been accused of spending vast sums of money in Syria and the Lebanon trying to gain to their side as many of those in the opposite camp as possible. See Iskandar Ryāshī, *Qabl wa Ba'd* [Before and After] (Beirut 1953), pp. 19-24; and Ḥarfūsh, p. 650.

30. See p. 28, above.

31. Ḥarfūsh, p. 584.

32. Ibrahīm Bey al-Aswad, *Tanwīr al-Adhān fī Ta'rīkh Lubnān* [vol. 3], p. 99. Ibrahīm Bey uses incorrect dates for the above-mentioned events. After the ceremony in Be'abda, Ibrahīm Bey, who was present, showed great interest in seeing the text of King Ḥusain's decree appointing Ḥabīb Pasha as

hoisted on the Serai at Be'abda. During that ceremony Ḥabīb Pasha swore allegiance to Faiṣal's Arab Government in Damascus. Later, he wrote to the Patriarch informing him of what had taken place and signed this letter: "Governor General of the Lebanon."[33] But the situation was in a state of constant change. A day before the "coup de théâtre" in Be'abda which had shocked the Maronites of Mount Lebanon, ships of the French navy, under Vice-Admiral Varney, coming from Port Sa'īd had entered the harbor of Beirut. The British arrived two days later, having marched up the coast from Haifa. On 8 October the Seventh Division reached Beirut, "to be received with acclamation by the inhabitants, who handed over about six hundred Turks to the British."[34] On the same day British Intelligence officers coming from Damascus arrived in Beirut and informed Shukrī Pasha that his mission was over. "He indignantly protested but eventually retired to his hotel." During the night, all Arab flags were removed.[35] "General [Edward] Bulfin established his headquarters at the principal hotel, the Deutscherhof, the same day. French military governors were appointed at Beirut, Sidon, and Tyre. Colonel de Piépape, commander of the D.F.P.S. ("Le Détachement Français de Palestine et de Syrie") being given this important position in Beirut."[36]

Governor of Lebanon. Shukrī Pasha told him that he had forgotten that document in his brief case in Beirut! "Then it became clear to me," adds Ibrahīm Bey "that the appointment had been arranged in Beirut."

33. Ḥarfūsh, p. 585.

34. Cyril Falls, p. 603. Dr. Bayard Dodge, the late President of the American University of Beirut, wrote in a letter from Beirut, dated 20 October 1918: "the army which has occupied and passed through Beirut has been most interesting. Countless British cavalry and automobiles, with even a greater number of Egyptian camel drivers, Indians of all types from the hill dwellers of the North to the Malayans of the Indies... all in one tremendous chase after the Turks and Germans who have evaporated like the mist...." — Bayard Dodge Papers, Archives of the American University of Beirut.

35. See Beckles Willson, "Our Amazing Syrian Adventure," and *Documents* 1:4, p. 412. See also Pichon, *Sur la Route des Indes*, pp. 157-158.

36. Cyril Falls, p. 604.

On the occasion of the evacuation of Beirut by the Sharifian forces, General Allenby gave certain "assurances" to the Emīr Faiṣal. On 17 October, Allenby reported to His Majesty's Government the terms of those "assurances" in the following communication:

"I gave the Emir Faisal an official assurance that whatever measures might

When Syria and the Lebanon were occupied by the Allied armies they had not been independent countries but part of the Ottoman Empire. Therefore, they were technically "occupied enemy territory" pending the signing of a peace treaty with Turkey, and indeed they were thus considered. On 23 October, General Allenby reported to the War Office that he had divided into three administrative areas the "enemy territory" in Syria and Palestine already in his hands or "likely to be occupied in the near future."[37] These areas were to be known as Occupied Enemy Territory South (O.E.T.S.), Occupied Enemy Territory North (O.E.T.N.), and Occupied Enemy Territory East (O.E.T.E.). The O.E.T.N. comprised the "Blue Zone" of the Sykes-Picot Agreement, extending from north of Acre to Alexandretta, and was to be administered by Colonel de Piépape. The O.E.T.E. which included portions of "Zone A" in which Faiṣal had already established his Arab Government in Damascus and of "zone B" came under the control of the British. For all the Zones, as long as the War lasted, supreme authority was vested in the Commander-in-Chief, General Allenby.

The French Government on the other hand had already appointed — on 9 April 1917 — M. Georges-Picot as their "Haut Commissaire en Palestine et Syrie." As M. Georges-Picot had not yet arrived Captain Coulondre was acting as his representative in Beirut. The French, already embittered by what they considered to be the anti-French attitude of British military and political officers in Damascus, took immediate steps to strengthen their position in the Lebanon. On 23 October, Coulondre visited officially the Maronite Patriarch in Bkerkī and discussed with him the future government of the Lebanon. It was agreed to leave

be taken during the period of military administration they were purely provisional and could not be allowed to prejudice the final settlement by the peace conference at which no doubt the Arabs would have a representative. I added that the instructions to the military governors would preclude their mixing in political affairs, and that I should remove them if I found any of them contravening these orders. I reminded the Emir Faisal that the Allies were in honour bound to endeavour to reach a settlement in accordance with the wishes of the peoples concerned, and urged him to place his trust wholeheartedly in their good faith."

Great Britain, Cmd. 5964 Miscellaneous No. 4 (1939): *Statements made on behalf of His Majesty's Government during the year 1918 in regard to the Future Status of certain parts of the Ottoman Empire*, pp. 6-7.

37. Cyril Falls, p. 607.

for the time being its administration in the hands of its Administrative Council and as Governor, to appoint temporarily a French Officer.[38] Two days later, this agreement was made public. On 25 October, another official ceremony took place in Be'abda. The members of the Lebanese Administrative Council with Ḥabīb Pasha al-Sa'd at its head, together with many Maronite notables received with great enthusiasm their new guests of honor, Colonel de Piépape and Captain Coulondre. But they were more than "guests" — they had come into their own "inheritance," the former as French Military Governor of O.E.T.N. which included all of the Lebanon and the latter as representative of the French Republic, "the deliverer of oppressed peoples." They had also come to officially undo the work of Shukrī Pasha — which, actually, neither they nor the Maronites had ever recognized — and to make it clear to the Lebanese and the Syrians and to all the Arabs beyond Syria that it was France who was Master in the Lebanon and not Faiṣal and his Arab Government.[39] The Military Governor in a warm and friendly speech praised Ḥabīb Pasha al-Sa'd and announced that he as Governor was now reinstating in office the Lebanese Administrative Council under the Presidency of Ḥabīb Pasha.[40] This was the same Ḥabīb Pasha who had been serving in that capacity less than a month before under the Turks and who not more than eighteen days earlier had sworn allegiance to Faiṣal's Arab Government in Damascus.[41]

Meanwhile, the British Army together with the Arab forces of Faiṣal commanded by Nūrī Pasha al-Sa'īd had been pursuing

38. Ḥarfūsh, p. 587.

39. A French monument at the Dog River, about 9 miles north of Beirut, has the following inscription on it: "Aux Libérateurs de la Syrie et du Liban — A la Gloire de l'Armée Française du Levant et de la Division Navale de Syrie."

40. This was actually in accordance with instructions contained in "G.H.Q. telegram No. O.A.M. 98 of October 22, 1918." In practice, the Administrative Council received its orders from and was responsible to the French Senior Military Administrator of the Lebanon. *Documents* 1:4, 1919, p. 293.

For a detailed account of this ceremony at Be'abda, see *Lisān al-Ḥāl* (Beirut), no. 7660/12 (26 October 1918), p. 2.

41. This, in a way, was a tribute to the outstanding position of leadership and great influence which Ḥabīb Pasha enjoyed in Mount Lebanon and which the Turkish, Arab. and French Governments recognized. He remained a staunch Maronite throughout his long career of service to the Lebanon.

the remnants of the Turkish Fourth Army northwards ever since the fall of Damascus. By 25 October Ḥoms, Ḥama, and Aleppo had fallen into Anglo-Arab hands. Five days later came the news of the armistice with Turkey.[42] By one of those striking ironies of history the final surrender of the Turkish army took place on the very plain of Marj Dābiq where almost exactly four hundred years earlier troops of Sultan Selīm won the decisive victory which had made the Ottomans masters of Syria. The armistice discussions with Turkey began on 26 October on board the British battleship H.M.S. *Agamemnon* in the harbor of Mudros at Lemnos in the Aegean Sea. After four days of "arduous and at times very painful discussion," the Armistice was signed at 9:40 p.m. on 30 October,[43] by Sir S. A. Gough-Calthorpe, the British Commander-in-Chief in the Mediterranean "acting under authority from the British Government, in agreement with their Allies." The 25th and last article of the Armistice read: "Hostilities between the Allies and Turkey shall cease from noon, local time, on Thursday, 31st October 1918." The only reference to "Syria" was in Article 16 which stipulated "the surrender of all garrisons in Hejaz, Assir, Yemen, Syria and Mesopotamia to the nearest Allied Commander."[44]

42. "In less than six weeks, Allenby's army had captured 75,000 prisoners and 360 guns, and had moved its front forward 350 miles." — Viscount Wavell, *Allenby, Soldier and Statesman* (London, 1946), p. 245.

43. Cyril Falls, Part 2, p. 620.

44. It is idle to deny that there was suspicion and rivalry between the British and French Governments in the Middle Eastern theatre of the War, simply because they were "Allies" and also because they had "settled" their differences by each secretly agreeing with the other upon its share in the "Sick Man's" heritage. The French were already vexed and irritated by British activities whether open or secret, in the Near East, particularly in Syria, and when the time came for the signing of Armistice with Turkey, they found themselves excluded by certain steps which the British Government has taken deliberately for that purpose. The negotiations for the Bulgarian Armistice signed on 29 September 1918, had been conducted entirely by the French. The terms were laid down by General Franchet d'Espéry who was Commander-in-Chief of Allied Forces in the Balkans. But the British Government were determined that the Armistice with Turkey should be the work of their representative. Consequently, when they realized that Turkey was on the point of surrender, they directed Sir S.A. Gough-Calthorpe, the British Commander-in-Chief in the Mediterranean to go to Mudros "where he was senior to the French Commander, Vice-Admiral Amet." They were equally determined that "when the Allied Fleet entered the Black Sea, it should be under the command of a British Admiral." Ibid., pp. 619-620.

The day of reckoning had at last dawned. The Ottoman Empire, which had once been the terror of Christendom in Europe over a long life of more than six hundred years, had finally collapsed in the greatest war that history had ever known. The German Empire built by Bismarck and the Kaiser, with all its might and pride was, after nearly four years of carnage of unprecedented magnitude and ferocity, about to be undone. The First World War was coming to an end. The victorious nations had now to face suddenly their greatest problem, the problem of building peace and security in the world.

This rivalry for power and prestige and this suspicion of motives and intentions not only embittered the relations of the two Powers during the next twenty-five years in the Middle East but actually weakened considerably their position in that area.

CHAPTER THREE

FAISAL, GREAT BRITAIN, AND FRANCE

"*He* ("*a slave:.. with silver-hilted sword in hand*") *led me to an inner court, on whose further side, framed between the uprights of a black doorway, stood a white figure waiting tensely for me. I felt at first glance that this was the man I had come to Arabia to seek — the leader who would bring the Arab Revolt to full glory. Feiṣal looked very tall and pillar-like, very slender, in his long white silk robes and his brown head-cloth bound with a brilliant scarlet and gold cord....*"

T. E. Lawrence, *Seven Pillars of Wisdom.*

"*On doit reconnaître qu'il y a en France beaucoup d'hommes qui n'ont ni la compréhension, ni l'équité, de l'Émir Faiçal.*"

Général Edmond Brémond, *Le Hedjaz dans la Guerre Mondiale.*

THE FIRST QUESTION THAT THE ARABS asked themselves when they learned of the Armistice with Turkey was: When would Great Britain carry out her wartime pledges and commitments? Had not General Sir Edmund Allenby given Faiṣal "an official assurance that whatever measures might be taken during the period of military administration they were surely provisional and could not be allowed to prejudice the final settlement by the peace conference, at which no doubt the Arabs would have a representative"? General Allenby in that same communication had "reminded the Amir Faisal that the Allies were in honour bound to endeavour to reach a settlement in accordance with the wishes of the peoples concerned and urged him to place his trust wholeheartedly in their good faith."[1] And what of the peace and the "Principles" of President Wilson with which the Arab leaders were by now familiar? In his Address to the Senate on 22 January 1917, the American President had said:

> No peace can last, or ought to last, which does not recognize and accept the principle that governments derive all their just powers from the consent of the governed, and that no right

1. See Chap. 1, n. 55.

> exists anywhere to hand peoples about from sovereignty to sovereignty as if they were property. . . . I am proposing government by the consent of the governed. . . .[2]

In addition to his Fourteen Points of 18 January 1918, President Wilson had told Congress on 11 February 1918:

> There shall be no annexations, no contributions, no punitive damage. . . . Self-determination is not a mere phrase. It is an imperative principle of action which statesmen will henceforth ignore at their peril. . . . Every territorial settlement involved in this war must be made in the interest and for the benefit of the populations concerned, and not as a part of any mere adjustment or compromise of claims amongst rival States.[3]

But the facts in themselves were very disturbing. At the time of Turkey's collapse Great Britain and to some extent France were in full possession and control of the Arab Near East. This crucial fact alone was perhaps more important than all the commitments and pledges given during the War. For the first time since the Crusades, Jerusalem and the whole coast of what was then known as "Syria" were once more occupied by foreign Christian forces, while Christian Powers had in their hands the destiny of the twin historic capitals of the once vast and mighty Muslim Empire: Damascus of Umayyad fame, and Baghdad of Abbasid grandeur.

When the news of the Armistice with Turkey became known, the Arabs were jubilant that their countries had been liberated from the horrors of war. But, politically, enough had happened between 1 and 3 October to fill them with misgivings and suspicion about the real intentions of Great Britain and France and with great anxiety about the future of their lands. They were face to face with a military and political West which occupied their countries. What guarantee was there that they were going to achieve their national hopes and aspirations? Hence it must have been with such Arab fears and suspicions in their minds that the "Policy makers" in Britain and France decided to issue early in

2. U.S., Department of State, *Papers Relating to the Foreign Relations of the United States, 1917, Supplement 1: The World War*, pp. 27 and 29.

3. John Maynard Keynes, *The Economic Consequences of the Peace* (London, 1919), pp. 57-58
See also the 12th of President Wilson's Fourteen Points of 8 January 1918.

November 1918 the now famous "Anglo-French Declaration." Indeed, Lloyd George himself has written that this joint Declaration was issued "in order to allay Arab susceptibilities."[4]

On 4 November, the French text of the Anglo-French Declaration was telegraphed to Sir Reginald Wingate, High Commissioner in Egypt. Four days later, it was published simultaneously in London, Paris, New York, and Cairo. The following is the English text as read in the House of Commons on 25 July 1921:

> The object aimed at by France and Great Britain in prosecuting in the East the war let loose by the ambition of Germany is the complete and definite emancipation of the peoples so long oppressed by the Turks and the establishment of national governments and administrations deriving their authority from the initiative and free choice of the indigenous populations.
>
> In order to carry out these intentions, France and Great Britain are at one in encouraging and assisting the establishment of indigenous Governments and administrations in Syria and Mesopotamia, now liberated by the Allies, and in the territories the liberation of which they are engaged in securing, and recognizing as soon as they are actually established.
>
> Far from wishing to impose on the populations of these regions any particular institutions, they are only concerned to ensure by their support and adequate assistance the regular working of Governments and administrations freely chosen by the populations themselves. To secure impartial and equal justice for all, to facilitate the economic development of the country by inspiring and encouraging local initiative, to favour the diffusion of education, to put an end to dissensions that have too long been taken advantage of by Turkish policy, such is the policy which the two Allied Governments uphold in the liberated territories.[5]

Sir Arnold Wilson wrote that on 8 November when the Declaration was published in London, Paris, New York, and Cairo, the India Office telegraphed him the French text *en clair*, "with instructions to give it the widest possible publicity." Sir Arnold adds: "This document, which derived from the doctrinairian genius

4. Lloyd George, *The Truth About Peace Treaties*, vol. 2, p. 1035.

5. Great Britain, *Parliamentary Debates, House of Commons, Fifth Series*, vol. 145, col. 36.

of President Wilson, profoundly modified the political outlook; among Syrians and Arabs it was regarded, rightly or wrongly, as superseding or at least qualifying the provisions of the Sykes-Picot Agreement. . . .[6]

On 11 November, Armistice Day, the Emīr Faiṣal was visiting the largest town in Syria and the most northerly — Aleppo. With its proximity to Turkish Anatolia and with its large volume of trade going north, Aleppo had always been known to have some pro-Turkish sympathies. In delivering an important speech on that day to the notables and the representatives of various communities in that town, Faiṣal began by painting a dark picture of Turkish misgovernment and oppression in Arab lands. The Turks also had not been loyal to Islam and its principles; hence the Arab Revolt against the Turks, led by his father, after agreement with the Allies. The Revolt was not due to the personal ambitions of the Sharif of Mecca nor was it an act of treason — "selling the Arab lands to the Westerners" — as the Turkish propaganda had alleged. Faiṣal then thanked warmly the Allied Governments, "particularly England and France," for their great help and support. At this point he read an Arabic translation of the Anglo-French Declaration which he said he had received on 8 November. Faiṣal called it "one of the great documents of history" which reflected "noble and humanitarian sentiments." All that the Arabs had to do now was to establish an orderly, well organized, just, and strong government. He said that their new political and

6. Wilson, *Mesopotamia, 1917-1920*, pp. 102-103.

Lloyd George wrote that the Anglo-French Declaration was "agreed upon on November 7th, 1918." As it was made public the next day, on the 8th, it has come to be associated almost always with that date. But actually the writer has definite evidence — and this may be significant of much — that the said document was already drafted in French by 30 *October*. It was then marked "Confidential." On 4 November, the text of that declaration "as finally agreed upon" was sent telegraphically to General Wingate with the request that it be "translated into Arabic at once and communicated to King Hussein and given widest possible circulation in native press." On the 6th, the Foreign office cabled Wingate again asking to postpone its publication until 8 November, at the request of the French Government. It is one of the little mysteries in the midst of greater mysteries, or perhaps confusions and uncertainties of that period, that the Declaration did not surface earlier. Was there possibly some hesitation, after it was drafted and made ready, on the part of one or both of its authors, to publish it at all? Private Papers of General Sir Reginald Wingate.

national life was still in its infancy. The mass of the people still did not understand the meaning of nationalism and political independence. Everything was still at its beginning. New laws had to be made to fit the new conditions and the new spirit of the times. Meanwhile, it was most important to keep law and order by obeying and serving the present Government, and every effort had to be made to develop and spread education in the country. The progress and enlightenment of the country depended upon sound education. Faiṣal's greatest appeal in his speech was to Arab unity, emphasizing the national rather than the religious aspect of unity. He was first and foremost an Arab before being anything else. The Arabs were all Arabs before being Muslim, Christian, or Jew. All religions taught justice and the brotherhood of man. Hence anyone who tried to sow dissension between Muslim, Christian, and Jew was not a true Arab. And as far as he was concerned, justice and justice alone was his only consideration, for in his view all were equal before the law.[7]

While Faiṣal was hoping to rally all the Arabs in Syria and the Lebanon around the new Arab Government in Damascus by appealing to them to unite through a new secular force, that of Arab nationalism, and thus reassure the Lebanese who might feel uncomfortable again as a religious minority in a preponderantly Muslim union. France was becoming more and more suspicious of British moves in Syria and of the anti-French policy of Faiṣal himself. Already on 6 November, M. Georges-Picot had landed in Beirut as "Haut-Commissaire de la République Française en Syrie et en Arménie." A few days earlier, during the course of a conversation concerning the Lebanon, Faiṣal had told Captain Mercier, the French liaison officer, that during the War a general reservation

7. For the Arabic text of Faiṣal's speech in Aleppo, see Sāṭiʿ al-Ḥuṣrī, pp. 195-201.

"... L'autorité de l'Émir Fayçal qui apparut à la fois comme le symbole et l'instrument de l'éviction de la France... Le gouvernement de l'Émir devenait le centre d'un mouvement nationaliste anti-français. La presse de Damas ne cessait, sous le régime de la censure, de vilipender la France." See M.R. de Caix, "La France dans le Levant — La Syrie," in Hanotaux and Martineau, *Histoire des Colonies françaises et l'expansion de la France dans le monde*, vol. 3 (Paris, 1931), pp. 493-494.

had been made concerning the coasts of Syria.[8] "England, France and I," Faiṣal is reported to have said, "are now like merchants in front of a merchandise which has no owner. Is it not logical that each one of us should try to appropriate it before the others?"[9] Hence it was that on 14 November, three days after Faiṣal had delivered in Aleppo his most important speech since the establishment of his Arab Government in Damascus, Georges-Picot cabled the French Government from Beirut that the only way to save France's position in Syria from being ruined was to send twenty thousand French troops, and ask England to leave to France the responsibility of organizing that country. Otherwise, the continued presence of the British army in that country would be considered as an encouragement to those who were hostile to France.[10]

From Aleppo, the Emīr continued his tour of the Syrian towns and visited Tripoli where he was the subject of a very warm welcome. He then went to Beirut where he arrived on Saturday afternoon, 16 November, accompanied among others by General Nūrī Pasha al-Sa'īd, Dr. Aḥmad Qādrī (his private physician), Taḥsīn Bey Qādrī, and Nasīb al-Bakrī.[11] Under the circumstances, it was natural that Beirut should receive Faiṣal with mixed feelings. The Muslims were jubilant and received him with great enthusiasm. He was given a great ovation. His carriage was stopped, the horses unharnessed, and young Muslims tied themselves to it and pulled it through the streets of the town, while hundreds of Muslim youths were shouting an old slogan used in Turkish days to express loyalty to the Sultan: "We will not have anyone (to rule us) except the Sultan,"[12] the "Sultan" in this case being, of course, Faiṣal.

8. A reference to the Correspondence between Sir Henry McMahon and the Sharīf of Mecca, particularly to McMahon's letter of 24 October 1915.

9. Brémond, pp. 307-308.

10. Ibid.; for the French text of the telegram, see. p. 308.

11. See *Lisān al-Ḥāl*, 18 November 1918.

Faiṣal had already complained to Major Cornwallis, then British liaison officer in Damascus that "agents of Captain Mercier" had summoned the "chief sheikhs of the Hawran Druses" and informed them that "a French protectorate will be shortly established here and that French Forces will arrive in a few days...." *The Wingate Papers*, Telegram of Cornwallis, No. C 198, of 2 November 1918.

12. The exact Arabic words were: "*Lā narḍā illa as-Sulṭān.*" For an eye-witness account, see *Beirut*, no. 2619, 5 October 1946.

The Christians, particularly the Maronites, were suspicious of Faiṣal's visit and considered it as part of his unceasing efforts to join the Lebanon with Syria.[13] The French were annoyed with the visit and almost ignored it. They attributed it to a British move calculated to encourage the pro-British and pro-Faiṣal elements in the Lebanon. Indeed, Faiṣal was the guest of General Sir Edward Bulfin, the British Commander of the 21st Army Corps, who gave an official dinner in honor of "His Royal Highness, the Emīr Feysal, Commander-in-Chief of the Arab Forces."[14]

On 20 November Faiṣal was back in Damascus, only to return a day later to Beirut to go straight on board the British cruiser H.M.S. *Gloucester* and leave for England. The invitation to visit Europe had come originally from the British Government — possibly on Lawrence's advice — and was sent to King Ḥusain. Faiṣal was to attend the Versailles Peace Conference as the representative of his father. It was while on the above-mentioned visit to Aleppo that he had received a telegram from King Ḥusain asking him to proceed forthwith to England and to France.[15] When the French Government learned that the Emīr was to land in Marseilles on 26 November they were irritated that King Ḥussain had not informed them officially of his son's visit. Upon instructions from Paris, Commandant Cousse, then in Jeddah, told King Ḥusain in gentle protest that while the Emīr Faiṣal would be received in France with the honor due to the son of a sovereign who was an ally and a friend of France, his Government was astonished that its representative, the French High Commissioner in Syria, had not been informed of this visit so that he might make the necessary arrangements for the Emīr's reception in Paris. Thus, it would be impossible to consider the Emīr in charge of any official mission in France, as the Government was uninformed about such a mission.[16]

When Faiṣal and his party landed in Marseilles on 26 November, the French Government delegated M. Bertrand and Colonel

13. Ibrāhīm Ḥarfūsh, p. 589.
14. Brémond, p. 308-309.
15. Erskine, *King Faisal of Iraq*, p. 97.
16. Brémond, p. 309.

Brémond[17] to receive him and act as his hosts during his stay in France. The Emīr was to be the guest of the French Government during that time. The following were among the instructions which Colonel Brémond received from M. Jean Gout, the Under-Secretary for Asia at the Ministry of Foreign Affairs:

> Treat the Emir Faisal as if he were a General and a distinguished person but without any diplomatic standing. Tell him that he has been badly advised. He should have talked to M. Georges-Picot [before coming here]. Tell him that the British Government does not do everything and should not have advised him to come here without consulting the French Government. Arrange matters in such a way as not to bring him to Paris without further instructions. . . . Take him round to see anything you like. Take him to General Gouraud who is with the IVth Army in Strasbourg and who will decorate the Emir with the insignia of the Order of "Grand-Officer". . . . With Lawrence, one must make things very clear and show him that he is on the wrong path. If he comes here as a British Colonel, in British uniform, we shall welcome him. But we shall not accept him if he comes as an Arab and remains disguised as such. . . .[18]

Faiṣal was accordingly taken round to Lyon, Belfort, Than, Colmar, and Strasbourg, from 26 November to 3 December without ever mentioning to him the date of his visit to Paris. On 3 December, the Emīr sent for Colonel Brémond and asked him very frankly to tell him whether the French Government did not really want him to go to Paris, for he did not want to lose any more time and preferred to return to Damascus. The following day Brémond received a telegram from Paris informing him that the President of the Republic would receive Faiṣal on the 7th at

17. M. Bertrand was the retired French Consul and later Minister at Jeddah in Arabia and Colonel Brémond, as Head of the French Mission in Arabia during the War, was the French counterpart of Colonel Lawrence.

18. Brémond, pp. 310-311.
When two days after his arrival Faiṣal learned of the attitude of the French Government towards Lawrence, he immediately sent for Lawrence (who was already in Faiṣal's company since the latter had landed in Marseilles) and asked him to leave that same evening. According to Brémond, Lawrence who was in his "étrange costume oriental blanc," went to M. Bertrand and told him: "You are expelling me. I shall leave this evening." Later, he returned to the French Government his Croix de Guerre. Brémond, p. 314.

5:00 p.m. Faiṣal was pleased. On the 5th, he was decorated with the "Croix de la Légion d'Honneur" as "Grand-Officer" during an impressive military ceremony. Then, after travelling to Metz and Verdun and visiting the battlefields there, Faiṣal finally arrived in Paris on the 7th, in the special railway coach which the Kaiser had used when travelling in Alsace, and was received at the Élysée by President Poincaré.[19] On the 9th there was a reception "pour rencontrer l'Émir Feysal" [20] at the Ministry of Foreign Affairs and that same evening Faiṣal and his party left Boulogne by ship for London.

Nearly fifteen years later, in 1933, the Emīr Faiṣal, then King of Iraq, gave his own version of that first visit to France. Mrs. Erskine, who had an interview with King Faiṣal in Baghdad, has reported in a résumé of her interview that the King told her:

> When I was in Aleppo in 1918, soon after the declaration of the Armistice, I received a telegram from my father asking me to represent him at the Peace Conference.
>
> On arrival at Marseilles, I found myself confronted by a sudden and disconcerting change of policy.[21] The French authorities met me with statements which can be summed up as follows: — "France has no information concerning the official mission with which you are charged at Versailles; consequently, it is undesirable for you to continue your journey to Paris."
>
> In order to save appearances, I was invited to visit the Western

19. Ibid., pp, 316-317. Professor Temperley must have inadvertently twisted his facts when he wrote that Faiṣal was received by President Poincaré "on the 6th December and subsequently shown over the French front . . . " (Temperley, vol. 6, p. 142). All that Poincaré has recorded in his diary about this meeting is the following: "L'Émir Feyçal, jeune, très brun, beaux yeux noirs, vient avec Ben Gabrit comme interprète. Échange de politesses banales, puisque aussi bien, je ne puis toucher au fond des choses." Poincaré, *Au Service de la France*, vol. 10, p. 435.

20. Brémond, who accompanied Faiṣal during his stay in France and who records the above-mentioned facts, remarks that the French used the British spelling of the word "Feysal" which, he adds, did not correspond to either the Arabic or the French pronounciation of that word.

21. It is difficult to know what Faiṣal meant when he said this. There was actually no change in policy unless Faiṣal had been misled by what he had been told before he landed in France. The French had been consistent all along in their policy towards Syria and their attitude towards Faiṣal.

front. Ten days later, I was able to go to Paris and thence to London, afterwards returning to Versailles.[22]

While Faiṣal was being shown over the muddy and shell-torn battlefields on the Western front, a most important meeting was taking place in London between Lloyd George and Clemenceau with far reaching consequences for Syria and the future of the Emīr himself. On 1 December, Marshal Ferdinand Foch, M. Georges Clemenceau, Signor Vittorio Emanuele Orlando, the Prime Minister of Italy, and Baron Sidney (Georgio) Sonnino, the Italian Minister of Foreign Affairs, arrived by the same train at Charing Cross Station in London. They were received at the Station by Lloyd George and many Cabinet members in the midst of an "extraordinary demonstration of popular enthusiasm."[23] According to the *Times*, "the chief business of Mr. Clemenceau and Marshal Foch during their stay in London will be to prepare, in consultation with allied statesmen, for the Inter-Allied Peace Preliminaries Conference which will presently meet in Paris... and to agree before hand upon the main lines of their peace policy."[24] There were several meetings at 10 Downing Street between 1 and 4 December, the day on which Marshal Foch and M. Clemenceau left by train for Paris. Some time during those days a most momentous meeting took place between Lloyd George and M. Clemenceau, in great privacy, during which the terms of the Sykes-Picot Agreement were modified. We shall probably never know exactly what passed at that meeting between the two statesmen, as their new "arrangement" was a "verbal agreement."[25] It is not possible to tell at what time the British Government started having its own regrets about the Sykes-Picot Agreement and decided to modify it at the earliest opportunity that presented itself. It appears now that on the day the Armistice with Turkey was signed, 30 October 1918, there was a meeting between

22. Erskine, p. 97.

23. *Times* (London), 2 December 1918, p. 9, col. 4.

24. Ibid. It is to be noted that the Americans were absent from this meeting of "allied statesmen" in London and that President Wilson had not yet arrived in Europe.

25. *Documents*, 1:4, p. 251. M. André Tardieu, *La Paix* (Paris, 1921), p. 117, refers to this meeting in London as "les entretiens privés de décembre."

Lloyd George and Colonel House who was acting as President Wilson's Special Representative.[26] During their conversation, "the British Premier extended feelers along the general lines of the Sykes-Picot Agreement, but in two areas he betrayed a crucial deflection from those war-time commitments to France about the future peace settlement." Britain was to assume a protectorate over Mesopotamia and "perhaps" Palestine. A month later the American Embassy in London received from the Foreign Office, unofficially, "an outline of the British Peace Plan for the Near East": Great Britain in Mesopotamia; America in Palestine, Constantinople and the Straits; France "probably" in Syria. All this meant a drastic modification, if not an actual scuttling, of the Sykes-Picot Agreement. Indeed, the Italian documents in the Archives of the Italian Ministry of Foreign Affairs seem to reveal that on 13 June 1918, over three and a half months before Lloyd George and Colonel House had their conversation, Mark Sykes had made an allusion to a possible American protectorate over Palestine in an informal conversation which he had with Marquis Imperiali, the Italian Ambassador in London.[27] Sykes must have known that the British Foreign Office was already seeking a major alternative to the provisions of the Sykes-Picot Agreement, partly because that Agreement was now considered to be unsatisfactory to the interests of Great Britain in the Middle East and partly to appease President Wilson and the United States Government, whose policy was opposed to all secret treaties and agreements, which were "follies of secrecy and blind self-interest."[28] He told Imperiali that "the secret treaty system of zones of influence would have to be refurbished in the light of new circumstances, especially the prestige of Wilson." Hence "it was thought that making America an integral part of a protectorate system might forestall Wilson's objections to zones of influence for the British and the French."[29] There is no evidence that the French Govern-

26. Frank E. Manuel, *The Realities of American-Palestine Relations*, pp. 215-216.

27. See Frank E. Manuel, "The Palestine Question in Italian Diplomacy, 1917-1920," *The Journal of Modern History*, vol. 27, no. 3 (September 1955), p. 273.

28. Edward Mandell House, *What Really Happened at Paris: The Story of the Peace Conference, 1918-1919*, p. 186.

29. Manuel, "The Palestine Question in Italian Diplomacy, 1917-1920," p. 273.

ment had been informed of any British proposition for an American protectorate over Palestine.[30] But when Lloyd George and Clemenceau met in London in the early days of December, as already stated, Clemenceau was asked to transfer both Mosul and Palestine to the British share of what they had planned to inherit from the Asiatic possessions of the "Sick Man (now dead) of Europe." Lloyd George himself has stated that "the British authorities were convinced that in at least two respects (Mosul and Palestine), amendment (to the Sykes-Picot Agreement) was essential" and in his own words has given the following version of what happened in London:

> When Clemenceau came to London after the War I drove with him to the French Embassy. . . . After we reached the Embassy he asked me what it was that I specially wanted from the French. I instantly replied that I wanted Mosul attached to Irak, and Palestine from Dan to Beersheba under British Control. Without any hesitation he agreed. . . .[31]

Nevertheless, Clemenceau's acceptance of the British Prime Minister's request was not as simple as the latter makes it appear. Professor Temperley, who admitted in 1920 that "the story is not fully known,"[32] wrote that according to André Tardieu, Clemenceau accepted on three conditions: (1) France to obtain some share in the oil of Mosul by modification of the agreement of May 1916; (2) full support of France against American objections; (3) if the Mandate system prevailed — Damascus and Aleppo, Alexandretta and Beirut were to be under one Mandate (the French).[33] It seems also that Clemenceau asked for certain concessions on the left bank of the Rhine.[34]

30. It should be remembered that, originally, in the Sykes-Picot Agreement, Palestine, with the exception of the ports of Haifa and Acre which were to be accorded to Great Britain, was the "Brown Area" in which "there shall be established an international administration. . . . "

31. Lloyd George, *The Truth About the Peace Treaties*, vol. 11, p. 1038.

32. Thirty-two years later, when the British Government published certain documents in Volume 4 of the First Series of *Documents on British Foreign Policy* to illustrate "the policy of His Majesty's Government in regard to Syria and Palestine," after the First World War, no document was included on the above mentioned episode.

33. Temperley, vol. 6, p. 182.

34. Henri Béranger, "Mosul," in *Dictionnaire Diplomatique*, vol. 2, p. 166.

Actually, because of the rising tension between the two Governments concerning the situation in Syria, what Clemenceau was most anxious to obtain from Lloyd George was a *confirmation* of the French rights in Syria and Cilicia as already laid down in the Sykes-Picot Agreement.[35] This confirmation was obtained at a price: Mosul and Palestine. Five months later at a Meeting of the Council of Four held at the Quai d'Orsay in Paris on 21 May 1919 Lloyd George reiterated the fact that on the occasion of the London visit he had promised Syria to France provided that Clemenceau gave up Mosul because Mosul was "in the same watershed as Mesopotamia" and "should form part of that country and go to Great Britain"[36]. Clemenceau's protest about losing Mosul[37] and his rejoinder that France had already had "a definite agreement before as to Syria" did not seem to have impressed Lloyd George.

However, as far as British interests were concerned, the British gained far more than the French did. France got "again" what she already had been promised by Britain, while the latter obtained

35. At a Meeting of the Big Four held at the Quai d'Orsay in Paris, on 20 March 1919, the French Minister of Foreign Affairs said: "As the difficulties between the two Governments continued, and as the French Government particularly did not wish them to reach a point where ultimate agreement would be compromised, the President of the Council, on his visit to London in December 1918, had asked Mr. Lloyd George to confirm the agreement between the two countries. Mr. Lloyd George had replied that he saw no difficulty about the rights of France in Syria and Cilicia, but he made demands for certains places which he thought should be included in the British Zone of influence, namely Mosul. He also asked for Palestine....". U.S., Department of State, *Papers Relating to the Foreign Relations of the United States*, vol. 5, p. 3.

36. Ibid., p. 763.

37. M. Jean Martet, at one time Clemenceau's secretary, has reported that on 17 May 1928, Clemenceau told him: "I should like to speak to you of another of my crimes — Yes — Mosul. I have been severely attacked because of Mosul and the oil fields. Well, yes, I gave up Mosul; but what they forget is that I used it as a bait in order to get Cilicia, which several of our good allies wanted us not to have. Cilicia was, it might again become, a very pleasant country.... I therefore said to the English, 'which would you rather have, Mosul or Cilicia...'?" Jean Martet, *Clemenceau*, trans. by Milton Waldman (London, 1930), pp. 190.

It has been asserted that giving Mosul to France was originally Sir Mark Sykes's idea, for according to his conception, "the primary object of the Sykes-Picot Agreement was to create a buffer state under French protection between Russian territory in the North and a British-protected Mesopotamia in the South." See Shane Leslie, *Mark Sykes: His Life and Letters*, p. 249, and A. Wilson, *Mesopotamia, 1917-1920: A Clash of Loyalties*, pp. 153-154.

what she did not have, namely Mosul and the strategic area of Palestine.[38] It was like selling the same goods twice to the same customer, perhaps with the excuse that the "company" was now under a different management[39].

On the other hand, the French had to face a fait accompli as far as Palestine and Mosul were concerned. The Balfour Declaration had already been issued on 2 November 1917 with its promise of a National Home for the Jews in Palestine, and the problem of Palestine was becoming more complicated with the Italians and the Vatican claiming to protect their own interests in the Holy Land. Mosul already had been occupied by British troops under General William Marshall, although at the time of the Mudros armistice it was in the possession of the Turks thirty miles north of the British line[40]. Moreover, as far as oil was concerned, France had recognized the exclusive right of the Turkish Petroleum Company to the oil in the vilayet of Mosul. Indeed at the time of the Lloyd George-Clemenceau meeting the whole position of France in the Near East was weak and uncertain, while Britain's military supremacy there was incontestable. France was militarily absent from an

38. It seems that at times Lloyd George muttered to himself his own thoughts. Sometime after his bargain with Clemenceau over Mosul and Palestine, he was heard muttering: "Mosul has oil, Palestine is Holy Land; Syria, what is Syria?"

39. At the time the French signed the Sykes-Picot Agreement, Sir Edward Grey was the Secretary of State for Foreign Affairs and Mr. Asquith, the Prime Minister.

40. This is not the place to discuss the question of Mosul, which embittered the relations of the Turks with the British Government for many years. But it may be of interest to state that after suspending hostilities on 31 October 1918 according to the terms of the Armistice, General Marshal, Commander-in-Chief of the British Forces in Iraq, invoking article 7 of that Armistice, wrote to 'Alī Iḥsān Pasha, commander of the Turkish 6th Army, asking him to evacuate the town. Article 7 said: "*Dans le cas où il surgirait une situation qui menacerait la sécurité des Alliés ceux-ci auront le droit d'occuper tout point stratégique.*" At first, 'Alī Iḥsān, supported by the Grand Vizier 'Izzet Pasha, rejected as unwarranted the request of General Marshal. Later, after much negotiation and under pressure from Vice-Admiral Calthorp in Constantinople, 'Izzet Pasha ordered 'Alī Iḥsān to surrender Mosul to General Marshall. Accordingly, the British forces occupied Mosul on 15 November at noon. See *La Question de Mosul : De la Signature du Traité d'Armistice de Moudros 30 Octobre 1918 au 1er Mars 1925* (Constantinople, 1925), pp. 15, 26-28, 34-37. See also the British *Blue Book* on Mosul, Turkey, No. 1 (1923): "Correspondence between Lord Curzon and Ismet Pacha respecting Mosul," and Toynbee, *Survey of International Affairs, 1925*, vol. 1, pp. 481-482.

area which though promised to her was conquered and effectively occupied by Britain. Hence, Clemenceau's anxiety that the Sykes-Picot Agreement of 1916 should under no circumstances be modifed as far as Syria was concerned.

Thus when Faiṣal arrived in London on 10 December the fate of Syria seemed to have been sealed and no political importance was given to his visit. The following day the *Times* in reporting in a few lines the arrival of the Emīr referred to him as the "Hero of the Arab epic" and to his "Romantic exploits as Commander-in-Chief of the Arab Northern Army." Faiṣal had come to England, said the *Times*, "to present the respects of his father to the King." [41] On 12 December Faiṣal was received by the King in Buckingham Palace and decorated with the Chain of Knight Grand Cross of the Royal Victorian Order. "It is understood that the King expressed to the prince his high appreciation of the assistance which the friendly Arabs had given to the British force operating on the Eastern front." [42] On that same day *L'Echo de Paris* was reporting a letter which Clemenceau had written to "the Syrian National Committee." Armed with the new assurances which he had received recently from Lloyd George in London the French Prime Minister had written that the present agreements with regard to Syria, including the Convention of 20 October, [43] were "transitory." A new territorial rearrangement was necessary in order "to end the dualism of French zones." However, as regards England, "the Agreement of 1916 will remain until a new agreement — which she desires as much as we — has been concluded." Clemenceau went on to say that as far as the British Cabinet in London was concerned, it had repeated that the interests of France must not suffer in the East "by reason of the concentration of our troops on the Western front;" nevertheless the situation in Syria was

41. *Times* (London), Wednesday, 11 December 1918, p. 8, col. 4. *The Times* added: "With the Emir also was Colonel Lawrence wearing a Mecca Headdress of crimson and gold." It should be recalled that on 9 December, Lawrence was waiting for Faiṣal at Boulogne on board the ship which brought them the next day from France to England.

42. Ibid., 13 December, p. 7, col. 5.

43. According to which the administrative divisions known as "Occupied Enemy Territory" had been created.

developing to the disadvantage of France. "In the East," concluded Clemenceau, "more than elsewhere, the absent are often in the wrong."[44]

Faiṣal remained in England until 7 January 1919 when he left for Paris to attend the Peace Conference. In the absence of official documents, it is not known exactly what went on between him and the British Foreign Office concerning the future of Syria. Temperley has stated that the Emīr was "advised to accept French control in Syria" for "it was made clear to him that Great Britain had no intention of falling out with France on Syrian questions."[45] There seems to be little doubt that Faiṣal became fully acquainted for the first time with the Sykes-Picot Agreement and its far-reaching implications. Probably it was during his London visit that he saw also the map of that Agreement which had "pushed the Arabs back into the desert"[46] and had to face, as he put it, "the bitter truth."[47] In desperation and as an alternative to Great Britain's support, Faiṣal seems to have for a while turned towards the United States of America. He also knew that the Zionists opposed vehemently France's desire to possess Palestine. Contact had already been established between Dr. Chaim Weizmann and the Emīr Faiṣal. At the suggestion of General Allenby, Dr. Weizmann had met the Emīr on 4 June 1918, "at the latter's Headquarters at Gueira between 'Aqaba and Ma'an" and "there was satisfactory inter-change of views."[48] Another meeting was now arranged in London at which Lawrence was also present as interpreter. "Feiṣal stressed the danger to Jewish and Arab interests presented by French policy and by the Sykes-Picot agreement."[49] The Emīr met other Jewish leaders at a banquet given in his honor by Lord Walter Rothschild.[50]

44. *Times* (London), 13 December, p. 7, col. 5.
45. Temperley, vol. 6, p. 142.
46. J. De Haas, *History of Palestine*, p. 481.
47. Erskine, p. 96.
48. Chaim Weizmann, *Trial and Error* (London, 1950), pp. 290-294; also De Haas, p. 480.
See also Esco Foundation for Palestine, Inc., *Palestine: A Study of Jewish, Arab and British Policies*, vol. 1, p. 130.
49. H.F. Frischwasser-Ra'anan, *The Frontiers of a Nation*, p. 104.
50. Esco Foundation, *Palestine*, vol. 1, p. 139.

The American attitude had already been made clear by President Wilson in his Addresses in 1917 and 1918 and in his Fourteen Points of 8 January 1918.[51] It seems that he had in mind a project for a Confederation of Arab States under the guidance and protection of the United States.[52]

Meanwhile Mark Sykes had returned to the Near East where Anglo-French relations were growing more strained and from where Georges-Picot was sending telegram after telegram to Paris complaining of the anti-French activities of British intelligence officers.[53] Sykes tried "to smooth out the rising chaos of passions and ambitions, promises and expectations which had been bequeathed by the war."[54] He met his old friend Georges-Picot again and together they went to Aleppo towards the end of December. According to Georges-Picot all the difficulties had not been settled between Britain and France but a great step forward had been taken.[55] Sykes spoke at receptions held in his honor at the Government House and at the Arab Club in Aleppo. On both occasions he praised the efforts of the French in the recent conquest of Syria and "suggested the helping power of France."

On 29 December, the French Foreign Minister M. Stephen Pichon, took the opportunity to reassert the rights of France in the Ottoman Empire, in the course of a debate in the French Chamber of Deputies. These rights were in Syria, in the Lebanon, in Cilicia, and in Palestine. They were based on history, on agreements, and on contracts.[56] When a Socialist deputy, M. Marcel Cachini, interrupted to say that the Syrians ask to be free and that was the essential contract of France, M. Pichon continued saying that

51. See pages 44 and 45, below.

52. Temperley, vol. 6, p. 144.

53. Brémond, p. 319.

54. Shane Leslie, p. 279.

55. See telegrams of Georges-Picot, Nos. 777, of 29 December 1918, and 789, of 1 January 1919, cited by Brémond, p. 319, n. 6.

56. "Nous avons dans leur empire des droits incontestables à sauvegarder; nous en avons en Syrie, dans le Liban, en Cilicie, en Palestine. Ils sont fondés sur des titres historiques, sur des accords, sur des contrats . . . . " France, *Journal Officiel, Chambre des Députés, Débats Parlementaires*, 2^d^ session of 29 December 1918, vol. 4, p. 3716, col. 1.

those rights were also founded on the aspirations and wishes of the populations (of those countries) who have been for a long time the "clients" of France. "The Peace Conference would be free to reach its own conclusions about the agreements which have already been made but we consider our agreements with England binding England and ourselves togther, and the rights which have been recognized to belong to us, to be ours already." Undoubtedly this was meant to be a broad hint directed towards France's ally across the Channel, at the time when Faiṣal was there, that France stuck to the Sykes-Picot Agreement and would not recognize any change which might affect France's rights in the Near East.

On 30 December, Faiṣal had lunch with the Lord Mayor and Lady Mayoress at the Mansion House. Among the prominent guests were Lord Rothschild and Sir Henry and Lady McMahon. "The Lord Mayor, proposing the Prince's health thanked him for the brilliant services his gallant troops had rendered in freeing the Holy Land from the detested rule of the Turk. The Prince, in reply, said that the Arabs were fighting for those great principles of freedom and justice which were so sacred to the Allies, and which were the antithesis of the Turkish sway. He rejoiced that, in that mission and cause, they had the true sympathy of the British people."[57] Thus, the year 1918 ended with France firmly attached to the Sykes-Picot Agreement, Britain trying to modify it, and Faiṣal talking about freedom and justice, while tension was all the time mounting in the Near East.

57. *Times* (London), 31 December 1918, p. 11, col. 2.

CHAPTER FOUR

THE PEACE CONFERENCE OF PARIS, 1919

"It was a picturesque scene, cast in the long Clock Room of the Quai d'Orsay, the conventional black of the majority of delegates broken by the horizon-blue uniform of Marshal Foch... and the white flowing robes and golden headdress of the Arabian Emīr Feiṣal...."

Charles Seymour, *Woodrow Wilson and the World War*, p. 261.

THE YEAR OPENED with the Peace Conference meeting in Paris, for the first time on 18 January. As far as Syria was concerned, two figures at this Conference, in their long-flowing Arab robes disconcerted and irritated Clemenceau. They were the Emīr Faiṣal and his "advisor" T.E. Lawrence.[1] Clemenceau distrusted both. He could not tolerate the presence of Lawrence at the Peace Conference and he considered Faiṣal thoroughly pro-British, doing whatever his British masters instructed him to do.[2] According to Wickham Steed, the Editor of the *Times*, the French showed their annoyance by "treating Faiṣal with studied contempt."[3]

1. The story is told of how, one day, Clemenceau himself decided to have a talk with "ce jeune homme." So, he called Lawrence to his room and told him that the French had historic interests in Syria and wanted that country. He asked Lawrence whether he knew that it was mainly the French who had fought in the Crusades. Whereupon Lawrence answered: "Yes, but the Crusaders had been defeated and the Crusades had failed." The conversation came to an abrupt end.

D.H. Miller wrote: "Col. Lawrence's attitude is distinctly anti-French; in fact, he said so to me as we walked home together." D.H. Miller, *My Diary at the Conference of Paris*, vol. 1, p. 74.

2. "The French Foreign Office... was very suspicious of our relations with Feisal, whom it was inclined to regard as merely a British puppet employed to queer the French pitch." Valentine Chirol, *Fifty Years in a Changing World*, p. 330. See also U.S., Department of State, *Papers Relating to the Foreign Relations of the United States*, vol. 5, p. 8, and R.S. Baker, *Woodrow Wilson and World Settlement*, vol. 3, p. 11.

3. Steed, vol. 2, p. 300.

T.E. Lawrence wrote in his "Diary of the Peace Conference": "Mr. Balfour completely forgot the Hejaz representatives at the first sitting. I got Mallet, Tyrell and Cecil to go and protest. Then I went to see Eric Drummond, and explained myself vigorously. He tried first to persuade me that we had no

Faiṣal had already submitted to the Peace Conference a Memorandum,[4] on 1 January, in which he had spoken of the aim of the Arab nationalist movements as being "to unite the Arabs eventually into one nation," of Syria as being "sufficiently advanced politically to manage her own internal affairs" and of his hope that the Powers will "find better means to give fuller effect to the aims of our national movement." "I came to Europe," he wrote, "on behalf of my father and the Arabs of Asia.... They expect the Powers to think of them as one potential people, jealous of their language and liberty, and ask that no steps be taken inconsistent with the prospect of an eventual union of these areas under one sovereign government." On the 29th, he submitted another Memorandum to the Peace Conference: "As representative of my father, who, by request of Britain and France, led the Arab rebellion against the Turks, I have come to ask that the Arabic-speaking peoples of Asia, from the line Alexandretta-Diarbekr southward to the Indian Ocean, be recognized as independent sovereign peoples, under the guarantee of the League of Nations.... I base my request on the principle enunciated by President Wilson (attached), and am confident that the Powers will attach more importance to the bodies and souls of the Arabic-speaking peoples than to their own material interests."[5]

standing, but later came round and promised to do his best. I dined with Mr. Balfour, and got his promise to the same effect, and loaded him full of ammunition. Meanwhile, I told Feisal that his question was not prejudiced, only postponed a day for production of necessary papers. Next day, Balfour proposed the Hejaz. Pichon protested. Clemenceau accepted one delegate, and Pichon said they could have no more since they were an embryo nationality, not an independent state. Balfour and Lloyd George countered sharply with the statement that they and France had recognised its independence, and the point — two delegates — was carried.

"Feisal had meanwhile been visited by Gout who told him his omission was intentional, and the English were only playing with him. He said France was strong, and the sooner Feisal ceased to listen to the mischief-makers in Mesopotamia and Syria who were working against France, the better it would be for him. They recognised no Arab army in Syria, and Allenby lied if he said they did. So Feisal saw that his representation was contested, and spent a very miserable night in consequence. I found him wandering about the hotel at 2 a.m. When we won, he took it as a good augury of all the future battles and was very joyful." Garnett, pp. 273-274.

4. Miller, vol. 4, Doc. 250, pp. 297-299. See Appendix C, below.

5. Ibid., Doc. 251, p. 300. See Appendix D, below.

Meanwhile, the "Intelligence Section" of the American Delegation to the Peace Conference, had "recommended" on 21 January to President Wilson and to the Plenipotentiaries:

(1) That there be established a Syrian State;

(2) That there be applied to the Syrian state the mandatory principle, but no recommendation is made as to the Power to be selected to carry out this principle;

(3) That no obstacle be interposed against the final incorporation of the Syrian State in an Arab confederation, if the tendency toward this solution should develop in the country.[6]

But, as far as we know, all that was officially decided about Syria during the first month of the year 1919[6] was a resolution adopted by the Representatives of the United States, Great Britain, France, Italy and Japan at a Conference held at the Quai d'Orsay on 30 January, to the effect that that country "must be completely severed from the Turkish Empire."[7]

It was not until 6 February that the Emīr Faiṣal, accompanied by Col. Lawrence, presented his case in person to the Peace Conference at the Quai d'Orsay.[8] He referred to his Memorandum of

On 19 January, the *Times* correspondent wrote from Paris: "...Colonel Lawrence, who accompanies the Emir as aide-de-camp, expects that Emir Feisal himself will be chosen as first delegate to the Kingdom of the Hedjaz, in order to give greater weight to an important proposal which is to be submitted to the Conference. The proposal will suggest the formation of a great federation of all the Arab States from the Red Sea to the Persian Gulf, free from any Turkish domination and under the protection of the United States. 'The Arabs of this most ancient race,' said Prince Feisal today, Colonel Lawrence acting as his interpreter, 'desire to become the youngest independent state in Asia, and they appeal to America as the most powerful protector of the freedom of man'." *Times* (London), 20 January 1919, p. 12, col. 4.

6. Ibid., Doc. 246, p. 262. See Appendix E, below.

7. U.S., Department of State, *Papers Relating to the Foreign Relations of the United States*, vol. 3, p. 795:

"2. — More particularly because of the historic misgovernment by the Turks of subject peoples and the terrible massacres of Armenians and others in recent years, the Allied and Associated Powers are agreed that Armenia, Syria, Mesopotamia, Palestine and Arabia must be completely severed from the Turkish Empire...."

8. Lloyd George, *The Truth About the Peace Treaties*, vol. 2, p. 1040.

"The Emir Faisal," wrote Harold Nicolson, "was granted an 'audition' before the Council of Ten. 'His voice,' records Mr. Lansing, 'seemed to breathe the perfume of frankincense'." Nicolson, *Peacemaking*, p. 142.

29 January in which he had asked that "the Arabic-speaking peoples of Asia, from the line Alexandretta-Diarbekr southward to the Indian Ocean, be recognized as independent sovereign peoples, under the guarantee of the League of Nations" — and now gave his reasons for this request. "His father" he said "did not risk his life and his kingdom by joining in the war at its most critical time to further any personal ambitions.... The Arabs were most grateful to England and France for the help given them to free their country. The Arabs now asked them to fulfill their promises of November 1918."

Then Faiṣal was given a hint — indeed it had the air of a fait accompli — when President Wilson asked him "whether, seeing that the plan of mandatories on behalf of the League of Nations had been adopted, he would prefer for his people a single mandatory, or several." This was certainly a far cry from Faiṣal's request for independence and sovereignty. And so Faiṣal did not answer the question directly. He said that he could not reply to that question without first consulting his father and the Arab people.

"He was here to ask for the independence of his people, and for their right to choose their own mandatory....

"Personally, he was afraid of partition. His principle was Arab unity. It was for this that the Arabs had fought. Any other solution would be regarded by the Arabs in the light of a division of spoils after a battle... The Arabs were an ancient people civilised and organised at a time when the nations represented in this room were unformed...."[9]

On 13 February, the question of Syria was discussed again, this time before a meeting of the Council of Ten held in M. Pichon's Room at the Quai d'Orsay. Dr. Howard S. Bliss, President of the Syrian Protestant College in Beirut (now the American University of Beirut) was called in to make his statement. Dr. Bliss's deep experience and knowledge of Syria and the Lebanon, the great esteem and respect with which he was held by Muslims and Christians alike and the genuine concern which he had shown for the future of those two countries right from the very first days of the arrival of the British and French troops, had led the State Depart-

9. Ibid., pp. 1043-44.

ment in Washington to invite him to Paris to present to the Peace Conference his views on the Syrian situation.[10] Dr. Bliss, after being welcomed by M. Clemenceau, read his statement in which he said in part: "My plea before this body in behalf of the people of Syria is this: that an Inter-Allied or a Neutral Commission be sent at once to Syria in order to give an opportunity to the people of Syria, including the Lebanon, to express in a perfectly untrammeled way their political wishes and aspirations, viz., as to what form of Government they desire and as to what Power, if any, should be their Mandatory Protecting Power.... The result of this inquiry will be, I am convinced, the discovery of a desire for the erection of a State or States looking eventually to complete independence but at present seeking the guardianship of a Mandatory Power."[11] In concluding his statement, Dr. Bliss brought to the

10. The text of the State Department's telegram was communicated to Dr. Bliss on 5 January and he left Beirut for Paris on the 9th. This text has been preserved among the Private Papers of Howard S. Bliss in the Archives of the American University of Beirut.

11. For the text of Dr. Bliss's Statement, see Appendix F. See also U.S., Department of State, *Papers Relating to the Foreign Relations of the United States,* vol. 3, pp. 1015-1918.

Before the meeting of 13 February, Dr. Bliss had already met in Paris, soon after his arrival, Mr. Robert Lansing, Mr. Henry White and all the other members of the American Peace Commission. He also put his views in writing and at their request to both Mr. Lansing, (on 26 January) and to Mr. White (on the 31st). To Lansing, he wrote: "Basing their claims upon the twelfth of the fourteen points of President Wilson (whom they regard as their Great Deliverer) and upon the Declaration of France and Great Britain of November 1918(a copy of which is appended) the people of Syria demand a fair, untrammeled opportunity to express their own desires as to their political future.... To fail to furnish the Syrians with such an opportunity to express their desires would be, in my belief, to compromise gravely and dangerously the honor of America, Great Britain and France.

"My suggestion would be that the Peace Conference appoint a Commission of wise, able and impartial men, back them with adequate power and charge them with ascertainting the desires of the people of Syria."

To White, Bliss conveyed the same thoughts and to both Lansing and White, he expressed the belief that Syria would choose as "Protective Power" first America, second Great Britain — America because of her "entire disinterestedness" and Great Britain because of her "capacity and justice." He did not believe that France would be chosen.

On 7 February, Dr. Bliss wrote a personal letter to President Wilson in which he said: "Having just come from Syria and from seeing many Syrians in Egypt, I beg to state to you how earnestly and even passionately the people of Syria are

attention of the Council of Ten the necessity of "an absolute separation between Religion and State." "The Government on the one hand," he added, "Religion on the other, can best pursue their majestic tasks apart."

After he had finished reading his statement, Dr. Bliss answered questions by M. Pichon, Mr. Balfour and Lord Milner. Then Dr. Bliss was followed by a "Syrian Commission" headed by "M. Chekri Ganem" (Shukrī Ghānim) founder of the "Comité Central Syrien." "M. Clemenceau having introduced the members of the Syrian Commission to the Conference called upon M. Chekri Ganem to make his statement."[12]

Shukrī Ghānim made a long and flowery speech. He said that he spoke "in the name of those whose members may be estimated at over one million." There were few small nations who had suffer-

depending upon your twelfth point and upon the Anglo-French Declaration of November 1918.

"They crave a fair opportunity to express their own political aspirations and they claim that this craving is justified by the above-mentioned documents.

"And such an opportunity they have not had. The censorship of the Press and Post Office and the difficulty of holding private and public gatherings have prevented it. . . ." *Private Papers of Howard S. Bliss.*

For a French point of view of the role which the Syrian Protestant College played in those days, it may be of some interest to quote the following passage:

"En Syrie même, la propagande américaine avait son centre dans l'Université américaine de Beyrouth, dite *Syrian Protestant College.* Cette vaste et superbe institution, merveilleusement outillée et dotée d'un personnel d'élite, jouit, à juste titre d'ailleurs, d'un rayonnement considérable parmi les milieux syriens, surtout auprès des musulmans. . . . Rien de surprenant, par conséquent, que l'Université américaine ait joué un rôle de premier plan dans la propagande." Gontaut-Biron, p. 247.

To the representative of *Outlook* (Paris), the Emīr Faiṣal said during an interview on 7 March 1919: "Dr. Daniel Bliss, the founder of the College at Beirut, was the grandfather of Syria; and his son Howard Bliss, the present President, is the father of Syria. Without the education that this college has given, the struggle for freedom would never have been won. The Arabs owe everything to these men." *Outlook*, 2 April 1919.

The first street sign of Beirut, set up by the Provisional Government of 'Umar Da'ūq in 1918, was *Shāri' Bliss* (Bliss street).

12. The other members of the Commission were: Anīs Sheḥādeh, Orthodox Greek; Jamīl Mardam Bey, Muslim; Dr. Georges Samné, Greek Melchite; Jamīl Bey Mukarzil, Maronite; Dr. Tawfīq Fārḥī, "Israelite Representative of the Committee." U.S., Department of State, *Papers Relating to the Foreign Relations of the United States*, vol. 3, p. 1024.

ed so much as the people of Syria "if one accepts the theory that the capacity for pain increases in proportion to moral development." He did not want the liberation of Syria to come from the Hijaz. He objected to Faiṣal as "representative of Hedjaz" to be speaking in the name of "all those who speak Arabic" and of Syria. "Damascus is at least 1500 kilometres from Mecca. What affinities exist between the nature of the Hedjazi and the Syrian, the nomad and the settler on the soil? Is there any such preponderance of Arab elements in Syria as might explain or justify this idea? To annex Syria to Arabia would be to do violence to the very soil from which the race and its history have sprung...." However, Syria needed foreign help. "For having broken our bonds, would you refuse us the support we need for our first steps? You would not raise us up only to leave us to stumble in the wreck of our fetters.... Gentlemen, both our interests and our reason lead us to admit that we shall need foreign collaboration."

As to consulting the people, No, under the circumstances, Mr. Ghānim did not advise it. "It would be more reasonable that the Powers, in their wisdom, should appoint that one among them which appears specially qualified to carry out the noble mission of helping a small country to lift itself up and of accustoming the eyes of its inhabitants to the light of liberty." Who was "that one" among the Powers?

"Even if the opinion of my colleagues and myself had differed from that of our mandatories, we should still have considered it our duty to execute our clear mission, which is to request your Excellencies, in the term of the documents submitted, that France may be charged with the reconstitution of an integral, independent, federated Syria.... She, alone, in our opinion, is competent to obtain the whole effect for which we hope.... She will be a guide speaking a language we understand, who will unite us towards our common destiny. She will be the arbiter before whom all mistrust will vanish and all conflict cease."

Then Mr. Ghānim ended his speech with an emotional appeal embodied in tragic sorrow and expressed first by a verse: "There was a day when I wept and now I weep for that day," and then by the following words:

"Gentlemen, will you, our only hope, who in our eyes represent right and human mercy, will you leave us to weep for our sad and grievous past?"[13]

According to Professor Shotwell, who was present at that meeting, the speech of Shukrī Ghānim defeated its own purpose. A month before that meeting, on 8 January, *The Manchester Guardian* had published an article under the title of "A Syrian Congress" in which this passage occurred: "There has just been held at Marseilles, under the auspice of the Syrian Committee of Paris a congress which passed a resolution to place Syria under the protection of France.[14] At the head of this movement stands a gentleman who, as Emir Feysal has remarked, has lived outside of Syria for about forty years." "This gentleman" was a reference to Shukrī Ghānim, described by Professor Shotwell as "an Arab-looking gentleman with a long, forked, grey beard," who had read "through his horn glasses" at the meeting of the Big Ten "a long account and plea which took two hours and a half to deliver and translate." "Just as he was starting," continues Professor Shotwell, "Westermann slipped a note to Wilson to tell him that Chekri Ganem had not been in Syria for the last thirty-five years, having spent all his time in France.[15] This hint was enough to destroy Wilson's interest in the long outpouring of pathetic eloquence which followed. Before long he got up from his chair, wandered over to the other side of the room, and stared out of the window with his hands in his coat-tails, clearly disconcerting the French. Clemenceau spoke over his shoulder to Pichon in a stage whisper, which carried to me as I was directly in line behind, asking savagely, 'What did you get the fellow here for, anyway?' Pichon spreading out his hands in impotent protest, said, 'Well, I didn't

13. Ibid., pp. 1024-38.

14. For an account of this Congress, see Gaulis, pp. 99-103.

15. T.E. Lawrence must have had men like Shukrī Ghānim in mind when he wrote in 1918: "Their political ideals were culled from books.... They formed committees in Cairo, Paris, London, New York, Beyrouth, Berlin and Berne, to influence European powers to deliver them from the Turks, and lend them the sinews to go on spinning real dreams. Their habits made Syria uncongenial, and most of them lived in foreign countries...."
"Syrian Cross Currents," in *Secret Despatches from Arabia*, p. 155.

know he was going to carry on this way'. It was a complete give-away."[16]

It may be worth noting, in passing, that a few days after the foregoing meeting an event occurred which, in a way difficult to assess, contributed most probably to a further weakening of the Arab case: Sir Mark Sykes died in Paris. Lloyd George has been reported to have said, soon after: "He was a worried, anxious man. That was the cause of his death."[17] Lord Hankey, in an interview with the author, said that Sir Mark Sykes was foremost among the small group of experts whose advice had guided Lloyd George in Arab affairs and that after his death there was no one to replace him.

On 26 February, the Minutes of the Daily Meetings of the (American) Commissioners Plenipotentiary record that Dr. Howard Bliss was called in and that he made a statement. "He declared that Syria was a small country, but that the principle involved was clear cut and one which affected the honor of the United States and her allies. Syria is depending on the Article of the President's declaration concerning the right of self-deter-

16. Shotwell, *At the Paris Peace Conference*, p. 178.

Two days later, on Saturday, 15 February, at another meeting of the Council of Ten in M. Pichon's room at the Quai d'Orsay, the question of Syria was brought up again for a short time, when a Lebanese Delegation was introduced to plead in favor of France's help for the Lebanon. The President of the Delegation, Daūd 'Ammūn, read a statement in which he said: "Conscious of the inability of the country, especially at the start, to develop its resources unaided, deprived as it is of financial means and technical advisors, the Government has sought the collaboration of a Great Power. One only could be thought of, France. Her liberal principles, her time honored traditions, the benefit Lebanon never failed to receive from her in hard times, the civilisation she diffused throughout made her prominent in the eyes of all the inhabitants of Lebanon. Consequently, the Administrative Council faithfully expressing public opinion, unanimously requested the collaboration of France." U.S., Department of State, *Papers Relating to the Foreign Relations of the United States*, vol. 4, p. 3.

17. In a conversation with Lord Riddell on 3 February 1919, Lloyd George said: "He was responsible for the agreement which is causing us all the trouble with the French.... Sykes saw the difficulties in which he had placed us, and was very worried in consequence. I said something to him about the Agreement and at once saw how I had cut him. I am sorry, I wish I had said nothing. I blame myself. He did his best...." *Lord Riddell's Intimate Diary of the Peace Conference and After, 1918-1923*, p. 25.

mination of race, and specifically of the twelfth point which refers to the Turkish affairs. France also made a declaration in November 1918 of which Dr. Bliss urged strongly the sending of an inter-Allied commission for examination in this matter, whatever might be its findings, it would satisfy the demands of honor. Mr. Lansing stated that he had made the same proposal but that it had been refused by Pichon under orders from Clemenceau. Mr. Lansing declared himself ready to press the matter provided he was sure of British assistance.

"Dr. Bliss declared that the country should certainly not be handed over before the wishes of the people were consulted, and both the Commissioners agreed." [18]

The next official record we have of any discussion about Syria comes to us from David Hunter Miller. On Monday, 10 March, a meeting was held at the Ministry of War in Paris between M. Clemenceau, Lloyd George, and Colonel House. Miller wrote:

"The Syrian question was discussed but no agreement arrived at because Clemenceau asked for more time. The French insist on getting all of Syria. Lloyd George said he would consent to give France the Lebanon but that there should be a break in the line north of the Lebanon so as to allow the English and the Arabs an outlet to the sea.[19] George does not want the French to occupy

18. U.S., Department of State, *Papers Relating to the Foreign Relations of the United States*, vol. 11, pp. 76-77.

19. Lloyd George may have taken this suggestion from Lord Milner who had now become Colonial Secretary and on whose lap the Syrian baby had been dropped to be quieted, if possible. On 8 March, he wrote to Lloyd George:

"You asked me last night what kind of compromise I thought possible. I therefore suggest a scheme.... But I defy any human being to get out of the Syrian tangle by any scheme which is not open to many objections, and I want to get out of it somehow without a row.

"The position is this. At present both parties, the French and Feisal, are in a hopless impasse....

"The compromise I suggest—the French to stop 'bossing' Feisal in the sense of full administrative control.... Let them give access to the sea at Tripoli....

"On the other hand, let Feisal on his side accept the French as the Mandatory Power for the whole of his territory not falling within the sphere of British influence, but as a mandatory power with the mildest form of mandate.... " Lloyd George, *The Truth About the Peace Treaties*, vol. 2, pp. 1047-1049.

any of the railroads running north and which Foch demands. Clemenceau asked for more time to consider this."[20]

Two days later, Colonel House who was present at the Ministry of War meeting, wrote in his diary:

"Another difficulty is Syria. George declares the French are making trouble for themselves and war is sure to come if they insist upon their present plans."[21]

But it seems that the first really important discussion which took place on Syria, after the visit that Clemenceau paid to London for a meeting of the Allied Supreme Council early in December 1918, was the Secret Conference of the Four Heads of States which met in Paris in Mr. Lloyd George's flat in the afternoon of 20th March. We have the Minutes of this Conference.[22]

The French Minister of Foreign Affairs, M. Pichon, began the discussion. He explained that "the origin of the question was the agreement of May 1916," i.e., the Sykes-Picot Agreement. According to M. Pichon, that Agreement had two objects. "First to detach the Arabs from the Turks; second, to decide the claims of Great Britain and France." After giving a summary of that Agreement and quoting the declaration of 8 November 1918, M. Pichon discussed the meeting of M. Clemenceau and Mr. Lloyd George in London in December 1918. He then gave an account of the "historic and traditional case" of France in Syria and added that "French opinion would not admit that France could be even partly excluded from Syria."

Mr. Lloyd George said that he was not departing from the 1916 agreement except as regards Mosul and Palestine. "M. Pichon had

20. Miller, vol. 6, Doc. 489, p. 317.

21. Seymour, *The Intimate Papers of Colonel House*, vol. 4, p. 371.

22. These Minutes were recorded by Sir Maurice (later Lord) Hankey. It was the practice to give copies of such Minutes to President Wilson or to the American Delegation. They first appeared in 1923 in R.S. Baker's *Woodrow Wilson and World Settlement*, vol. 3, pp. 1-19 which has the subtitle "Written from his unpublished and personal material." In 1946, the State Department published them in *Papers Relating to the Foreign Relations of the United States: The Paris Conference, 1919*, vol. 5, pp. 1-14.

The following were present at this meeting: President Wilson, Lloyd George, Clemenceau, Balfour, Pichon, Berthelot, Orlando, Sonnino, General Allenby, General Bols, Lt.-Col. Sir Maurice Hankey. The interpreter was Prof. P.J. Mantoux.

omitted in his lucid statement to explain that the blue area in which France was allowed to establish such direct or indirect administration or control as they may desire and as they may think fit to arrange with the Arab State or Confederation of Arab States did not include Damascus, Homs, Hama or Aleppo. In area A, France was 'prepared to recognise and uphold an independent Arab State or Confederation of Arab States... under the suzerainty of an Arab Chief'. Also in area A, France would 'have priority of right of enterprise and local loans'... and... 'shall alone supply advisers or foreign functionaries at the request of the Arab State or Confederation of Arab States'. Was France prepared to accept that? This, however, was not a question between Great Britain and France. It was a question between France and an agreement which we had signed with King Husain.

"M. Pichon said he wished to say one word. If a mandate were granted by the League of Nations over these territories, all that he asked was that France should have this part put aside for her.

"M. Lloyd George said that we could not do that. The League of Nations could not be used for putting aside our bargain with King Hussein. He asked if M. Pichon intended to occupy Damascus with French troops? If he did, it would clearly be a violation of the Treaty with the Arabs.

"M. Pichon said that France had no convention with King Hussein.

"Mr. Lloyd George said that the whole of the agreement of 1916 (Sykes-Picot) was based on a letter from Sir Henry McMahon to King Hussein from which he quoted the following extract:

"The districts of Mersina and Alexandretta, and portions of Syria lying to the west of the districts of Damascus, Homs, Hama and Aleppo, cannot be said to be purely Arab, and should be excluded from the proposed limits of boundaries. With the above modifications, and without prejudice to our existing treaties with Arab Chiefs, we accept these limits of boundaries; and in regard to those portions of the territories therein in which Great Britain is free to act without detriment to the interests of her ally France, I am empowered, in the name of the Government of Great Britain, to give the following reply to your letter:

'Subject to the above modifications Great Britain is prepared to recognise and support independence of Arabs within territories included in the limits of boundaries proposed by the Sherif of Mecca'.

'(Extract from a letter from Sir H. McMahon to King Hussein, Oct. 24, 19)'.

"M. Pichon said that the undertaking had been made by Great Britain (Angleterre) alone, France had never seen it until a few weeks before when Sir Maurice Hankey had handed him a copy.

"Mr. Lloyd George said the Agreement might have been made by England (Angleterre) alone, but it was England (Angleterre) who had organised the whole of the Syrian campaign. There would have been no question of Syria but for England (Angleterre). Great Britain had put from 900,000 to 1,000,000 men in the field against Turkey; but Arab help had been essential; that was a point on which General Allenby could speak.

"General Allenby said that it had been invaluable.

"Mr. Lloyd George, continuing, said that it was on the basis of the above quoted letter that King Hussein had put all his resources into the field, which had helped us most materially to win the victory. France had for practical purposes accepted our undertaking to King Hussein in signing the 1916 agreement. This had not been M. Pichon but his predecessors. He was bound to say that if the British Government now agreed that Damascus, Homs, Hama and Aleppo should be included in the sphere of direct French influence, they would be breaking faith with the Arabs and that they could not face this.

"He was particularly anxious for M. Clemenceau to follow this. The agreement of 1916 had been signed subsequent to the letter to King Hussein."

Not even a small measure of agreement could be reached between France and Great Britain. President Wilson in an exasperated mood intervened to say that "the point of view of the United States of America was, however, indifferent to the claims both of Great Britain and France over peoples unless those peoples wanted them. One of the fundamental principles to which the United States of America adhered was the consent of the governed...."

The only way to deal with this question was "to discover the desires of the population of these regions." So, President Wilson suggested that "the fittest men that could be obtained should be selected to form an Inter-Allied Commission to go to Syria, extending their inquiries, if they led them, beyond the confines of Syria. . . ." Then, at Mr. Lloyd George's request, "President Wilson undertook to draft Terms of Reference to the Commission."

No one came out that meeting any wiser than he had been when he entered it as to how the Syrian question was going to be solved. Wickham Steed who was in Paris then and who was very much interested in Arab affairs, referring to that Secret Conference of 20 March, later wrote: "The meeting discussed the question of Syria and the Franco-British agreements in regard to it, as well as the Secret Treaties in general, with the result that confusion became more confounded. President Wilson came out of the meeting cursing everybody and everything saying that he had done nothing but talk for forty-eight hours and was getting disgusted with the whole business."[23]

There seemed to be no way out of the impasse, no way of reconciling the divergence of views between France and Great Britain. Faiṣal who had now been for nearly three months in Paris was getting ready to leave for Damascus. It was at this point that "in order to avoid the breach," Wickham Steed made an effort "to bring together these exponents of the British and French views." They met in Mr. Steed's rooms. "For nearly six hours," continues Mr. Steed, "we discussed the question in all its aspects and reached so large a measure of agreement that Colonel Lawrence undertook to advise Feisal not to leave Paris, while the French undertook to get into direct touch with Feisal. In this way, it was hoped to avoid the necessity of sending out a special Commission from the Conference to Syria, and to settle the question in Paris."[24]

Immediately afterwards, a Memorandum of the conversations which took place at that informal meeting was prepared by Mr. Steed for the American Delegation, which handed it to President Wilson. It is almost certain that it is this Memorandum that David Henry

23. Steed, *Through Thirty Years, 1892-1922,* vol. 2, p. 298.
24. Ibid., vol. 2, pp. 169-170.

Miller has recorded in his Diary as Document No. 608.[25] Apparently, it was as a result of the decisions reached at that meeting that M. Clemenceau and the Emīr Faiṣal met at the Ministry of War in Paris, on 16 April. Sāṭiʿ al-Ḥuṣrī, a friend and trusted adviser of the Emīr, gives the following account of the conversations which took place between M. Clemenceau and Faiṣal, based on the personal diary of the Emīr himself:

"Clemenceau — The British (troops) will be withdrawing from Damascus and Aleppo and I would like to have our troops replace them in those two towns.

"Faiṣal — (replies immediately) I cannot agree with this idea. Syria has no need of foreign troops. Should it be in need of such troops in future, it would not hesitate to ask for help....

"Clemenceau — I do not wish to conquer the country. But I am telling you this because of the present circumstances. If the matter lay in my hands, I would not disagree with you for one minute. On the contrary, I would agree with everything you want. But the French nation cannot agree that there shall be no sign of her in Syria to indicate her presence there. If France is not represented in Syria by its flag and by its soldiers, the French nation will consider it as a national humiliation, as the desertion of a soldier from the battlefield.... However, we do not want to send a large force but only a few men.... and there will be no objection to have your flag side by side with ours...."[26]

Next day, the draft of a letter written by Clemenceau was communicated to Faiṣal, "with a request to communicate the answer which it was proposed to return." When Faiṣal's draft reply was received, it was rejected by M. Robert de Caix (acting for M. Clemenceau) and therefore M. Clemenceau's letter was never sent to him. Faiṣal's draft reply was "a frank statement of what the Syrians wanted from the Powers and were willing to offer France."[27]

25. Miller, vol. 7, pp. 169-170. Curiously, Miller makes no mention of Steed.

26. Al-Ḥuṣrī, *Yawm Maisalūn* [The Day of Maisalūn], p. 101. In 1927, Pierre Bonardi wrote that France went to Syria "pour y venir au secours de notre prestige séculaire" and "nous n'avions pas d'objectif plus précis que le flamboiement de notre auréole." Bonardi, *L'Imbroglio Syrien*, p. 44.

27. F.O. Despatch No. 3475 of 26 May 1919: Earl Curzon to Mr. Balfour (Paris) — See *Documents*, 1:4, p. 253.

M. Clemenceau's draft letter contained the following statement:

"Le Gouvernement français, désireux d'assurer à la Syrie comme à l'Arménie, à la Mésopotamie et aux autres pays d'Orient délivrés par la victoire de l'Entente, le régime de liberté et de progrès conforme aux principes dont il s'est toujours inspiré et qui sont la base des délibérations de la Conférence de la Paix, déclare reconnaître le droit de la Syrie à l'indépendance sous la forme d'une fédération d'autonomies locales répondant aux traditions et aux vœux des populations.

"La France est toute prête à donner son aide matérielle et morale à cette émancipation de la Syrie."[28]

Faiṣal wrote another letter to Mr. Clemenceau on 29 April, a day before his departure for Syria. It contained pleasant generalities and was noncommittal. He pointed out that "The deep sympathy that exists between the people of France and the people of Syria is founded on a tradition which you may rest assured I will do my best to confirm." The next paragraph contained a broad hint which would obviously irritate Clemenceau:

"I was deeply impressed by the disinterested friendliness of your statements to me while I was in Paris and must thank you for your having been the first to suggest the despatch of the Inter-Allied Commission, which is to leave shortly for the East to ascertain the wishes of the local peoples as to the future organisation of the country. I am sure that the people of Syria will know how to show you their gratitude."[29]

Actually, Faiṣal had written to President Wilson on 24 March "expressing his gratitude for the formation of the Commission," and asking for an interview. Laurence Evans wrote: "Wilson was far too busy at this time to see the Arab leader, but five days later House held a conversation with him at the Crillon, T.E. Lawrence acting as interpreter. Faisal said that he had come to say good-bye as he was leaving for Syria soon. House asked him what he thought of the Commission to Syria; Faisal replied that it was 'the best

28. F.O. Despatch No. 628 of 30 April 1919: Communicated to Curzon by Balfour — Ibid., p. 252.

29. F.O. Despatch No. 628 of 30 April 1919: Communicated to Curzon by Balfour — *Documents,* 1:4. pp. 252-253.

thing he had ever heard of', and went on to say that, though he liked the British, since there was friction between them and the French was there any possibility of the United States becoming the mandatory? House expressed doubt and Faisal added that the Arabs would die rather than accept a French mandate. . . ." [30]

Matters dragged on and the deadlock about Syria continued. "Lloyd George and Clemenceau were still at logger-heads about it and Colonel Lawrence was not helpful. The French Foreign Office was pertinaciously obstructive." [31] At the end of April, Robert de Caix told Mr. Steed that "Lloyd George had promised Clemenceau to tell the Emir Feisal that in future he must agree with France, who would pay him his subsidy; but apparently Lloyd George had done nothing of the kind." [32]

Meanwhile Faiṣal had left for Syria [33] and, immediately upon his return to Damascus, he issued a Statement on 1 May to the "Sons of dear Syria" in which he announced to them that it had been agreed, en principe, in Paris, to grant Syria its independence and to send an International Commission of inquiry. This was a great achievement on the external plane, "thanks to the attachment of the four Great Governments to their noble principles." The internal problems were the responsibility of the nation itself. This nation had to prove to the International Commission that it deserved independence and was capable of governing itself. For this purpose, it was necessary to be united, determined and law-abiding. [34]

On 5 May, Faiṣal addressed a large gathering of notables and heads of various communities, in the Town Hall of Damascus. They had come from different parts of Syria and also from certain sections of the Lebanon. After referring briefly to the history and purpose of the Arab Revolt, he spoke of his "defence of Arab lands" at the Peace Conference of Paris where he had gone on behalf of his father. His defence, he said, was in two parts:

30. Laurence Evans, *United States Policy and the Partition of Turkey, 1914-1924*, p. 141, citing Wilson Papers, Series 8 A, Box 27; in Arabic with translation.
31. Steed, p. 323.
32. Ibid.
33. Faiṣal returned to Beirut on the French cruiser *Paris* on 30 April.
34. Al-Ḥuṣrī, pp. 201-202.

(1) The Arab countries should not be divided;

(2) Syria, the Hejaz and Iraq had to have each its own separate independence—as the time was not yet ripe for all the Arab countries to be united under one Government, although the Arabs constituted one nation ("Ummah"). Faiṣal claimed that when the Western nations learned through him the aims of the Syrians, "they agreed to grant them all their wishes." He then asked all those who were present and who "morally represented" the nation to state whether they approved of what he had done. Amid great applause and acclamation, they all answered: "Well done, well done; we approve, we approve." When individually every "delegate" stood up to express his opinion, the response varied from "full confidence" in the Emīr to "our possessions and souls are in your hands."[35]

35. Ibid., pp. 202-213. See also *Documents*, 1:4, pp. 267-272. The date of Faiṣal's address is erroneously given in the *Documents*, 1:4, as 9 May.

CHAPTER FIVE

THE CONFLICT BETWEEN LLOYD GEORGE AND CLEMENCEAU

"Clemenceau was by far the most eminent member of the Council of Four.... Mr. Lloyd George came to occupy an ostensibly middle position.... Let (the reader) remember the Prime Minister's incurable love of a deal; his readiness to surrender the substance for the shadow; his intense desire, as the months dragged on, to get a conclusion and be back to England again. What wonder that in the eventual settlement the real victor was Clemenceau."

John Maynard Keynes, *Essay in Biography*.

IN PARIS, the month of May was a month of bitter complaints and violent recriminations: Clemenceau and Pichon taking the "offensive," while Lloyd George's attitude seemed to be stiffening more and more against the French claims in Syria.

On 4 May, Clemenceau sent for Wickham Steed and "complained bitterly that Lloyd George had continually failed to keep his word to him." He added: "At first Lloyd George expressed himself entirely in favour of a French mandate for Syria and said that the only obstacle was Wilson. 'Agree with Wilson', he added, 'and I will help you in every way, provided that you do not want to conquer Syria, that you give up your claims to Cilicia and that you leave Mosul in the British sphere'. All this, I had done; but after I agreed with Wilson and House, Lloyd George did nothing."[1]

At about this time, the French wanting apparently to find a short-cut path to their goal through the tangled maze of Allied "Agreements" and British "pledges" to the Arabs, began openly to ask for a French mandate over Syria but Lloyd George refused at first to entertain such an idea. The Minutes of the Allied Supreme Council show that the Mandatory System was discussed at its meeting of 30 January 1919.[2] The first hint came from M. Pichon at the secret Conference of the four great Powers which was held on

1. Steed, vol. 2, p. 323.
2. Miller, vol. 21, pp. 557-569.

20 March. M. Pichon said: "If France was promised a mandate for Syria, she would undertake to do nothing except in agreement with the Arab State or Confederation of States. This is the role which France demanded in Syria".[3] On 11 May, M. Clemenceau asked Mr. Steed whether Steed "could not get the British to agree to a French mandate for Syria and to the substitution of French for British garrisons there, with the good will and assistance of the British authorities."[4]

Meanwhile, Faiṣal stated very frankly his attitude towards France to the British authorities. On 12 May, General Clayton had an interview with the Emīr in Damascus. A day later, he reported the result of his interview to General Allenby who, in turn, communicated it to Lord Curzon of Kedleston (George Nathaniel) telegraphically on 21 May, from Cairo. The following is the important text of Allenby's cable:

"I have received following from my Chief Political Officer, General Clayton; Begins:

" 'I had interview with Feisal yesterday and today. He raised the question of his policy towards the French. He informed me that on the advice of Lawrence he had agreed verbally with Clemenceau to use his efforts with the people to secure a French mandate for Syria on the understanding that France recognised Syrian independence. Feisal stated frankly that he had never any intention of carrying out the arrangement and that Syria was bitterly opposed to French penetration in any form whatever. He said that Great Britain would be welcomed as mandatory Power but that he was unable to ask for a British mandate as he could not ascertain whether or not Great Britain would accept a mandate if offered. He had asked the Prime Minister the question but had received no direct reply. Feisal was obviously nervous as to the result of such an underhanded policy towards the French and asked for my advice. I told him that in my opinion a policy of intrigue and deception would only recoil upon himself and might easily endanger Franco-British relations and as a consequence relations between Great Britain and the Arabs.

3. Baker, vol. 3, p. 11.
4. Steed, vol. 2, p. 325.

" 'Feisal has now decided to await the arrival of the Peace Conference Commission and to ask definitely for the following:

" '1. The independence (of Syria) as the ruling principle of any mandate which the Peace Conference may decide to give.

" '2. Advice and assistance to the Syrian State to be given by Great Britain; should they refuse, by America; if America refuses, by Great Britain, America and France; in no case by France alone (?).

" 'This is in accordance with the impressions I have gained when (? in Damascus on) May 12.'. "[5]

Meanwhile, the attitude of the Arabs in Syria towards France was growing steadily worse. In his Report on the "Political situation in Arabia" dated 16 May, Lt. Col. Kinahan Cornwallis wrote: "The politicians (in Damascus) have only two convictions; firstly, that they want independence, and secondly, that they do not want France. Anti-French feeling is surprisingly strong amongst the people who count...."[6]

The next day, the *Times* reported:[7] "An article by 'Pertinax' in this morning's *Echo de Paris* reveals the anxiety of the French about the future of Syria, which has found expression in the French Press on more than one occasion during the Conference. His theme is that a French diplomacy, too much occupied with the situation on the Western front to trouble about affairs in the East, has allowed French influence in Syria to be usurped by Great Britain. Today, when the distribution among the Great Powers of mandates for various portions of the Ottoman Empire has to be decided, we find, says 'Pertinax' the Emir Feisul, a vassal of Great Britain, settled in Damascus and Syria garrisoned almost exclusively by British or Hedjaz troops."

The *Times* added, significantly: "There should be no reason for the minds of our Allies to be perturbed about our policy in the Levant. Great Britain has always recognised France's right to Syria as a sphere of influence.... Now, some Power has got to have the

5. *Documents*, 1:4, p. 265.

6. Ibid., p. 265

7. *Times* (London), 17 May 1919, p. 13, col. 6.

Mandate for Syria. Great Britain does not want it. Mr. Lloyd George has told the world so. The only other Power interested is France...."

By this time Clemenceau was getting exasperated at the meager progress which was made in arriving at some definite and final decision about Syria. He was worried lest his own political career should be jeopardized by the criticisms against him in the French conservative and religious circles that he lacked zeal for Syria.[8] So, at the meeting of the Council of Four (sitting as the "Three"),[9] M. Clemenceau "delivered an angry speech" when, on 21 and 22 May, the Council discussed Syria again.

According to the Minutes of this meeting:[10]

"M. Clemenceau complained that Mr. Lloyd George's promises to him had not been kept. When L.G. asked 'in what way the promises made to him had not been kept, M. Clemenceau said that in the Autumn of 1918 when he saw how the British were acting in Syria, he had come to London and had asked Mr. Lloyd George to say exactly what he wanted. Mr. Lloyd George had said Mosul and Palestine. He had returned to Paris, and in spite of the objections of M. Pichon and the Quai d'Orsay, he had conceded it. Then Mr. Lloyd George had said that France and Great Britain would get along alright. M. Clemenceau also complained that nothing had been done about the evacuation of Syria by British troops and their replacement by French troops. Also, Lord Milner had promised to help M. Clemenceau with Emir Feisal. He had never carried out his promise...."

M. Clemenceau then made an emotional appeal for the necessity of preserving Anglo-French and Franco-American solidarity.

Mr. Lloyd George said that "as regards the charge of a breach of faith, this was without any foundation."

8. "He did not belong to that section of political or religious French opinion which took a fanatical interest in Syria. He never joined the chorus of 'Partant pour la Syrie'." Lloyd George, *The Truth About the Peace Treaties*, vol. 2, p. 1076.

9. The meeting was held in President Wilson's house in Paris. Those present were President Wilson, Mr. Lloyd George and M. Clemenceau.

10. See *Papers Relating to the Foreign Relations of the United States*, vol. 5, pp. 756-766 and 807-812, See also Paul Mantoux, *Les Délibérations du Conseil des Quatre*, vol. 2, pp. 137-143 and 159-164.

M. Clemenceau remarked that France had had "a definite agreement before as to Syria."

"Mr. Lloyd George said that in London it had been agreed that Syria should go to France and Mesopotamia to Great Britain, but that Mosul which was in the same watershed as Mesopotamia, should form part of that country and go to Great Britain."

Perhaps the most significant development of this meeting was the Memorandum submitted by Mr. Lloyd George, entitled "Scheme for Settlement in the Turkish Empire," points 7 and 8 of which were:

7 — "France to have a provisional mandate over Syria pending the report of the Commission which is proceeding to the Near East," and

8 — "Great Britain to have a provisional mandate over Mesopotamia and Palestine pending the report of the Commission that is proceeding to the Near East."

But M. Clemenceau was far from being satisfied. He did not like the word "provisional" and the conditional phrase: "pending the report of the Commission," a Commission to which he had objected right from the beginning and in which he was not at all interested.

When the Council of Four met again the next day, Mr. Lloyd George said:

"The territory in dispute was, under the Sykes-Picot Agreement, not allotted to France, but was entirely Arab. The same applied to Damascus, Aleppo and Homs, which were to be entirely Arab. Under the Sykes-Picot Agreement, they were not included in Syria, and France was only to have the littoral. If that arrangement was to stand, he would be glad to know. He thought it was agreed that the Sykes-Picot Agreement had been a bad one. He wanted to know whether it existed or not. If it exists, France has no right to hoist a flag or put a soldier in the Arab zone; they had only the right to provide advisors."

Then he advanced an added argument—but a psychologically ill-chosen argument which immensely hurt Clemenceau — to the effect that the British effort in overthrowing Turkey had been much greater than France's effort. The British "white casualties" in the

Turkish campaign had been 125,000. France's help had been "negligible" — "perhaps 2,000 men out of 200,000, 1 per cent." A further irritating reminder came with his words that the best attack would have been from Alexandretta. Lord Kitchener wanted to do so. France had opposed it. "The French had been in the position of not going there themselves and not letting us go."

"M. Clemenceau said that the Sykes-Picot Agreement held. He adhered to it. Mr. Lloyd George interrupted to ask "whether this included Damascus?" M. Clemenceau said, "of course when he gave Mosul he realised he would share in Damascus and Aleppo on corresponding terms. Of course, he recognised that Damascus was Arab.... If he had not agreed to cede Mosul in London, the present controversy would never have arisen.... The British were in (military) occupation... He was not willing, however, to accept the line now proposed.... He thought that Mr. Lloyd George was wrong, but he would take every care not to push matters so far as to make trouble between the Entente...."

At such moments, when the discussion got to a delicate and critical point, President Wilson could not be helpful. He would not and possibly could not understand the "Secret Diplomacy" of the 19th century. Anyway, he did not want to have anything to do with it. He had no compromise to suggest for the Near Eastern tangle. Instead of attempting to solve the problem, he wanted to do away with it altogether on the basis of the principle of his Fourteen Points which he had announced to the world on 8 January 1918 and of his Address at Mount Vernon on 4 July of the same year.[11]

11. Point 5 of the Fourteen Points said:
"A free, open-minded, and absolutely impartial adjustment of all colonial claims based upon a strict observance of the principle that in determining all such questions of sovereignty the interests of the populations concerned must have equal weight with the equitable claims of the government whose title is to be determined."

Point 2 of President Wilson's Address at Mount Vernon was:
"The settlement of every question, whether of territory, of sovereignty, of economic arrangement, or of political relationship, (to be) upon the basis of the free acceptance of that settlement by the people immediately concerned, and not upon the basis of the material interest or advantages of any other nation or people, which may desire a different settlement for the sake of its own exterior influence or mastery."

Miller, vol. 4, Doc. 251, Appendix, p. 301.

Indeed, the American Peace Commissioners had already put on record at their meeting on 18 February 1919 that the United States intended to completely ignore the London Agreement of April 1915 and the Sykes-Picot Agreement in the discussion of the Near East problems, "unless by chance, they happen to contain provisions which we consider to be just and proper, in accordance with our declared principles." Thus, when he got tired of listening to Clemenceau and Lloyd George and became impatient at their claims and counter claims, he enquired, according to the above-mentioned Minutes, "as to what part he was asked to play in this affair. He himself had never been able to see by what right France and Great Britain gave the country away to anyone." Lloyd George seeking the alliance of the President against Clemenceau and having nothing to lose in this case, said very shrewdly, that "he was quite willing to abide by the decision of the inhabitants as interpreted by the Commission." This seemed to please the President who added that "that was necessarily his own point of view.... He did not think that these peoples could be left entirely to themselves. They required guidance and some intimate superintendence, but this should be conducted in their interests and not in the interests of the mandatory." But at this point, Lloyd George, not willing to infuriate Clemenceau beyond a certain point and having himself never thought seriously of sending a Commission to Syria, said "he could not send Commissioners if the French would not send any, but the American Commissioners could go alone." Whereupon, President Wilson said that his "Commissioners were absolutely disinterested. He proposed that the question should now be adjourned for further consideration."

Nine days later, the Council of Four again had Syria on its agenda. It met in M. Pichon's Room at the Quai d'Orsay. "Mr. Lloyd George read a telegram he had received from General Allen-

Lord Hankey told the author that in his black Despatch Box which he carried with him to every Conference and every Council meeting, he kept a set of standard reference material to produce or to refer to whenever necessary. Among these reference materials he always kept the Fourteen Points of President Wilson. Lord Hankey called the Fourteen Points a sort of "moral background" to the politics of the time. Interview with Lord Hankey, in London, in March 1951.

by, indicating that the situation in Syria would be extremely grave unless the Commission of the Peace Conference should come to Syria.... Hence, the moment had come to decide."[12]

Clemenceau, however, remained, adamant. "As long as Syria remained entirely in British military occupation," he said, "it was useless to send French Commissioners. Lloyd George was equally emphatic: "He would not send Commissioners if the French did not...."[13]

This was a great relief for Clemenceau: no Anglo-American Commission was going out to Syria. Meanwhile, the "American Section of the International Commission on Mandates in Turkey" had already left for the Near East[14]. The two principal members of

12. Allenby cabled to Balfour, in Paris:

"Cairo, 30th May.

"I look on the situation as extremely grave.... It is certain that Feisal will raise the Arabs against the French and ourselves unless he (Feisal) can be officially reassured that the Commission is going out to decide the future of the country....

"The Political Officer at Damascus adds that the situation at once becomes most dangerous if Feisal's interpretation of the decision of the Peace Conference be correct: namely, that the British troops are to be withdrawn from Syria in favour of France, without consulting Syria's wishes. Joyce agreed with him that Feisal is in dead earnest and that, even if willing, he will be unable to prevent bloodshed on a large scale; indeed he will probably identify himself with any rising unless the news is contradicted....

"A rising of the Bedouins would bring against us all the tribes of the Sinai peninsula and serious trouble would certainly break out in Egypt and the Sudan. In such a case, I shall be totally unable to handle the situation with the troops at my disposal." *Documents*, 1:4, p. 256.

At the same time, General Allenby, as Commander-in-Chief of the Occupation Troops in the Near East sent a cable to Faiṣal giving him a stern warning which was more in the nature of an ultimatum. Allenby said: "...I count upon you in the meantime to maintain order and discipline and to restrain any action that might endanger future of your country. Any hasty action that would bring you into conflict with my troops would put an end to all your national aspiration at once." Ibid.

13. See U.S., Department of State, *Papers Relating to the Foreign Relations of the United States*, vol. 5, p. 812. "M. Clemenceau — Je suis prêt à envoyer mes représentants en Syrie dès que la relève des troupes d'occupation aura commencé. Mais je trouve qu'il est inutile à envoyer une commission en Syrie pour faire une enquête sous la dictature du général Allenby." Mantoux, pp. 143 and 263-264.

14. "After the failure of Clemenceau and Lloyd George to agree to a joint inter-allied Commission to Syria... President Wilson instructed the Americans to go forward at once. They left Paris May 25 and 29...." Baker, vol. 2, p. 206.

this Commission were Dr. Henry Churchill King and Mr. Charles R. Crane.[15]

The British had nominated Sir Henry McMahon and Dr. David Hogarth as their delegates for the Commission, with Prof. Arnold J. Toynbee as its secretary. Brigadier Longrigg has written that Lloyd George was "also influenced by doubts as to the desirability of the Commission proceeding also to Iraq (upon which the French very naturally insisted) and by some degree of Zionist pressure, since the unpopularity of that movement in Palestine was known to be growing rapidly." Stephen Hemsley Longrigg, *Syria and Lebanon under French Mandate* (London, 1958), p. 89, n. 1.

This "Zionist pressure" was a further complication in the stormy waters through which the appointment of an Inter-Allied Commission sailed. Between 8 and 16 May 1919, an exchange of four letters took place between Professor Felix Frankfurter and President Wilson. "On 8 May, Professor Felix Frankfurter, in behalf of the Zionist Organization, wrote to President Wilson expressing his fears lest the appointment of the Inter-Allied Commission would postpone the Near Eastern settlement beyond Wilson's stay in Paris and lead ultimately to a disposition of the problem contrary to the Balfour Declaration, on which Zionist hopes had centered. Wilson did not reply until some days later, and finally, in response to Frankfurter's request for a reassuring word, remarked that he had never dreamed that a renewed assurance of his adhesion to the Balfour Declaration was necessary." Harry N. Howard, "An American Experiment in Peace-making: the King-Crane Commission," *Muslim World*, vol. 32, no. 2 (April 1942), p. 131.

15. Among other members of the American group were Professor Albert J. Lybyer as "General Technical Adviser" and Captain William Yale as "Technical Adviser for The Southern Regions of Turkey." Dr. Henry Churchill King was President of Oberlin College and "Director of religious work for the Y.M. C.A." in 1918-19; Mr. Charles R. Crane, was a well-known manufacturer from Chicago and a member of President Wilson's Special Diplomatic Commission to Russia in 1917. In 1919, both Dr. King and Mr. Crane were appointed to serve in the American Section of the Peace Conference, Inter-Allied Commission on Mandates in Turkey. In the "Minutes of the Daily Meetings of the Commissioners Plenipotentiary," it has been recorded that President Wilson felt Dr. King and Mr. Crane "were particularly qualified to go to Syria because they knew nothing about it. . . . " See *Editor and Publisher*, vol. 55, no. 27, 2d sec. (2 December 1922), p. 4, and *Papers Relating to the Foreign Relations of the United States*, vol. 11, p. 133.

"It was a letter from President Howard Bliss of the American University of Beirut, on February, 7, 1919 to President Wilson which seems to have laid the essential foundations for the sending of a Commission of Inquiry to the East." — Howard, "An American Experiment in Peace-making," and idem, *The King-Crane Commission*, pp. 25-26. p. 124.

It is not certain whether the Italians were seriously considering to send an Italian commission to Syria but the following conversation reported by Professor Mantoux is worth nothing: "M. Lloyd George . . . L'Italie enverra-t-elle ses commissaires en Syrie?

More warnings came to the Foreign Office from the British Representatives in the Near East assuring the Government of the certainty of hostile action by Faiṣal and the Syrians against France and even against British troops stationed in that area.

During the month of June, Faiṣal did everything he could to keep the British in Syria in order to prevent a French occupation of the country. But the British Government made it categorically clear that they were not going to take the Mandate for Syria in spite of the desperate appeals of Faiṣal that they should take it. They tried, however, to allay his fears by assuring him that they were not abandoning either him or the Arab Cause, for they "earnestly desired to support both."

The following documents give a brief account of the main events of June.

Towards the beginning of this month, the French Ambassador visited Curzon and referred to "strong feelings" between the Prime Ministers of France and Great Britain in Paris, on the future of Syria. In his reply, Lord Curzon told the Ambassador:

"If there was any region in which France had good cause to be grateful for our support, it was in Syria itself. Not only had Mr. Lloyd George in the Councils of Paris openly declared that Great Britain neither desired nor would accept, if it were offered to her, a mandate for Syria, but we had actually telegraphed an intimation to the same effect to the Emir Faisal."[16]

This intimation was given to Faiṣal by General Allenby in a cable which he sent from Cairo, dated 12 June:

"His Majesty's Government have expressed unwillingness to accept a mandate for Syria but will give fullest weight to advice of Commission in the Council of Allied and Associated Powers."[17] There is no evidence to support the last part of General Allenby's

"M. Orlando — J'attendrai les autres.

"Le Président Wilson — La commission américaine est déjà partie.

"M. Clemenceau — M. Lloyd George vient de dire qu'il n'enverra personne en Syrie si nos représentants n'y vont pas.

"M. Orlando — Je ferai la même chose que vous." Mantoux, p. 264.

16. *Documents* 1:4, p. 184.

17. Ibid., p. 276.

statement. In all probability it was added to lessen the anxiety of Faiṣal. On 14 June, Faiṣal's reply said:

"Telegram received. I have noted Great Britain's expression of unwillingness to take mandate for Syria. Its intention to give the fullest weight to advice of Peace Commission however is cheerfully understood by us all. The Syrians will be unanimous in expressing to Commission their wish to have Britain and no other, for reasons I am going to set before a Conference to be held shortly at Damascus comprised of Delegations from every part of Syria strongly backed by public opinion. I wish to inform your Excellency of all this, hoping that this national feeling of mutual love and esteem and confidence will last forever, profoundly trusting British honour will never permit those who pray for its assistance to be thrown away into strange arms." [18]

Meanwhile, the "Inter-Allied" or "the Neutral Commission" for which Dr. Bliss had pleaded to be sent to Syria, arrived in Jaffa, Palestine, as an American Commission, on 10 June. The Commission had come to institute an inquiry as to the actual desires of the inhabitants and report to the Peace Conference. [19] Unfortunately, the Commission added to the complications of an already entangled situation by raising false hopes and strengthening previous illusions. Their arrival was awaited with much eagerness as the people believed this was their only means by which they could make their aspirations known to the Peace Conference. The Commissioners gave the impression that the Syrians could count on President Wilson and the American people "who recognise that they

18. Ibid., p. 277.

19. General Clayton to Earl Curzon:

"Cairo, June 1, 1919.

"Have seen Picot today. He tells me Syria is being divided without reference to Feisal and that American Commission is only coming out to keep Feisal in the dark while partition of Syria is being arranged. This, Picot professes to know for certain from French Official sources. He and I agree that it if true, this is dangerous game to play. If Feisal finds that the fate of Syria has been decided without his knowledge and before Commission has made its report, he will undoubtedly take hostile action. M. Picot tells me while he was in Paris it was decided to send international Commission to Syria and Palestine. If this is true, I would suggest that I ought to have been so informed by you." Ibid., p. 263.

have responsibilities for just settlements under the League of Nations with a view to securing permanent peace."[20] "The King-Crane Commission...," wrote Sir Ronald Storrs who was at that time the Military Governor of Jerusalem, "forthwith descended upon O.E.T.'s East and West, and South."

In an illuminating Report sent by General Clayton to Earl Curzon on 23 June, giving "a summary of the situation up to date in Syria," Clayton wrote:

"His (Faiṣal's) great difficulty now is what he considers the extraordinary attitude of Britain; after liberating the Arabic-speaking countries at an immense cost in blood and treasure and after four years' unbroken friendship with the Emir and the Arabs, England has suddenly cooled, refuses to say whether she is going to help anymore, and is now giving the impression that she has sold the Arabs to suit the exigencies of politics in Europe.... France, to all appearances, relies solely on England and America for her future existence; this the Emir knows full well, and he cannot understand why England should be so afraid of doing anything to offend the country which should logically be prepared to make almost any sacrifice to avoid alienating England....

"A French mandate is regarded as a national death. It will bring French colonists and French citizenship and French hegemony. The Emir and his Arabs did not make their revolution to see the fairest part of their country handed to France, whom they regard as nothing less than an enemy, and whom they fully intend to resist by force of arms should she attempt to exercise a protectorate over Syria....

"If England is not going to accept the mandate, the sooner this is widely known the better. If England will accept Syria, the cry for complete independence and the immediate recruiting of troops will be at once dropped. If England is determined to avoid further

20. Ibid., p. 286. In a Statement which the Commissioners issued when they arrived in Palestine they said, in part: "American section (of the International Commission) is now arrived with a view to ascertaining the desires of all peoples and sections in order that full knowledge may be at the disposal of President Wilson and American people when they are called upon to act in the Peace Conference or subsequently in the League of Nations." Ibid.

responsibilities in Syria... then Syria wants complete independence...."[21]

As it was evident that Great Britain was going to stay in Mesopotamia, Faiṣal and his advisers thought now of a new way of keeping her in Syria by proposing that Mesopotamia and Syria should form "one united government." So, on 24 June, the Ḥejāzian Delegation in Paris transmitted to Mr. Lloyd George a Memorandum, dated 23 June, by General Nurī Pasha al-Sa'īd, Chief Aide-de-Camp to the Emīr Faiṣal. "This Memorandum was designed to prove the necessity of forming one united government of the liberated Arab provinces of Syria and Mesopotamia.... The overwhelming majority of the inhabitants of Syria and Mesopotamia looks forward to the formation of one single government composed of a group of united states.... The desire to separate Syria and Mesopotamia is based in part on the imperialistic policy of certain parties in Europe.... The best solution of the Arab question, and it is the only solution which will meet with the approval of the majority, is to form one government composed of federal states on the same lines as the United States of America; each state of which should have some sort of self-government compatible with the traditions, habits and degree of development of its inhabitants."[22]

As Faiṣal continued to hope that Great Britain might take the Mandate for Syria, partly by personal conviction and partly, perhaps, by the attitudes of Generals Allenby and Clayton, who it seems, were not themselves quite certain that Great Britain was leaving Syria, bag and baggage, Mr. Balfour sent the following cable from Paris to General Allenby in Cairo, on 26 June:

"... H.M.G. have not departed from view expressed orally by Prime Minister, I think in your presence, to M. Clemenceau in the presence of President Wilson, Signor Orlando and myself that in no circumstances would Great Britain become mandatory for Syria;

21. Ibid., pp. 291-292.

22. Ibid., p. 296.

"*Les Vœux du Peuple Arabe — Le Peuple Entier Revendique l'Indépendance Entière, Sans Restriction, de la Syrie et de la Mésopotamie. Pas de Mandat! Pas de Tutelle! Pas de Protectorat! Mais l'Unité Arabe et l'Indépendance Entière!*" The above headlines appeared in thick letters on page 1 of *L'Indépendance: Organe Arabe* (Damascus), no. 23, Saturday, 28 June 1919.

and this has been repeated explicitly in telegram No. 16 to General Clayton which runs as follows:

" 'You can reply to Feisal that His Majesty's Government are determined not to take a mandate for Syria'.

"I feel confident that Feisal was told the same thing when he was here though I can find no record of this having been done.... But... he is quite without justification in thinking that this refusal constitutes an abandonment of either himself or of the Arab Cause. We earnestly desire to support both."[23]

Thus, by the end of June, the French had scored one more point in favor of the realization of their ambitions in Syria: Great Britain was "determined not to take the mandate for Syria".

Indeed, on 2 July, in a Memorandum transmitted by Mr. Balfour, from Paris, to Mr. Lloyd George on the subject of "Disposal of Turkish Territories," Mr. Balfour gave his own personal view which he had "more than once expressed", of a new arrangement of the "Turkish settlement." "I venture briefly," he said, "to recapitulate it:

" (1) All Arab speaking parts of the Ottoman Empire should be permanently severed from it, and should be put under Mandatories. The precise power of these Mandatories has still to be determined.

" (2) The French should be the mandatory for Syria, the British for Mesopotamia, the American (s) or English for Palestine, the Americans for Armenia and the Straits (Constantinople), Italy perhaps for the Caucasus.

" (3) The French Mandatory should include Alexandretta, though historically this can hardly be said to belong to Syria. I should however be sorry to see any important extension of the French Mandatory westwards along the Anatolian coast, not because I grudge this to the French, but because everything that the French gain in the Eastern Mediterranean is made the basis of a fresh claim by Italy.

"This in roughest outline is the territorial arrangement of the Turkish Empire outside Europe, which I should be disposed to

23. *Documents,* 1:4, p. 298.

recommend. If that could be combined with a settlement of all the small but irritating questions which are perpetually raising points of difference between French, Italians and British in Africa and the East and if (by) such an arrangement all petty jealousies and intrigues between these Allied Nations could be finally put an end to, not merely those three Allied coutries but all the world would greatly gain. I cannot think that such a consummation is wholly beyond our reach, but if its to be attained, we should set to work to do it at once."[24]

Notwithstanding the British refusal to take part in the Commission of Inquiry and the British determination not to have a Mandate over Syria, French anxiety as to the recognition of their claims in Syria seems in no way to have been lessened. "British officers and officials in the Near East were openly charged with influencing the native population against France," and "French public opinion, turned always with passionate regard towards Syria, saw in the continued British occupation only a sinister agency — an agency which alone prevented the immediate transformation of a romantic national dream into actuality most happy and desirable."[25]

What added fuel to the flame and infuriated the French was the news from Syria, as reported by the American Commission, of the unfavorable attitude of the Syrians towards a French Mandate. In their cable from Beirut, dated 10 July, to the Peace Conference, the Commissioners said:

"Certain points are unmistakable. Intense desire for unity of all Syria and Palestine and for as early independence as possible. Unexpected(ly) strong expressions of national feeling. Singular(ly) determined repulsion to becoming a mere colony of any power and against any kind of French Mandate. Only marked exceptions to

24. Ibid., pp. 302-303. This Memorandum was minuted as follows by Lord Curzon: "This Memo is generally, as it appears to me, on sound lines.... Much turns on whether the American Congress will allow President Wilson to accept a mandate for anything. I rather doubt. Better not circulate at present. (C. 5/7)" Ibid.

25. Temperley, vol. 6, p. 150.

this statement are found in strong parties of Lebanese who demand complete separation of Lebanon with French collaboration." [26]

Accordingly, the French press launched a series of bitter attacks against Great Britain, accusing her of conducting anti-French propaganda in Syria. On 26 July, Sir G. Grahame, Minister at His Majesty's Embassy in Paris, reported to Earl Curzon the gist of two articles which may be considered as typical of these French accusations. Sir G. Grahame wrote:

"The *Bulletin de l'Asie Française* for July contains an article by a well-known publicist, M. Robert de Caix, violently attacking British propaganda against France in the Levant.

"According to M. de Caix, the object of this propaganda is to eliminate French influence in Syria. It was for this purpose, he says, that British occupation encouraged pan-Arabism in Syria and despatched the Emir Feisal to Paris with an exaggerated programme. England, he says, justified her attitude towards the King of Hedjaz by promises made to him at the end of 1915. These promises were contradictory to engagements taken by England towards France in 1916, and he complains that promises made to 'the King of the Arabs, should have prevailed over those made to France, and attributes this to British self-interest."

"*Temps* of to-day's date publishes most of de Caix's article and practically endorses his view, adding that it is in interest of two countries so closely allied as France and Great Britain to be loyally frank with one another....

"*Temps* then refers to work of American Mission in Syria and expresses belief that result of its report is unfavourable as regards France's Mandate. If, it adds, this is so, this view is due to the skilful propaganda during past six months aimed exclusively against France." [27]

26. *Papers Relating to the Foreign Relations of the United States*, vol. 12, p. 749.

27. *Documents*, 1:4, pp. 318-320.

"Notre situation en Syrie fut aggravée de deux ordres de faits:

D'abord la sinistre bouffonnerie de la Commission américaine. Dirigée exclusivement contre la France, elle n'alla ni à Baghdad, ni à Mossoul, où elle aurait pu constater une opposition très vive à l'Angleterre....
Son enquête fut une odieuse comédie. Elle ne reçut que les délégations présentées par les Britanniques et les Chérifiens se refusant à recevoir celles

M. Clemenceau himself joined in these accusations. Nearly two months earlier, on 11 May, he had complained to Steed about the anti-French attitude of Britain in Syria: "All we now want," he told Steed, "is that the British should agree with us and that instructions should be given to the local British officers not to stir up the population against us."[28] And then in July, at the Meeting of the Heads of Delegations of the Five Great Powers which was held at the Quai d'Orsay, on the 18th of that month, M. Clemenceau said, in anger: "General Allenby had acted as a British General and not as an 'Allied Commander-in-Chief'. The effect of his activities was distinctly anti-French. This ambiguous situation was unsatisfactory. As an Allied Commander-in-Chief, he refused to allow French troops to enter Syria. He placed them in Cilicia, knowing that the mandate of Cilicia was likely to go to the Americans. All his agents were consistently against the French. On every occasion, he said that the unpopularity of the French troops rendered their relief or their stationing in Syria undesirable."[29]

Needless to say that the British Government vehemently refuted all these allegations. Replying to Clemenceau. Mr. Balfour said that "he felt sure that no responsible British officer desired to impair French popularity in Syria. They knew that under no circumstances would Great Britain accept a mandate in Syria. The British Government, therefore, had no motive for creating difficulties in the path of others."[30]

favorables à la France, ou si elle s'y trouvait obligée, les rudoyant grossièrement. . . ." Brémond, *Le Hedjaz dans la Guerre Mondiale*, p. 327.

28. From "Notes of a Meeting of the Heads of Delegations of the Five Great Powers held at the Quai d'Orsay," in *Documents*, 1:1, p. 134.

29. Ibid.

30. Ibid. On the other hand, William Yale reported:

"The British intend, if possible, to keep Palestine and would like to control Syria. They do not wish the French even in Mount Lebanon. However, realizing that without an open break with France, they cannot single handed force France to give up her claims they would be pleased if the United States stepped in and took Syria. They have allowed and encouraged the Young Arabs to carry on a United Syria propaganda even though it might cost the British Palestine, in order to create a situation which would force the United States to take the Mandate over all Syria. . . ."

From "A Report on Syria, Palestine, and Mount Lebanon for the American Commissioners prepared by Captain William Yale, Technical Advisor to The

As the clamour of the French Colonial Party for Syria became noisier and the controversy seemed to threaten the Franco-British Entente, Mr. Balfour, while in Paris, wrote a Memorandum "respecting Syria, Palestine and Mesopotamia."

In its penetrating analysis of the problem, in its clear exposition of political motives, in its frank admission that "the literal fulfilment" of the promises made by the Allies is "impossible," in its honesty and courage to state the truth and face the facts of a highly unpleasant situation, this Memorandum stands out among all other documents on British-French-Arab relations, supreme and unrivalled. Suffice it here to quote from it the following passages:

"The effect which the Syrian question is producing on Anglo-French relations is causing me considerable anxiety — an anxiety not diminished by the fact that very little is openly said about it, much is hinted.... "This brings into clear relief what I fear is the unhappy truth, namely, that France, England and America have got themselves into a position over the Syrian problem so inextricably confused that no really neat and satisfactory is issue now possible for any of them."

The Memorandum proceeds to discuss the difficulties of the Secret Agreements made during the war and dwells in particular on the Sykes-Picot Agreement. According to Mr. Balfour, those who framed that Agreement "started from the view that France had ancient interests and aspirations in Western Syria; that Britain had obvious claims in Baghdad and Southern Mesopotamia... they never supposed themselves to be dealing with three nations already in existence, ready for 'provisional recognition', only requiring the removal of the Turk, the advice of a mandatory, and a little time to enable them to 'stand alone'. It never occurred to them that they had to deal at all with nations in the modern and Western sense of the term."

Mr. Balfour admits that "the literal fulfilment of all our declarations is impossible, partly because they are incompatible with each other and partly because they are incompatible with facts....

American Section of the International Commission on Mandates in Turkey," dated 26 July 1919, pp. 14-15. See U.S., and Records Service, Department of State, Record Group 59.

As part of a new scheme, Balfour then suggests that "the fundamental conception underlying the Sykes-Picot Agreement should be maintained — namely, a French sphere centring round Syria, a British sphere centring round the Euphrates and the Tigris, and a home for the Jews in the valley of Jordan."[31]

Meanwhile, the French press continued throughout the month of August its anti-British campaign in connection with Syria. The British Cabinet, by this time annoyed by these French attacks, instructed Sir G. Grahame to call upon M. Pichon, the French Minister for Foreign Affairs and try "to shake his belief" in "the anti-French action of British agents in Syria." However, M. Pichon's belief could not be shaken. Sir G. Grahame reported to Lord Curzon:

"M. Pichon, speaking at first heatedly, declared that his *dossiers* were full of reports of anti-French propaganda carried on by Anglo-Syrian agents. He received them almost daily and they formed a formidable mass of evidence. These reports were so detailed and concordant that it was absolutely impossible for the French Government not to believe that they were well-founded.... I interrupted his Excellency at this point to tell him... that the French were entirely mistaken in thinking that we were working against them there.... M. Pichon listened to me but maintained his view that contrary information was reaching him from many quarters, which he could not possibly disregard...."[32]

M. Pichon was also convinced that His Majesty's Government were "not fully aware of the intense feeling about Syria" in France, and the "passionate interest" which the French took in this question. "If the Government laid themselves open to the charge of not properly defending French interests, they would be swept away. They would not get ten votes in the Chamber if they tried to thwart this sentiment...."[33]

31. For the full text of this document, see *Documents*, 1:4, pp. 340-349.
32. Ibid., pp. 349-350.
33. Ibid., p. 350.

T.E. Lawrence (Lawrence of Arabia).

British troops (The Australian Light Horse Brigade) passing through Damascus, 1 October 1918. The building in the background is the Turkish Hamidiyyah barracks.

The Emīr Faiṣal leaves Hotel Victoria in Damascus after conference with General Allenby, 3 October 1918.

General Sir Edmund Allenby (3rd from right) with a number of his staff officers standing in front of a British inscription at the Dog River, near Beirut, Lebanon. The inscription reads: "The XXI British Army Corps with Le Détachement Français de Palestine et de Syrie occupied Beirut and Tripoli October 1918."

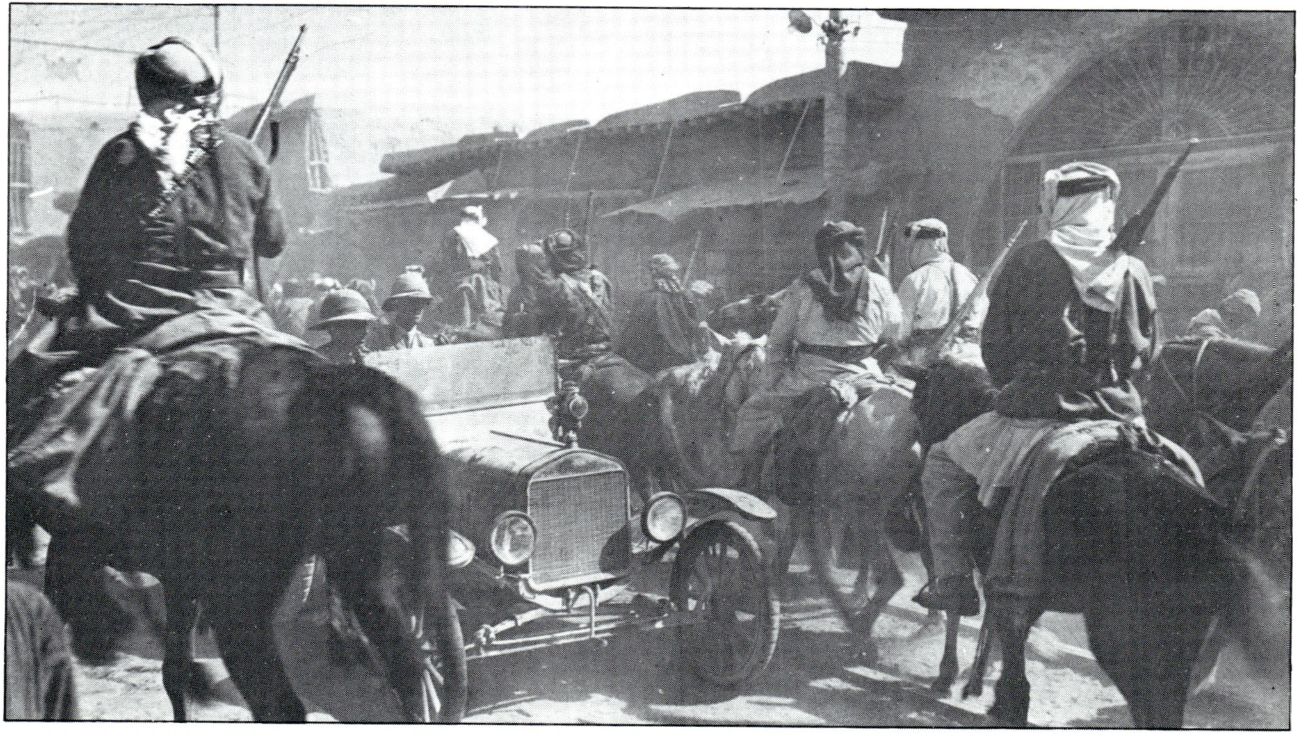

Regular Arab cavalry entering Damascus on 1 October 1918. Captain Hodgekinson is seen here in a Model T automobile.

Irregular Arab troops in Damascus, October 1918.

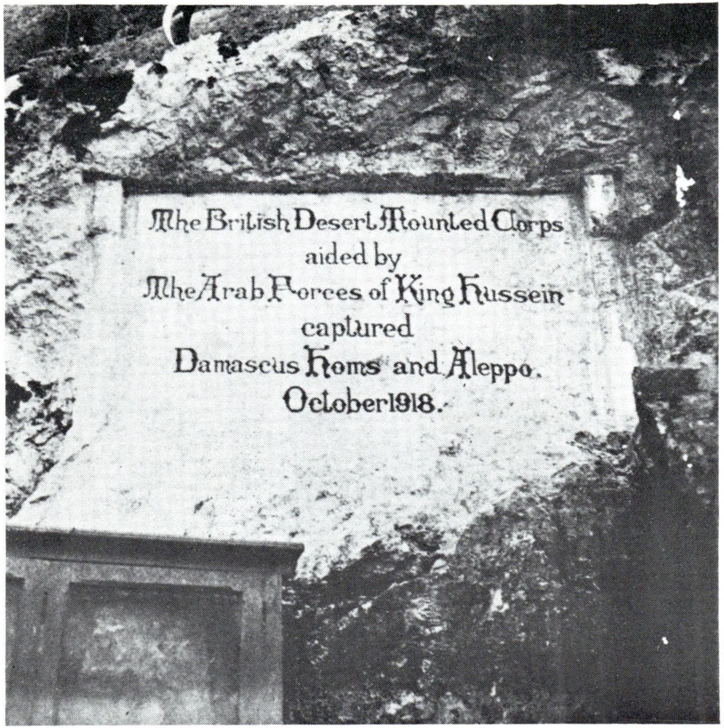

An inscription on the left bank of the Dog River, about 15 kms north-east of Beirut, Lebanon.

General Sir Edmund Allenby, Commander in Chief of the Egyptian Expeditionary Force.

The Sharīf Ḥusain of Mecca, King of the Hejaz.

King Faisal I of Syria and, later, of Iraq.

CHAPTER SIX

THE SETTLEMENT OF THE "SYRIAN QUESTION" 1919

"*The French stood by their bond. The American* Deus ex Machina *failed. Faisal had our support in debate but not in action; and having pushed him into the Councils of Paris, as the accredited representative of an allied nation, we let him return to tell his nation that except Hejaz, its independence was to be, in fact, dependence on two alien Powers for an indefinite period.*"

D. G. Hogarth in *The Quarterly Review*, No. 464, October 1920.

BY THE MIDDLE OF AUGUST, the British Government seems to have become almost desperate about finding a basis of settlement for the Eastern Question. On the 20th, Lord Curzon wrote in a letter to Lady Curzon: "This morning at the end of our third Cabinet — it lasted 3 1/2 hours — the Cabinet led by the P.M. unanimously asked me to go out to Paris and take in hand the Eastern Question and *gave me authority for any settlement that I might like to effect....*"[1]

On 31 August, the Emīr Faiṣal made a Statement to the Chief of the General Staff, Egyptian Expeditionary Force and the Political Officer in Damascus. In simple and clear language, the Statement is perhaps the best brief summary of the Arab case which we have. Faiṣal said: "My father, King Ḥussein, received a message from the High Commissioner, Egypt, Sir Henry MacMahon, through a certain agent, in which promises were made by the High

1. Earl of Ronaldshay, *The Life of Lord Curzon*, vol. 3, 204. Author's italics.
At about this time (23 August), Lord Riddell wrote in his diary: "Kerr arrived from Paris, evidently impressed with the necessity of making concessions to the French in the Eastern Mediterranean. L.G. angry with the French for their attitude concerning Syria. He said that the Syrians would not have the French, and asked how the Allies could compel them to accept mandatories who were distasteful. He added, 'I shall have to make a public statement'. His attitude to the French has changed greatly since the end of 1918. He continually refers to their greed."
Lord Riddell, *Lord Riddell's Intimate Diary of the Peace Conference and After, 1918-1923*, 112.

Commissioner that Great Britain would assist the Arabs, if the latter threw in their lot with her.

"Accordingly, my father relying on this promise, took up arms against the Turks, who had at that time proclaimed a Holy War against the Allies and against Great Britain in particular, and accepted willingly the responsibility of war.

"We, the Arabs, were formerly with the Turks and fought against them, not with the intention of dividing the country by giving a share to the French and a portion to the British. . . ."[2]

Nevertheless, thirteen days later, the most important turning point in the future fate of Syria was reached when an agreement was concluded between Lloyd George and Clemenceau, on 13 September, "by which the evacuation of the British Army in Syria was to be concluded by November 1st, 1919. . . ."[3] The British troops should at that time hand the garrisons of Damascus, Ḥoms, Ḥama and Aleppo over to the Emīr Faiṣal, while west of the Sykes-Picot line, in Syria, "the garrisons would be handed over to the French troops."[4] This was undoubtedly a momentous decision of far-reaching consequences. "The Agreement between Messieurs Clemenceau and Lloyd George," wrote Professor William Yale,[5] "by which British troops will on November 1st be withdrawn from Cilicia, Syria and Mount Lebanon, to be replaced by French troops in Cilicia and along the Syrian Littoral and by Arab troops in the four cities of Damascus, Ḥoms, Ḥamah and Aleppo, is a most pernicious one.

"Superficially this is not a political move, but simply a change in the status of the military situation in 'Occupied Enemy's Territory'. Actually it not only seriously compromises the political future

2. *Documents*, 1:4, Appendix 2.

3. Lloyd George, 2: 1081. See also, Appendix D, below.

4. *Documents*, 1:1, p. 690.

5. William Yale was at this time a member of the American Commission to Negotiate Peace, in Paris. Earlier, he "had worked for Standard Oil of New Jersey in the Near East, first as explorer and then as resident agent in Jerusalem from 1915-1917." After the break in diplomatic relations with Turkey he returned to Washington. The State Department then sent him back to Cairo to report on the situation in the Near East, "a key area in the general peace settlement." See Manuel, p. 180.

of the Arab Provinces, but also seriously jeopardises the peace of the near and Middle East."[6]

As a result of the Agreement of 13 September, the Heads of the Delegations of the Five Great Powers met in M. Clemenceau's room at the War Office in Paris, on 15 September.[7] Lloyd George's "*Aide-Mémoire* in regard to the Occupation of Syria, Palestine and Mesopotamia pending the Decision in regard to Mandates," was handed round to those present. The whole Syrian affair was discussed once more, beginning again with the Sykes-Picot Agreement. "Under the Sykes-Picot Agreement," said Lloyd George, "Damascus, Ḥoms, Ḥama and Aleppo had been included within the boundaries of the Arab State." He therefore proposed that the British troops should hand the garrisons of these towns over to the Emīr Faiṣal. In other parts of Syria, west of the Sykes-Picot line, the garrisons would be handed over to the French troops." The second important point in Lloyd George's *Aide-Mémoire* was the statement that "the Sykes-Picot Agreement had also been based on the engagements of the British Government with the Arabs." But the British Government could not accept the view that by that Agreement they had given away something which was promised to the Arabs. "In their communications with King Ḥussein, they had always made it clear that in their view the country west of Damascus, Ḥoms, Ḥama and Aleppo was not Arab in character." The Prime Minister admitted, however, that as a result of "certain engagements" entered into with King Ḥusain, the latter had given "strong support" to the British forces. "In consequence of these engagements, the Arabs had greatly harassed the Turks, and had kept some thirty or forty thousand of them constantly occupied and given us every material assistance in conquering the country. *The Arabs had fulfilled their engagements and we were bound to fulfil ours.*"[8]

In M. Clemenceau's view, "the question of an Arab Empire raised great difficulties, and the governments concerned must take time to consider it...." There was one pressing question, at this

6. Garnett, p. 283.

7. For a full study of the discussion which took place at that meeting, see *Documents*, 1:1, pp. 685-701.

8. Author's italics.

meeting, on which he wished to have an answer from Mr. Lloyd George. Would the occupation by French troops of Syria be considered as the fulfilment of a part of the Sykes-Picot Agreement or as a definite acceptance of the whole of that Agreement? If it meant accepting the whole Agreement (and thus admitting Arab rights to Syria proper and the four towns of Damascus, Ḥoms, Ḥama and Aleppo), Clemenceau could not undertake to send troops. Lloyd George's reply was that M. Clemenceau would not be committed to the whole agreement by sending troops.[9]

At this time the Emīr Faiṣal was on his way to Europe, having been urgently invited by Lloyd George with the hope that some satisfactory solution of the Syrian problem might be reached between them all. When Faiṣal arrived in France, Clemenceau, who like the rest of his Government was in "an extremely suspicious frame of mind on the whole of the Syrian question" and extremely angry with the British Government for alleged duplicity and bad faith, refused to see him.[10] This refusal was communicated to Lloyd George in the strongest possible terms. Whereupon, the British Prime Minister invited Faiṣal to proceed immediately to London.[11]

9. The Agreement of 13 September was, indeed, a triumph for Clemenceau and his Government who for months past had insisted on their "rights to Syria." Soon after the acceptance of the British proposal, "the (French) Ministry of War," Brigadier Longrigg has written, "proceeded to the dispatch of reinforcements to Syria and Cilicia, consisting of French African troops, and that of Foreign Affairs selected General Gouraud to command them and to become France's supreme representative in the Levant." Longrigg adds: "Clemenceau used the occasion to address to the Syrian nation a promise that a regime of 'liberty, order and progress according to the wishes and interests of its people' would be theirs. To French opinion, the arrangement was an instalment, on acceptable lines if greatly overdue; but it was no comprehensive settlement, and seemed ominously to leave the Amir more free than ever to oppose the full attainment of French 'right'." Stephen H. Longrigg, *Syria and Lebanon under the French Mandate*, p. 94.

10. Lloyd George, 2: 1081-1083 and 1095. See *also Documents*, 1:1, pp. 685-686.

11. "The British Government are so impressed with the importance of bringing about an understanding between the Arabs and the French that they did not communicate your message to the Emir Feisal in the somewhat insulting form in which it reached them. Had they done so, there would, in their opinion have been but little chance for a peaceable settlement of the Syrian question." Lloyd George to Clemenceau, 18 October 1919 (See Lloyd George, 2:, 1097).

Faiṣal arrived in London on 18 September, and the following day, the Prime Minister invited him to attend a special meeting at 10 Downing Street, "with the object of inducing him to accept the proposal about occupation as assented to in Paris." [12] No sooner had Faiṣal been informed officially of the Franco-British Agreement of 13 September than he raised the strongest objection. He said that the Arabs were vehemently opposed to any partition of Arab territory in any form and the Syrians to any partition of Syria. Moreover, the Syrians did not recognize the right of France to any mandate over Syria. The Emīr was not appeased by the Prime Minister's assurance that His Majesty's Government stood by every one of their engagements with King Ḥusain and would redeem their pledges as "the Arab forces had redeemed the pledges they gave to Great Britain." Faiṣal said that "he could not stand before the Moslem world and say that he had been asked to wage a war against the Kaliph of the Moslems and now see the European Powers divide the Arab country. . . .' [13]

On 21 September, Faiṣal wrote a long letter to Lloyd George commenting on the latter's Memorandum, which had been handed to him at the previous meeting, embodying the Agreement of the 13th and asked for its complete abrogation. He condemned it as a return to the unjust policy of colonialism, warned the Prime Minister that the Arabs would defend, to the utmost of their ability, their unity and their existence and washed his hands from all responsibility towards the British Government and towards the whole world. He concluded by asserting that it would be far better either

12. Lloyd George wrote to Clemenceau concerning this meeting:

"Despite very great difficulties the British Government put the strongest pressure on the Emir Feisal to accept the arrangement and to come to terms with the French Government."

In the course of this meeting, the Prime Minister also informed Faiṣal that "the French Government were prepared to undertake the payment of one half of the subsidy to the Arab Administration of Occupied Enemy Territory Administration East." On 7 November, Lord Curzon wrote to the British Ambassador in Paris, requesting him "to inform both the French Government and His Highness the Emir that with effect from the 1st November 1919 the monthly subsidy of £ 150,000 hitherto paid by His Majesty's Government will be reduced to £ 75,000." *Documents*, 1:4, p. 509.

13. For the discussion which took place at the Meeting of 19 September, at 10 Downing Street, see *Documents*, 1:4, pp. 395-404.

to leave the situation in its present form or to withdraw all the European troops until a final settlement was concluded.[14] Two days later Faiṣal wrote again to the Prime Minister informing him that the day before, he had refused to discuss with the Commander-in-Chief of the Allied Forces in Syria, the subject of the withdrawal of British troops.[15] He now asked for one of the following two alternatives: either the return of the coastal districts to the Arab forces as in the early days of the occupation of Syria (before the British themselves removed the Arab flags from the Government buildings in Beirut) or the preservation of the status quo until final agreement was reached.[16]

On 9 October, Faiṣal wrote once more to the Prime Minister, who had not yet answered his previous letter of 21 September, appealing to him to cancel the "Paris Agreement" of 13 September or at least to postpone acting on it. The withdrawal of the British forces from Syria was a "great catastrophe" for the Arab world. He asked for the whole question to be placed before the Peace Conference or to be studied by a Committee composed of British, French and Arab members, under the chairmanship of an

14. For the original Arabic text of Faiṣal's letter, see Wahbah, pp. 373-376.

15. Ibid., p. 377.

16. During an interview which William Yale had with the Emīr Faiṣal, in October 1919, "Faisal said that he could not accept a change in the military occupation of Syria, that should Great Britain withdraw her troops he would make a final appeal to the United States, and if America refused to take any action he would return to Syria to lead his people to armed resistance of foreign occupation. He would not state the minimum that he would accept but declared that he would accept any solution the United States imposed."

After other interviews which Yale had with responsible men among the British, the French, the Arabs and the Zionists, he drew up his own solution for Palestine, the Lebanon, Syria and Mesopotamia. It appears that the British Cabinet was ready to adopt the "Yale Plan" but "when Yale returned to Paris and explained to his chiefs in the American Commission to Negotiate Peace what he had been doing, they refused him permision to put forward his Plan to the French as President Wilson on his final return to the United States had left them without authority to make any decisions or to take any action."

As far as the Lebanon and Syria were concerned, Yale had proposed: "Mount Lebanon to be a separate political unit under the mandate of France; Syria from Maan to Akaba to Aleppo with the ports of Tripoli and Latakia to be considered as a 'provisionally' independent state with an Arab government representative of its inhabitants. This Arab state was to be under the mandate of France." David Garnett, pp. 282-286.

American who would then report its decisions to that Conference. But he emphasised that the most vital necessity for reaching a satisfactory solution was first the abrogation of the Paris agreement.[17] On that same day, Lord Curzon wrote a long letter to the Emīr in answer to his communication of 21 September. He recapitulated the pledges and the commitments of His Majesty's Government during the War both to the Sharīf Ḥusain and to the French Government and said that they established two definite points: (1) the British Government had undertaken obligations towards King Ḥusain to set up "an Arab independent Kingdom" which would include within its boundaries the four towns of Damascus, Ḥoms, Ḥama, and Aleppo and (2) the British Government had made it very clear, "without any vagueness," to King Ḥusain, before the Arabs entered the War, that France had special rights in that portion of the area lying west of these towns.

Lord Curzon then tried to explain the reason the Cabinet had decided to withdraw the British troops from Syria. The British Government had borne the greatest share, in men and money, in the defeat of Turkey. She had employed a total of over 1,400,000 troops and incurred an expenditure of £750,000,000. The peoples of the British Empire had lost more than 950,000 and suffered a staggering debt of £9,000,000,000. Moreover, it was not possible until then — despite the British Government's hopes — to find a speedy and satisfactory solution for all the difficult problems concerning the future of the Middle East. But it would not be fair to impose a heavier burden on the British taxpayer than he had borne hitherto. Consequently, His Majesty's Government had decided to withdraw its troops from Syria, beginning 1 November.

The next part of Lord Curzon's letter concerning France deserves to be quoted in full. It says: "In so far as the occupation by France of the rest of Syria is concerned, they would ask Your Highness to remember that the Arabs owe their freedom in a large measure to the supreme sacrifices made by the French people in the late War. It is true that the French contribution in Syria itself was not great for France was deeply pre-occupied in the War on other fronts. But on these greater and vital battle-fields of Europe they

17. Wahbah, pp. 378-379.

lost 1,400,000 in dead, and incurred a debt not far short of that incurred by Great Britain in overthrowing the power which sustained the Turkish tyranny and without whose support the Turkish military power could not have continued the war more than a few weeks."[18]

Finally, Lord Curzon advised that it was to the best interests of the Arabs to accept this "temporary measure" and to join with their Allies, Great Britain and France, in friendly and practical ways of enforcing it. He wanted the Emīr to be assured that this question of the military occupation in those areas which formerly belonged to Turkey was not in any way an "Agreement" between the French and British Governments, but simply "proposals" put forward by the British Government of its own accord until the Peace Conference reached a final decision about the future of those areas. The British Government as a sincere friend of the Arabs, invited them to accept these "proposals" and urged His Highness the Emīr to discuss them immediately with French Government.[19]

If Faiṣal was still nourishing even a slight hope of a least postponing the evil day, that hope was shattered by the letter which he received the next day, 10 October. It came from 10 Downing Street, was dated 10 October 1919 and signed by the Prime Minister himself, David Lloyd George. The Prime Minister rejected the two request of Faiṣal made in his letter of the previous day. He was also not prepared to discuss this matter again as it had already been clarified enough in the letter which the Emīr had received from the Secretary of State for Foreign Affairs.[20]

"His Majesty's Government have made up their mind," wrote the Prime Minister, that it is impossible for them to continue the occupation of Syria by British troops. Six months ago they announced to the Peace Conference and to yourself that under no circumstances would they accept a mandate for Syria.... It is therefore impossible for His Majesty's Government to withdraw the proposals which they have made for dealing with the Syrian

18. Cited by Lloyd George in his letter of 18 October to Clemenceau. Lloyd George, 2: 1095-1096.

19. For the Arabic text of this important letter found among the private papers of King Ḥusain, in Mecca, see Wahbah, pp. 381-388.

20. A reference to Lord Curzon's letter of 9 October cited above.

problem in the interim period until the Peace Conference can settle it...."[21]

Meanwhile, the French continued to feel that Great Britain's protection of Faiṣal's independence in the French zone was an irreconcilable intrusion in the Anglo-French agreements concerning the Syrian Mandate.[22] According to Pichon and Clemenceau the position of France and England ("*l'Angleterre*") in the Arab region of the Near East was defined essentially by two agreements: the Sykes-Picot Agreement of 1916 and the necessity recognized by the Peace Conference of conferring upon a European Power a mandate over the Arabs ("*un mandat sur les Arabes*"), who were considered incapable of governing themselves by themselves in Syria as well as in Mesopotamia. Moreover, the position of France in Syria and her relations with the Arabs in her zone could not but be identical with the position of England in Mesopotamia and her relations with the Arabs in her zone. Clemenceau complained that the French Government could not come to a direct understanding with Faiṣal as long as the latter was the "client" of the British and was protected by them.

Between 10 and 18 October, Clemenceau sent to Lloyd George, first a telegram, then a latter, in reply to the latter's *aide-mémoire* of 13 September. Both messages showed that he was "angry, extremely angry." His telegram, dated 14 October was, in the words of Lloyd George, "a strongly worded telegram in a temper of acrid resent- and full of insinuations against British good faith."[23] So, on the 18th, the Prime Minister wrote a long letter to "*Monsieur le Président*

21. F.O. 406/41, N° 114. *The Prime Minister of Great Britain to His Highness Sherif Feisal*, 10 October 1919.

22. *Documents*, 1:4, pp. 452-454.

23. "I received from M. Clemenceau a strongly worded telegram written in a temper of acrid resentment.... Smarting under the hornets and gnats of the Chauvinist and clerical Press, and of Parliamentarians who accused him of betraying the historical interests of France in Syria, the Tiger lashed his tail furiously and bit his best friends." Lloyd George, 2: 1081-1082.

Lord Curzon pointed out to the French Ambassador in London on 22 October, that insulting messages had been handed in by the French Government in the course of the last six months, "culminating in the recent exchange of high explosive shells between M. Clemenceau and Mr. Lloyd George." *Documents* 1:4, p. 496.

du Conseil," recapitulating once more the whole history of the "Syrian Question," going over the pledges of Great Britain to the Arabs and to the French in the Sharīf Ḥusain-McMahon Correspondence and the Sykes-Picot Agreement, the Anglo-French declaration of 8 November 1918, and the declaration of Great Britain made to the Council of Four on 20 March 1919 stating that under no circumstances would Great Britain accept the mandate for Syria. He wanted to assure M. Clemenceau that the British Government was "not forgetful of France's rights and claims" while discussing with Faiṣal the evacuation of the British Army from Syria and its replacement by French and Arab troops. Here, the Prime Minister quoted an extract from the letter of Lord Curzon to Faiṣal concerning the debt which the Arabs owed to France for their freedom.[24] But he wanted the French Prime Minister to know that the British Government was "under solemn obligation both to the Arabs and to the French Government." The Emīr Faiṣal was not to be dealt with a high hand. When he goes to Paris, the British Government expected that he would be treated "with the courtesy and consideration which one of the Allies deserves." "They would remind you," continued the Prime Minister, "that he initiated a revolt against Turkish rule at a time when the Allied fortunes were at a very low ebb, that he was loyal to the Alliance to the end, and that he and his followers played an indispensable part in overthrowing Turkey, which was the prelude to the collapse of the German combination. The Emir Feisal is the representative of a proud and historic race with whom it is essential that both the British and the French should live in relations of cordial amity."[25]

These were the last strong words that Lloyd George used to defend Faiṣal and the Arab cause. But they were of no avail and Faiṣal was finally abandoned to the French, "with all the best wishes" of the British Government. It was the beginning of the end for Arab independence under Faiṣal in Syria. One might say that in the Anglo-French rivalry in the Near East, the British Government "won" in October 1918 when they established and supported

24. Cited pp. 105-106, above.
25. Lloyd George, 2: 1097.

an Arab Government in Damascus under the Emīr Faiṣal but in October 1919, almost exactly a year later, the British Cabinet finally retreated before the relentless and continuous pressure of the French Government. There were also other important contributory factors, in addition to the French pressure, which led Lloyd George to his decision of 13 September. Egypt was in open revolt and the situation in Iraq was deteriorating. Then there was the "Moroccan Question" and the French threat to the internationalization of Tangier. The British Government refused to entertain the French tendency, very evident in France at this time, "to treat Morocco as a country in which France possesses a supreme — not to say exclusive — interest." Perhaps British rights in Morocco could be put on a secure basis if Lloyd George agreed to a *quid pro quo* in Syria for France. At the same time, the situation in Asia Minor, in Russia and in Germany, to mention only three danger areas, required the urgent attention of the British Government. A number of causes of dissatisfaction on the "home-front" in England were also threatening to precipitate a crisis of the first magnitude. The Irish problem was growing worse and the Sinn Fein movement was creating grave disquiet in the ranks of the Coalition Cabinet. There was continuous industrial unrest and the acute threat of a political General Strike. The finances of the country were in bad shape and Lloyd George decided to cut ruthlessly the expenditures of the government departments.[26] These problems are mentioned here in passing, simply to point out the interrelation and the multiplicity of

26. In October 1919, the Government issued a White Paper containing a "Revised Statement of Revenue and Expenditure" for the current year. The deficit for the year, "originally estimated at 250 millions," showed an increase of £ 223,645,000 and thus mounted to a total of £ 473,645,000.

The Times expressed severe criticism of Lloyd George and his Cabinet of 20 Ministers, in its issue of 28 October: "During the War, the government had not been responsible except in name. It is not responsible except in name, today. The Prime Minister gradually assumed during the War a quasi-Presidential position, quite incompatible with the genius and the normal working of the Constitution.... It was not disagreeable to him and he has hitherto maintained it."

On 30 October, the Government motion on finance was carried in the House of Commons. The next day, referring to the speech of Lloyd George in the House as "a display of rhetorical fireworks," *The Times* wrote again: "The genius of the speech was unmistakable, but it was the genius of an unrivalled performer on the auditory nerves, not that of a statesman bent on unravelling our difficulties and applying himself to the grave problems of the hour."

all the problems that the statesmen of those days were called upon to discuss and to settle in different areas of the world. Thus, Lloyd George and his Cabinet had other momentous decisions to take beside the one on Syria. Indeed, it had become necessary to put the Syrian Question out of the way as soon as possible in order to avoid continuous friction and misunderstanding with France.

On 20 October, Faiṣal arrived in Paris. On that same day, M. Maurice Barrès, well-known author, Deputy, and member of the French Academy contributed an article in *L'Echo de Paris* strongly criticizing both Great Britain and Faiṣal. "If we consider Syria," wrote Monsieur Barrès, "no one can doubt the right of France to receive a mandate for the four towns of Damascus. Ḥoms, Ḥama and Aleppo. French public opinion will not for a moment allow us to be driven out. France learns with amazement that General Gouraud is not to occupy these towns. The Feisal comedy has gone far enough. No nation other than France possesses in so high a degree the particular kind of friendship and genius which is required to deal with the Arabs.... The British theory of installing in Syria an Arab Government of the Hedjaz is untenable. The Emir Feisal has no right to be in Damascus, Ḥoms Ḥama or Aleppo. France knows how to give these towns a Syrian Government. What is Feisal to us or to the Syrians? A man of straw set up by England, without a title, without influence.... If England wishes to give a kingdom to this Emir, let her set him up in Bagdad."[27]

Faiṣal stayed in Paris for over two and a half months, doing his best, as he wrote to Lloyd George, "to keep on good terms with the French Government, endeavouring to eliminate misunderstandings and to meet our mutual interests."[28] In November, he had

27. *Documents,* 1:4, p. 491. In his Report to the American Commissioners, dated 26 July 1919, William Yale wrote: "The French since the beginning of the war have looked upon Syria as the booty which they would secure on a successful conclusion of hostilities. It is unnecessary to expatiate on the fundamental reasons which lie under French claims to Syria; they are commercial, imperialistic and sentimental. The British outwitted the French when they secured partial control of the Young Arab Movement by their relations with King Hussein and Emir Faisal." U.S., National Archives and Records Service, Department of State, Records Group 59.

28. *Documents,* 1:4, p. 510.

conversations with M. Clemenceau, M. Berthelot, M. Gout, General Gouraud and other French officials at the Quai d'Orsay.[29] There was also an exchange of correspondence between him and Clemenceau, expressing his anxiety about an eventual partition of Syria and the internal troubles that may ensue. Clemenceau assured Faiṣal that his anxieties were not well founded. Neither the political condition of Syria nor its future boundaries were in question. Should there by any internal trouble, the French forces would immediately answer Faiṣal's appeal for help.[30] The Emīr still remained unconvinced. He appealed to the Supreme Council of the Peace Conference to give "fresh consideration" to the suggested project of the relief of British by French troops. He explained fully all his fears about that "suggested project" and its effects on "the over-excited feeling now prevailing in the Arab provinces, as well as in other Moslem provinces of the Ottoman Empire in Asia." It was based on the secret Sykes-Picot Agreement "which dealt with the country as if it were a private estate or a mere parcel of goods" and which neither the Arabs nor the United States Government had recognized. He was also afraid of an outburst of Muslim-Christian fanaticism. "I personally throughout the war," he wrote, "have been fighting fanaticism every time and at every place... Our unity was national and not religious. A great number of men who are working with me now in this national cause do not belong to my religion." On the 9th, Clemenceau wrote to Lloyd George thanking him for advising Faiṣal to go to Paris and reach an understanding with the French. Clemenceau's letter contained two significant

29. While expressing his sympathy to Faiṣal, General Gouraud said that "he would be obliged to carry out all orders he might receive. He further said that although he disapproved of bloodshed, he could not hesitate to meet it if his orders required it." Ibid., p. 511.

General Henry J. E. Gouraud had been appointed by the French Government on 9 October as French High Commissioner for Syria and Cilicia and as "Chef de l'Armée du Levant."

30. "Dans les régions où les soldats français prendront la place des soldats anglais, j'ai la certitude que nos chefs militaires sauront rassurer les populations et maintenir l'ordre. Il vous appartient, avec votre haute autorité, d'agir de même à Damas et à Alep: je suis tout prêt à venir à votre premier appel pour vous aider à maintenir l'ordre, s'il venait à être troublé par des agitateurs qui ne pourraient que compromettre les intérêts des Arabes et diminuer la confiance que la Conférence est prête à leur accorder." Clemenceau to the Emīr Faiṣal, Paris, 2 November 1919, in *Documents,* 1:4, p. 512.

sentences, one referring to the past and the other presaging the shape of things to come. "In point of fact," wrote the French Premier, "if this procedure had been followed at once at the beginning, that is to say, at the time of the occupation of Damascus a year ago, the recent misunderstandings would, without doubt, have been avoided. I am pleased to think that henceforth there is no chance of their recurring between us, and that the Peace Conference will have nothing to do but to sanction our agreement for the French mandate in Syria and the British mandate in Mesopotamia."[31]

Meanwhile, a Lebanese Delegation, headed by the Maronite Patriarch himself, Monseigneur Hoyek, had arrived in the French capital on 22 August 1919 and was actively working to preserve Lebanese independence under French protection.[32] The Delegation was received by M. Poincaré and M. Clemenceau, and presented a Memorandum to the Peace Conference on the 27th containing the Lebanese aspirations. In a letter which the Patriarch had written to M. Clemenceau on the 25th, he had summarized those aspirations as being: (1) the recognition of the independence of the Lebanon with full sovereignty, "internal and external;"[33] (2) the restitution of her natural, historical and economic frontiers, and (3) the help and support of France for the achievement of those aspirations in the light of the tradition of friendship which the Lebanon had always maintained towards France.[34] On 10 November, Clemenceau himself wrote to the Patriarch assuring him that France was in full agreement with the Lebanese aspirations and would give them the full support. But there were certain limitations within which this Lebanese independence was going to be exercised. They could not be defined for the time being before the mandate over Syria had been granted to France.[35]

31. *Documents*, 1:4, pp. 520-521.

32. See K.T. Khairallah, *Les Régions Arabes Libérées*, p. 75, and Lyne Laheac, pp. 74-76,

33. "Le peuple libanais demande en premier lieu, la reconnaissance de son indépendance, impliquant sa pleine souveraineté intérieure et extérieure." Bkerkī Archives.

34. See Yūsuf al-Saudā, *Fī Sabīl al-Istiqlāl*, pp. 206-207. See also Lyne Loheac, pp. 77-81.

35. "Le désir des Libanais de conserver un Gouvernement autonome et

It is unfortunate that the evacuation of the British forces from Syria began at the time when Faiṣal was still in Paris. Had he been in Syria, he might — though this is by no means certain — have allayed the fears and suspicions of the populations and rallied around him the more moderate and reasonable influences. But every item of news which he was now receiving from Damascus showed that a helpless administration was being carried along by a public opinion inflamed by national and religious feelings. Syria was already in ferment. All the political factions, Syrian, Mesopotamian and Palestinian were now not only anti-French in feeling but anti-European — "with hostile allusions made to the English." [36] Turkish propaganda was becoming at the same time very active. King Ḥusain in a telegram to Faiṣal assured him that "people North-West of Aleppo are in negotiation with Kemal Pasha." A wave of pro-Turkish sympathy which had really never died at the end of the War, was now sweeping across the country skilfully fed by Turkish circulars issued by the "Mustapha Kemal Party" in Aleppo and tacitly encouraged by the disillusioned Arab officers formerly serving in the Turkish armies.[37] The British political agents believed that Yāsīn Pasha himself, "the leading spirit in Syria," was "in cor-

un Statut national indépendant s'accorde parfaitement avec les traditions libérales de la France." Ibid. For the full text of this letter see Appendix H.

36. *Documents,* 1:4, p. 524.

On 7 September 1919 Meinertzhagen wrote: ". . . At present Feisal is actively planning to fight the French. . . as the Arabs completely mistrust the French . . . . The French, on the other hand, mistrust the Arabs . . . . They are, moreover, determined to impose themselves on Syria, whilst Feisal is equally determined that France shall not rule in Syria . . . " (Meinertzhagen, Richard, *Middle East Diary,* p. 44).

37. Extract from one of these circulars:

"Mustapha Kemal's proclamation to the Syrians.

"As a co-Religionist I pray you not to heed the strife stirred amongst us and which has separated us; we must remove all misunderstanding and let us all aim our arms against the treacherous parties who want to divide our country . . . .

"The Mujahids (Fighters for a Religious cause) who trust in the Right will soon be the visitors of their Arab brethren, and will scatter away the enemy. Let us live as brethren in religion and may our enemies perish." *Documents,* 1:4, p. 478, and F.O. 406/41, N° 191. Colonel Meinertzhagen to Earl Curzon, General Headquarters, Egyptian Expeditionary Force, Cairo, 2 December 1919. Appendix 2: A letter to the Syrians (in Turkish). See also Ja'far Pasha al-'Askarī, p. 125.

respondence with Mustapha Kemal." It was even alleged that he aimed at "reinstituting Turkish rule in Syria."[38]

At this time there was confusion and chaos in the Biqāʿ Valley and all along the eastern boundary of the Lebanon with Syria. Arab military posts in the districts of Zaḥleh, Baʿalbek and Zebedānī were attacked by organized bands with the purpose of forcing the Syrian troops to withdraw beyond the Sykes-Picot line of the Blue Zone. It must be said in all fairness that the activities of these bands were not limited to one side of the boundary only. The French were meanwhile bringing strong forces into the Biqāʿ, which they were determined to occupy, as General Gouraud himself informed General Allenby on 27 November. Gouraud's decision received the full approval of Allenby.[39] The Arab garrison, a token force of about three hundred men was finally forced to withdraw to Damascus.[40] Warnings and fears that the Arabs would rise and defend their freedom expressed by Faiṣal in letters to Lloyd George, Clemenceau and Lord Curzon, did not seem to have been taken seriously or to have produced any appreciable effects. The British and French military authorities, who knew the extent of their own strength and of the weakness of the Arabs, could not worry about such threats

38. F.O. 406/41, N°. 173. Colonel Meinertzhagen to Earl Curzon, General Headquarters Egyptian Expeditionary Force, Cairo, 10 November 1919. Meinertzhagen's long report on the situation in Syria and Palestine begins with the following words:

"The temperament of the inhabitants, already strained by uncertainty and delay, is rendered doubly suspicious and alarmed by the commencement of the evacuation and the increasingly violent tone of Turkish propaganda. Turkish influence is gradually creeping back, and signs are not wanting of a rejuvenated popularity of Turkish rule with all its forgotten disadvantages. The main theme of all propaganda is the religious argument, which is producing an anti-European and pan-Islamic feeling. This is not confined to Syria alone, but has been recently traced in Jerusalem and other Palestinian centers."

39. Ibid., pp. 590-91.

40. The Commanding Officer of that area, ʿAlī Jawdat Bey al-Ayyūbī, related to the author, during an interview, that his house was twice surrounded, once by French troops with machine guns at Muʿallaqat-Zaḥleh and the second time by about 250 civilians armed by the French, when he had withdrawn to Rayak. He was also told by General Congreve and Colonel Cousse that according to an agreement reached between the British and French Governments, he had to evacuate that district. For a detailed account of the Syrian occupation of the Biqāʿ and its subsequent evacuation, see ʿAlī Jawdat, *Dhikrayāt*, pp. 79-87.

as found in a telegram from the Emīr Zeid to Faiṣal: "I cannot stop revolution.... If French advance one span from boundaries, battles will start. If you like no bloodshed, do best to keep French in present zone...."[41] Or, of King Ḥusain's words in a letter to Faiṣal: "Moreover, if Syrians decide to fight for their liberty and independence I will not hesitate to go over to them to cooperate with them in my capacity as an individual Arab so that they may know that I did not betray them."[42]

Damascus city was evacuated by the British forces on 26 November, and by the first week in December the British withdrawal from Syria was complete. There was nothing more that the British Government could say to Faiṣal or could do for him. Already, on 21 November, when Faiṣal had a long interview with the British Ambassador in Paris, the Earl of Derby, the latter had written to Lord Curzon: "He (Faiṣal) was very anxious to know what I thought of position. I was very careful to say nothing to him."[43] Then, when on 19 December, Faiṣal wrote to Lord Curzon that French troops had invaded the Biqā', that he had asked the French Government for "the immediate withdrawal of their troops" and that he trusted "the British Government in this critical situation will not refrain from giving their indispensable assistance to secure peace in the East," he received no written reply. Instead, he received a verbal message from Mr. G. J. Kidston of the Foreign Office to the effect that he (Kidston) did "not see how we can help or intervene in any way. We should very strongly resent any French protest as to our action in Mesopotamia or even in the Vilayet of Mosul or on its borders and the French position with regard to the Bekaa is somewhat analogous."[44]

It is not in any way clear just what happened in Paris during the next three weeks between the Emir Faiṣal and the French Government. We know that Faiṣal had planned to leave for Syria on Sunday night, 21 December, but he did not, although the British

41. *Documents,* 1:4, p. 533.
42. Ibid., p. 549.
43. *Documents,* 1:4, p. 544.
44. Ibid., p. 592.

Ambassador advised him to go.[45] British and French documents on the activities of the Emīr during that period are unavailable. Arabic sources are non-existent. We have, however, one document of prime importane and great significance. The Earl of Derby informed Lord Curzon about it on 20 December and sent him a copy of it by courier the next day. This document was a copy of a proposed agreement between the French Government and the Emīr Faiṣal. The agreement contained eight articles and its main provisions were as follows:

1. The French Government offered to help in every way the "Syrian nation" ("*la nation syrienne*") and to guarantee its independence against all aggression.

2. The Emīr Faiṣal would ask the French Government, and only this Government ("*et à ce gouvernement seul*"), to appoint councillors, instructors and technicians to organize all civil and military administrations and to control certain of its branches such as the Departments of Finance and Public Works.

3. The Emīr Faiṣal will have a representative ("*un agent plénipotentiaire*") in Paris, who will have under his orders a delegate in London, in Rome and in Washington within the framework ("*le cadre*") of the French Embassy in those capitals. In other countries, Syrian interests will be entrusted to diplomatic and consular representatives of France.

4. The Emīr will recognize the independence of the Lebanon under the French Mandate.

5. The Emīr will facilitate the formation of an autonomous organization for the Druses of the Ḥūrān within the State of Syria.

6. Syria will give every assistance, with all its forces and on all occasions, to France.

7. The Arabic language will be recognized as the official language in administration and in schools. The French language will be taught as an auxiliary language.

8. Damascus will be the capital of Syria. The French High-Commissioner will reside in Aleppo. But both the Syrian Head of

45. Ibid., p. 593.

State and the French Representative will have a winter residence in Beirut, which will enjoy its own municipal autonomy.

A note at the end stated that this agreement would remain secret between the two contracting parties until the signature of the final and detailed agreement, which would be drawn up as soon as the Emīr Faiṣal would have returned to France and would be submitted at the appropriate time to the Peace Conference.[46]

Thus, the year 1919 came to an end and Faiṣal finally decided to return to Syria. The crowded and significant events of this year must not appear to be merely a succession of "newsreels." Their main trends and underlying currents should not be missed. The year began with Great Britain and France at loggerheads over the future of Syria. Long and bitter controversies followed. Lloyd George appeared to give his full support to Faiṣal and to an independent Arab Government in Syria. But after three momentous occasions — on 13 February, 20 March and 13 September — Lloyd George finally gave way to Clemenceau's uncompromising attitude and the year ended with France firmly "in possession" of Syria.

46. For the French text of this agreement, for the counterdraft which the Emīr Faiṣal proposed, changing slightly some of the articles, adding that no foreign troops would be stationed on Syrian territory and fixing a time limit of ten years for the duration of the agreement and for a modified form of that agreement, communicated secretly to Colonel Gibbon by the representative of Faiṣal in Paris, General Ḥaddād Pasha, see *Documents*, 1:4, pp. 592-595 and 624-626. To the French, this agreement was simply a project of a provisional agreement but they were very pleased about it. At the same time, General Ḥaddād stated definitely that the agreement was a French draft which Faiṣal had not signed but had taken with him to Syria. p. 627.

At a meeting of the Supreme Council of the Allies held in London on 17 February 1920, M. Berthelot, at the request of Mr. Lloyd George, gave a resumé of the terms of the above-mentioned provisional agreement. See Lloyd George, 2: 1106-1107.

CHAPTER SEVEN

FAIṢAL PROCLAIMED KING OF "UNITED KINGDOM OF SYRIA"

"*We, members of this Congress (the Syrian Congress) as representatives of the Syrian nation* (Al-Umma al-Sūriyah), *proclaim unanimously the independence of our country Syria with its natural boundaries... and we have chosen His Excellency Emīr Faiṣal, the son of His Majesty King Ḥusain... as Constitutional King over Syria with the title of His Majesty Faiṣal I....*"

Al-Ḥuṣrī, *Yōm Maisalūn,* Translated from the Arabic text of the resolution adopted by the Syrian Congress on 7 March 1920.

FAIṢAL left Paris for Beirut on 7 January 1920. He had stayed in Europe nearly four months. This long absence from Damascus, at a time when tension was mounting and anti-French agitation increasing, had a disastrous effect on Faiṣal's regime in Syria. The resentment of the extreme nationalists against France had grown louder as well as deeper. They were now looking for a strong-handed leader who would "open hostilities against the French, and probably make an open alliance with Turkey."[1] *Le Temps* made things worse for Faiṣal by publishing an "apparently authoritative statement" to the effect that "a complete agreement" had been reached between the Emīr and the French Government. "We understand that the general lines of that agreement, which was submitted to the approval of the Conference, are as follows. The Emīr agrees to a French mandate for the whole of Syria. In return, France consents to the formation of an Arab state to include the four towns of Damascus, Ḥama, Ḥoms and Aleppo, and to be administered by the

1. Yasīn Pasha, who was the Chief of Staff of Faiṣal's Arab army, had been arrested recently by the British military authorities at the request of General Gouraud. "According to a communication by the Director of Military Intelligence (transmitted to Foreign Office on 8 December 1919) the reasons for Yasīn Pasha's arrest 'are that he was conducting active anti-French propaganda and making military preparations to resist French occupation of the Blue Area'." *Documents,* 1:4, pp. 564, n. 2 and 615.

Emīr with the assistance of French advisers and inspectors."[2] That statement settled the fate of Faiṣal with the extremists.

On 13 January, it was reported to Lord Curzon that it was unlikely for Faiṣal to return to his old position in Damascus because of his recent agreement with the French. His three alternatives were "to throw in his lot with the extremists, to allow hismelf to be reinstated in Damascus by French bayonets, or to abandon his position in favour of an extremist leader."[3] When Faiṣal arrived in Beirut on 14 January, he told Colonel Waters Taylor that he had not signed the agreement with the French, but had brought it with him to obtain the consent of his people to its clauses. He added that the agreement was largely distasteful to him and would be unpopular with his people, but the attitude of the British authorities left him no other choice.

Faiṣal found the situation in Syria most turbulent and unstable. Even his closest friends and collaborators were in a state of great anxiety and agitation. The news of the replacement of British by French troops and of his negotiations with Clemenceau had preceded Faiṣal and filled the country with the wildest rumours. The Head of the Syrian Government, they reasoned, had gone to the Peace Conference to put an end to the anomalous position of his Government and his country as "Enemy Occupied Territory," while theoretically independent, to ask for the withdrawal of all foreign troops from Syria and to obtain its full and unconditional independence. He had, instead, compromised with the enemy and "sold" the country. The chasm between Faiṣal and the Syrians had disastrously widened. Men of all parties thought that he had made a crucial blunder. From newspapers, platforms and the streets of Damascus came a swelling chorus of criticism.[4] The blow to the position of leadership and the prestige of Faiṣal was irreparable. Meanwhile, the new situation had created fertile ground for the growth and success of pro-French activities. A small group of in-

2. Cited in *Documents* 1:4, p. 615.

3. Ibid.

4. Already, on 12 December, there had been demonstrations in Damascus against Faiṣal and the Emīr Zaid. On the 14th the Chief Administrator, al-Rikābī Pasha, had been forced to resign and his place had been taken by 'Abdul Ḥamīd Pasha who also resigned soon after taking office. Ibid., p. 614.

fluential Syrians had come to the conclusion that a French occupation of Syria was eventually inevitable and that it would be wise to establish good relations with France.[5] Taking all the circumstances into consideration, the nationalists, the political thinkers and Faiṣal's army officers, became convinced that an armed rebellion against France was unavoidable. It was the only way to clear the French out of the country. A decree instituting compulsory military service had been unanimously approved by the Syrian Congress in December 1919, before the return of Faiṣal. The Government was thinking seriously of the defense of Syria and of the necessity of proclaiming its full independence immediately, thus confronting the French with a *chose jugée* and a *fait accompli.*[6] When Faiṣal realized the emotional tempo of the country, he at first hesitated, for at heart he still believed that it was very useful to come to an agreement with France. But soon, he surrendered to the emotional torrent that surged around him, a torrent in which eventually the independence of Syria foundered.

On 22 January, Faiṣal decided to answer his critics publicly and to allay their fears and dismay. In a speech delivered at "*An-Nādī al-'Arabī*" (the Arab Club) in Damascus in the presence of a great gathering of notables, nationalists and army officers, he said that he had not changed, but was the same Faiṣal they had always known. He still had one supreme aim; the independence of not only Syria but of all the Arab lands "because all Arab lands are my land." He wanted to restore "our past glories." He had expressed himself in the same way in the West. There was no one in the Arab countries who would accept enslavement by any foreign Power. But words were not enough. For a year and a half the Arabs had been simply talking. The time had now come for action. The great national enthusiasm which he had found upon his return from

5. Ibid., p. 565.

6. This psychology of "*fait accompli*" seems to have been greatly inspired by the example of the Italian poet and aviator, Gabriele D'Annunzio. French and British troops had occupied Fiume. It will be recalled that D'Annunzio at the head of a corps of volunteers marched into that town on 12 September, 1919, and took possession of it in the name of Italy. The Allied force withdrew at short notice and without fighting. This exploit appeared very significant and encouraging to the Arab nationalists.

Europe was not enough in itself. He now called upon the nation to act. But they had to rely upon the Government and have full confidence in Faiṣal himself, who was the Government. The Emīr reminded his audience that the Syrian Government was still a temporary military government not elected by the people. He also underlined the gravity of their immediate situation and hinted at the necessity of reducing their attacks on France by saying that they should not belittle any Power because then they would be belittling themselves. For reasons which he could not discuss for the moment he was postponing the formation of a Government elected by the people until he had succeeded in presenting them with the "gift of independence." Faiṣal concluded by asking again for their confidence in himself and for their support of his Government.[7]

Faiṣal's closest advisers and friends were now pressing upon him the necessity of declaring to the whole world the independence of Syria and proclaiming himself as its King. Faiṣal was tired and worried. He was suspected by his own people, warned by his father not to compromise the independence of Syria, and harassed by deputation after deputation which came to see him and urge immediate action.[8] A crisis of great magnitude was rapidly developing all over the country, a crisis which he could no more direct or control effectively. Lawlessness and disorder were increasing in various districts. Parties of Bedouins attacked various village in the valley of the Biqā' and on the vague border between Syria and the Lebanon. In the Marj-'Ayūn district there were murders and bloodshed, looting and destruction and the French losses were serious.

It is to be noted that Faiṣal's closest associates and advisers were Iraqis, Syrians, Palestinians and even Lebanese. The Iraqis had their grievances against Great Britain, who had occupied Iraq; the Syrians were against the French and the British, who had now abandoned them to France; the Palestinians, after the Balfour Declaration, accused Britain of having "sold" Palestine to the

7. For the Arabic text of Faiṣal's speech, see al-Ḥusrī, pp. 218-220.

8. Faiṣal had already been bitterly criticized by his father, King Ḥusain, for having negotiated with the French in Paris. Originally, King Ḥusain wanted to go in person to Syria, then travel to Paris and represent the Arabs at the Peace Conference. See al-Raiḥānī, vol. 1, p. 52.

Zionists, and some Lebanese were shocked by France's direct and full intervention in their affairs. Each faction considered its own problem the most important and urged Faiṣal not only to solve it but to give it priority over the others. Meanwhile, King Ḥusain of the Ḥijaz was vexed that his son was dealing with regional groups and in terms of separate geographic units. He wanted to obtain the independence of the whole of the Arab *Ummah* and the restoration of the past glories of the Arab Empire. The late King 'Abdallah told the author that the Arabs have "two histories," an old history, which ended with the decline and fall of their empire and a new history, which began with the Revolt of his father, the Sharīf Ḥusain of Mecca against the Ottomans during the first World War. "The main purpose of that Revolt," 'Abdallah emphasized, "was the creation of one Arab nation which would become the bearer of the honor of the Arab East a second time and live side by side with the living nations of the world. This Arab nation was to be ruled by one Arab king."

In January 1920, King Ḥusain was in great distress about the situation in Syria. When Field-Marshal Viscount Allenby had an interview with him in Jeddah on 8 January concerning his relations with Ibn Sa'ūd, the King said: "His Majesty's Government has sent me a message regarding the question of Ibn Sa'ūd: this question I regard as of minor importance, my mind is full of the problems of Syria and my own position as regards the Arabs.... The policy which Great Britain is following now in handing over Syria to her ally, France, is rendering useless all the work which Great Britain and the Arabs have accomplished as allies.... The Arabs look to me now, ask why Great Britain has deserted them and call on me to act as their spokesman with her...." Allenby's reply was that he had not come to discuss matters affecting Syria or the leadership of the Arabs but "to facilitate a settlement of the Ibn Sa'ūd question."[9] Sometime later, Lieutenant Colonel C.E. Vickery, the British Agent in Jeddah, had an interview with King Ḥusain under instructions from Cairo to read personally the original copy (i.e., its translation in Arabic) of Sir Henry McMahon's letter of 24 October 1915 to Sharīf Ḥusain. The King produced

9. *Documents,* 1:4, pp. 617-618.

a letter, then, according to Vickery, frequently and vehemently pointed out the following excerpt in the letter: "*Bil Niābat 'an al-ḥukūmat al-brīṭānīyat al-'aẓīmah ana aqbal bi-kull maṭālibukum* (On behalf of the Great British Government I accept all your requests)." Colonel Vickery was given the letter and told by the King: "Read yourself, O light of my eye." Vickery noted that the letter was not written in scholarly Arabic, had no English translation in the margin and the above-mentioned sentence, "worded unfortunately," referred to the requests for munitions of war.[10] "I can say definitely," wrote Vickery, "that the whole of the King's demands were centred round Syria and only round Syria."[11]

Meanwhile, the Peace Conference of Paris had closed on 21 January without the United States taking part in the postwar settlements of the Near East. The Conference was followed by an intermittent series of international conferences the first of which was the meeting of the Supreme Council of the Allies in London from 12 to 17 February to resume discussion on the Turkish Treaty.[12] At this time, M. Clemenceau had already disappeared from the political scene, having resigned as a result of his defeat in the French elections. M. Alexandre Millerand had become the new Prime Minister. He did not attend the London Conference, but sent M. Bertholet, "much the ablest official in the Quai

10. This reference was not only to munitions of war but also to money in gold and to rice, flour, barley, coffee and sugar. See Letter No. 9, Sharīf Ḥusain to McMahon 18 February 1916, in Cmd. 5957, pp. 15-16. For the Arabic original of this letter see Plates at end of volume.

11. See C.E. Vickery's letter in *The Times*, 21 February 1939. The above Arabic quotation in Vickery's letter is from McMahon's letter of 10 March 1916 in reply to the Sharīf's of 18 February 1916. It does not occur in McMahon's letter of 24 October 1915. Vickery must have reproduced it from memory when he wrote to *The Times*. The words are not the exact words of the English translation but convey the same misleading meaning which King Ḥusain had understood from them. In the English text, the full sentence reads: "I am pleased to be able to inform you that His Majesty's Government have approved of meeting your requests. . . ." See Cmd. 5957, p. 17. The original Arabic translation of that letter, which was sent to Sharīf Ḥusain and which the author has seen, contains the following Arabic version of the above sentence: "*wa qad yasurrunī an ukhbirukum bi an ḥukūmat Jalālat al-malik ṣādaqat 'alā jamī' maṭālibukum. . . .*" It is to be noted that the word *jamī'* (all) has been added, in the Arabic version, before the words "your requests."

12. Lloyd George, 2, 1108-09.

d'Orsay," according to Lloyd George. At the request of the British Prime Minister, M. Bertholet stated the terms of the Agreement entered into between the French and the Emīr Faiṣal and added that "the Emir left Paris perfectly satisfied with the agreement which had been reached and his loyalty to the French Government, as an Oriental, appeared to be irreproachable. He, personally, placed the greatest confidence in his good faith. He fully realised that the Emir possessed a weak character and that his position would be a difficult one, on account of his being surrounded in Damascus by a group of enemies, who entertained anti-French sentiments. But, should the Emir lose authority owing to his weakness, it was understood that all agreements entered into with him would, *ipso facto* lapse."[13]

The situation in Syria was going from bad to worse. Faiṣal's policy of moderation was looked upon by many of his followers with great suspicion and had indeed already failed. He himself was steadily losing his power and prestige. Percival Phillips of the *Daily Express* wrote from Damascus on 13 February:

"He (the Emīr) impressed me in my last interview as being on the verge of absolute despair, because he is doubted by everyone. The French distrust him, suspecting intrigues for repudiation of the agreement and a declaration of an independent Syria. The King of the Hedjaz distrusts him, thinking it possible that the Emir has delivered himself and his country into vassalage by an agreement unknown to Mecca."[14] At a previous interview on 8 February, Faiṣal had admitted to Percival Phillips his agreement with France because "The British Government insisted on my doing so."

13. Toynbee, *Survey of International Affairs, 1920-1923* (London, 1925), p. 9.

14. *The Daily Express* (London), 1 March 1920.

In the same issue, the paper's Correspondent reported an account of an interview with the Druze Chiefs of Jabal ed-Drūz ('Abdu'l-Ghaffār Bey al-Atrash, Nasīb Bey al-Atrash, 'Abdu'l-Qāsim Bey al-Atrash and Wahīb Bey Ṭalī'). They expressed great disappointment at the turn of events. They vehemently rejected a French Mandate as being a "policy of colonisation." Nasīb Bey's final words were a prophecy which was fulfilled a few years later: "... Tell England that if the Mandate of France is imposed on us there will be continual warfare throughout the country, because the people believe that Syria will become a French colony."

But Faiṣal added: "Even my best friends are opposing the Agreement."[15]

It was useless for Faiṣal to point out to his zealous but unpractical advisers that while "right" was on their side, "might" was on the French side and that if it came to a showdown, the issue would be decided by the force of arms.[16]

On 6 March, the General Syrian Congress met in Damascus. This Congress had originally been convoked by Faiṣal before the arrival of the American King-Crane Commission.[17] It had already decided on the drastic step which it was going to take. Faiṣal addressed them briefly asking them to decide on the future course of the Arab lands in the light of the doctrine of self-determination and the freedom of nations which President Wilson and the Allies had announced. He reminded them that the Arabs had fought during the War for their freedom and national independence. Theirs was a great responsibility and a grave duty, today. They had to decide on the form which their new country was going to take and lay down a constitution for it. He also reminded them, in conclusion, that their Iraqi brethren had fought and served well the national patrimony. For their future strength and happiness, cooperation between them all was most essential.[18]

15. *The Daily Express* (London), 24 February 1920.

In *L'Humanité* (Paris), 25 February 1920, M. Marcel Cachin wrote that "les populations syriennes qui viennent d'être libérées d'un joug insupportable et qui aspirent désormais à vivre indépendantes, ne veulent, ni de notre 'protectorat', ni de notre 'mandat'."

16. A well-known French journalist with a penetrating knowledge of Near Eastern history, Mme Berthe-Georges Gaulis, was in Damascus in 1920. She had already met the Emīr Faiṣal several times in Paris and in Beirut. Mme Gaulis has written that during the Emīr's absence in Paris: "A Damas, les esprits s'échauffaient; de loin, l'Emir laissait dire et laissait faire, le nationalisme syrien prenait corps et sur Hama, Homs, Alep, Bagdad, le même souffle d'extrémisme passait." And she adds: "Encouragés par ces désunions apparentes, les partis extrêmes soulevaient l'opinion publique orientale, cette force latente dont nous persistons à nier l'existence." Gaulis, p. 109.

17. See below, Appendix F, and al-Ḥusrī, p. 245.

18. For the original Arabic text of that speech, see al-Ḥusrī, pp. 220-223. For the reply of the Congress, expressing full support for Faiṣal and announcing to him their decision to proclaim him "constitutional King" over "all parts of Syria with its natural boundaries" on 8 March, see again al-Ḥuṣrī, pp. 255-259.

The following day, 7 March, the General Syrian Congress "representing the Syrian Arab nation" drew up a historic resolution. After reviewing the purpose of the Arab Revolt, the sacrifices of the Arabs during the War, the promises of the Allied leaders on the principle of self-determination, the division of Syria into three enemy occupied zones, the resolution went on to say that the people of Syria wanted to put an end to their doubts and uncertainties and obtain their independence. Consequently, the Syrian Congress was unanimous in proclaiming the full independence of Syria with "its natural boundaries." including Palestine in which they rejected the claim of the Zionists for a National Home for the Jews. "We have, accordingly," said the resolution, "chosen His Highness the Emīr Faiṣal, the son of His Majesty King Ḥusain.... a constitutional King over Syria with the title of His Majesty King Faiṣal I, and we hereby declare the termination of the present occupying military governments in the three Zones. They will be replaced by a constitutional monarchy." The national aspirations of the Lebanese were to be respected. The Lebanon will have its autonomy within its old prewar frontiers provided it keeps away from any foreign influence. As the purpose of the Arab Revolt was to liberate the Arab nation from Turkish rule, "We ask for the full independence of Iraq", the resolution proclaimed with the understanding that there will be a political and economic union between Syria and Iraq.[19]

The resolution ended with an assurance that friendship with the Allies would be maintained and their interests respected, and with the hope that the Allied Governments and all the other countries would recognize the independence of Syria.

The next day, 8 March, the foregoing resolution was read to the populace at about three o'clock in the afternoon from the balcony of the town hall in Damascus, the Emīr having arrived there riding through cheering crowds. Faiṣal was proclaimed as King of the "United Kingdom of Syria," i.e., of Syria, the Lebanon and Palestine,[20] while one hundred and one salvoes greeted the

19. For the original Arabic text of this Resolution, see al-Ḥuṣrī, pp. 261-265.

20. The President of the Congress, Hāshim al-Atāsī, sent a letter the next day, 9 March, to King Ḥusain, informing him of the Resolution taken by the Congress and of the fact that his son, the Emīr Faiṣal, had been proclaimed "King of the Syrian countries," and conveying to him the gratitude of the

birth of the new Kingdom and its new flag was unfurled.[21] A few minutes later and from the same balcony another proclamation was read declaring the "complete independence of Iraq" under the sovereignty of Faiṣal's brother, the Emīr 'Abdallah. This decision had been taken by an "Iraqi Congress" meeting in Damascus and working in cooperation with the General Syrian Congress.[22]

It is to be noted that the proclamation of the United Kingdom of Syria was contrary to the original aim of Sharīf Ḥusain, which was the independence of all the Arabs and Arab countries in the Near East under his kingship. But the Arab leaders assembled in Damascus found the former step more in line with the exigencies of the time. However, the late King 'Abdallah of Jordan frankly criticized the proclamation of his brother as King of Syria. It was done against the advice of his father, who wanted it postponed until after the treaty of peace with Turkey had been signed and the latter had renounced its rights in all the Arab lands. The Arab policy of recognizing and proclaiming an independent Syria and an independent Iraq was, according to King 'Abdallah, one of the greatest mistakes of the Arabs after the First World War. It destroyed Arab unity and led directly to the establishment of Mandates in those two countries. He believed that it was brought about by the influence of those Arab leaders who had for years served under the Turks and who were still thinking in terms of "Decentralization," which was then the principal objective of Arab independence.[23]

On 9 March, Riḍā 'Alī Pasha al-Rikābī became the first Prime Minister of the new Kingdom of Syria and formed his first Minis-

"faithful sons of Syria" for having "opened the door of independence" for their country. For the Arabic text of this letter see *Al-Ḥayāt* (Beirut), no. 2405, 7 March 1954, p. 1.

21. A white star was added in the middle of the red triangle. For an account of the ceremony and the various proclamations, see the Syrian Government's official journal *Al-'Aṣimah* (Damascus), no. 107, 8 March 1920, and no. 103, 11 March 1920. Also, in commemoration of this historic occasion, a new gold dinar was struck and put in circulation and the Syrian stamps were overprinted in Arabic: "In commemoration of the independence of United Syria, 8th March, 1920."

22. Al-Ḥuṣrī, p. 83. For the Arabic text of this proclamation, see *Al-Qiblah* (Mecca), no. 373, 8 April 1920, pp. 1-2.

23. 'Abdullah, pp. 167 and 242-248.

try.[24] He wrote immediately to the Allied Governments notifying them of the proclamation of Syrian independence, sending them a copy of the resolution taken by the General Syrian Congress, explaining the good intentions of the new Syrian Government and trusting that the Allies would recognize the new Syrian Kingdom.[25] Faiṣal himself sent personal letters and cables to President Wilson, Lord Curzon, General Allenby and General Gouraud, explaining why it had become necessary to proclaim the unity and independence of Syria, emphasizing that this was not against the interests of the Allies and assuring them of the friendship and cooperation of the new State of Syria.[26] Lord Curzon sent an immediate telegraphic reply on 9 March in the name of the British and French Governments, protesting strongly. He stated that the Arab Congress was not a legal body, that it had acted against the wishes of the British and the French Governments, and that the proclamation of independence would complicate the settling of the Turkish question at the Peace Conference. Moreover, he added that Great Britain did not recognize the right of any group of people in Damascus to speak on behalf of Palestine and Iraq.[27] It should be stated that, on 7 March, Faiṣal had informed the British Government of the resolution taken on that same day by the General Arab

24. Al-Ḥuṣrī, p. 234.

25. For the original Arabic text, see al-Ḥuṣrī, pp. 265-268.

26. Ibid., pp. 268-273. Also, *Al-'Aṣimah*, no. 114, 5 April 1920.
"What Allenby's answer was, is not known, but Gouraud dispatched a very courteous telegram in which, while emphasizing that as a High Commissioner of the French Republic he could not in any way recognize the action which had occurred, he tendered to the new king his personal congratulations." Jeffries, p. 320.

According to an article in the *Temps*, under the Beirut dateline of 11 March and cited in *The Daily Telegraph* (London), 16, March 1920, it appears that Faiṣal had informed Gouraud of what was going to take place, "but pointing out that his proclamation as King would in no way affect the friendship of France and Syria."

General Gouraud's opinion of Faiṣal is worth nothing here: " 'C'est une personnalité des plus frappantes', me disait le général Gouraud, à Beyrouth, la veille de mon départ pour Damas.... De l'avis de tous, l'émir Fayçal est un caractère, une personnalité. Il est intelligent et fin, assimilateur à l'extrême, sans vanité, travailleur acharné...." B.G. Gaulis, *La Question Arabe*, pp. 107 and 123.

27. Al-Ḥuṣrī, pp. 85 and 261.

Congress, but as he was proclaimed King the following day, there was no time for the British Government to communicate to him their views. But when Faiṣal cabled again to Lord Curzon, through Colonel Easton, the British Liaison Officer in Damascus, justifying the action taken by the Congress, the British Government refused to recognise Faiṣal as anything more than a "Hashimite Emīr" and the Head of a Provisional Arab Government under the supreme authority of General Allenby as Commander-in-Chief of the Occupied Enemy Territories. Any permanent settlement had to wait the final decision of the Peace Conference. The French Government, Press and public opinion were greatly irritated, particularly at the inclusion of the Lebanon in the Faiṣal Kingdom, as he had no right, they said, to meddle in areas "*soumis à l'influence directe de la France.*" To a telegram from the French Prime Minister, M. Millerand, to the British Government stating that if Faiṣal was recognized as King, it would be an unfriendly ("*inamical*") act towards France, the British expressed regret at what had taken place and their readiness to protest to the Emīr.[28]

As to the United States, Faiṣal did not succeed in securing American recognition of his proclamation as King of Syria. When the American Consul at Damascus, as reported by Laurence Evans, cabled on 11 March "for instructions if he were invited to attend the coronation," the reply said that "unless the British and French Consuls attend the ceremony he was to absent himself from Damascus for the period of the ceremonies, ostensibly going to Beirut to consult his colleagues there on 'urgent business'."[29]

The British, French, and American press showed much interest in the affairs of Syria at this time. In *The Times* of 13 March, its diplomatic correspondent wrote that Faiṣal had always expressed readiness to accept a French Mandate over the Lebanon and a British one over Palestine, but "apparently events have proved too strong for him. The proclamation of Faiṣal as "King of an independent and integral Syria, to include Northern Mesopotamia, the Lebanon and Palestine... was far from unexpected. But the rapidity with which it has been rushed to an accomplished fact is decidedly

28. Ḥarfūsh, p. 621.
29. Evans, *United States Policy*, pp. 253-54.

disconcerting, and is held to reinforce its character as a challenge to the upholders of the Anglo-French agreements." Mr. Ernest Smith, correspondent of the *Daily News*, wrote from Cairo, on 20 March: "If the Emir Feisul had not come down on the independence side of the fence, his authority would have been entirely lost, carrying with it probably also the loss of the Hedjaz."

Faiṣal also accorded a number of interviews to the representatives of the foreign press. J.M.N. Jeffries (as representative of *The Daily Mail*) has reported at length on his visit to Damascus and his meeting with Faiṣal.[30] "It was the first opportunity he had as King," wrote Jeffries, "to speak to the British and European public, and my interview was endowed with some formality." Faiṣal is reported to have said on this occasion: "Our action was quite justified. Long ago, the Allies promised us an independent Arab State where we have proclaimed it. But what immediately forced Congress to take the step of proclamation was the never-ending delay of the Peace Conference in coming to a decision concerning us.... Men (i.e, the Arabs) have lost their confidence: they are convinced that the Allies mean to leave Syria divided into three parts as it is now, and that the promised union of the Arab people in an Arab kingdom or confederation is a myth. The result is that the most dangerous public opinion has been formed in the country and will not hear of further postponments." When Faiṣal was asked what would be his attitude towards a Mandate, he smiled and said: "I've not yet arrived at a clear understanding of what a Mandate means. It may mean nothing but friendly support and relations; it may mean colonization. It is too elastic a phrase. Everything depends upon how the 'Mandate' would be exercised." Jeffries' comment on what Faiṣal told him was: "It disposes absolutely of any idea that he accepted the permanent division of Syria into zones, or that he stood for anything less than the independence of the whole area of Syrian soil."

On 18 March, answering a question asked by Mr. Ormsby-Gore in the House of Commons about the "recent political and military developments in Syria," the Prime Minister said:

30. Jeffries, pp. 322-327.

"It appears that the Emir Feisul was proclaimed King of Syria, including apparently Palestine and Syria, by a Congress at Damascus on March 8th.... As it is obvious that the future of these territories which have been conquered from the Ottoman Empire can only be properly determined by the Allied Powers who are at present assembled in Conference for the purpose, the Emir Feisul has been informed by the British and the French that they cannot recognise the validity of these proceedings, and the Emir has been invited to come to Europe to state his case." [31]

A word should be said about the reaction of the Lebanon to the proclamation of Faiṣal as King of United Syria. The Lebanese Delegation headed by Patriarch Hoyek had returned to Beirut on 10 October 1919. But soon after the arrival of Faiṣal in Damascus in January 1920, Maronite public opinion became greatly perplexed and apprehensive by the turn of events in Syria, particularly when it became evident that, as a result of the pressure of extremists, Faiṣal had abandoned the idea of signing an agreement with France. Whereupon the Patriarch sent a new Delegation to Paris headed by Bishop (*Monseigneur*) 'Abdullah Khūrī. [32] The Delegation arrived in the French capital on 11 February and started immediately the next day on its task of "saving the independence of Lebanon," by contacting the Ministry of Foreign Affairs. When the news of 8 March reached Beirut, protests began to pour in at the Maronite Patriarchate from all over the Lebanon, rejecting the claim of the fifteen prominent Muslims of Beirut, who had joined the Syrian Congress as "representatives of Lebanon," and vehemently objecting to the inclusion of the Lebanon in the new Kingdom of Faiṣal without consulting previously the wishes of its inhabitants. [33] On 15 March, the Lebanese Delegation in Paris, which had already redoubled its activities, learned that the Patriarch himself had sent a telegram to the Prime Minister,

31. Great Britain, *Parliamentary Debates*, Fifth Ser., vol. 126, 18 March 1920, pp. 2359-2360.

32. The members of the Delegation who accompanied the Bishop were the Emīr Tawfīq Arslān, Shaikh Yūsuf Gemayel and Mr. Emile Eddeh.

33. See *Lisān al-Ḥāl* (Beirut), nos. 355/8005 and 356/8006, 10 and 11 March 1920.

M. Millerand, protesting against the Emīr Faiṣal proclaiming himself as "King over Lebanon."[34] A day earlier, on the 14th, 'Abdullah Khūrī, after consultation with the Ministry of Foreign Affairs and with its approval, had sent a telegram to the Patriarch — through General Gouraud — assuring him that no modification had taken place in the intentions of France towards the Lebanon. General Gouraud incorporated that telegram in a letter which he wrote expressing his own pleasure that the French Government had renewed its intention of standing by the people of the Lebanon.[35]

Three days later, 'Abdullah Khūrī addressed an appeal to M. Millerand to protect the interests of the Lebanon, which were so closely tied with those of France.[36] On the 20th, the Lebanese Delegation was received by the French Prime Minister and assured

34. Ḥarfūsh, p. 620.

35. Owing to the importance of this letter, it may not be out of place to cite it here in toto:

"Haut Commissaire de la République
Française en Syrie et Cilicie.

Beyrouth, le 16 mars, 1920
Le Général Gouraud, Haut-Commissaire de la République Française en Syrie et Cilicie et Chef de l'Armée du Levant.

A Sa Béatitude Monseigneur
Hoyek, Patriarche Maronite.

Monseigneur,

J'ai reçu le télégramme suivant émanant de Monseigneur Abdallah Khouri et destiné à Votre Béatitude:

'Recevons du Ministre des Affaires Étrangères l'assurance que rien n'est modifié dans les intentions du Gouvernement Français en ce qui concerne le Liban depuis le départ de Monseigneur Hoyek, les assurances envers le patriarche sont intégralement maintenues.

'Les manifestations qui viennent d'avoir lieu à Damas sont considérées comme ne pouvant en rien modifier la politique que le gouvernement français poursuit en Syrie. Poursuivons actuellement ici nos démarches en parfait accord. Trouvons partout accueil encourageant. Signé, Abdallah Khouri.'

Je tiens à vous l'adresser moi-même et à vous dire en même temps que j'ai été très heureux de voir le Gouvernement français renouveler les déclarations si fermes que M. Clemenceau a déjà faites au peuple libanais.

Veuillez agréer, Monseigneur, les assurances de ma haute considération."

(Sgd.) Gouraud

For the original text of the above-mentioned letter, see the Private Archives of the Maronite Patriarchate at Bkerkī.

36. The letter to M. Millerand contains a typical expression of the Maronite point of view. Its first and last paragraphs are as follows:

that the French Government considered the letter of M. Clemenceau to the Maronite Patriarch as a binding agreement which the Government intended to carry out.[37] However, for the time being, the French Government did not feel free to comply with the request of the Lebanese Delegation and act unilaterally to add any new territory to the Lebanon (the plain of the Biqā' and the towns of Ḥasbaya and Ba'albek), without consulting other Powers.

Meanwhile, the situation in Mesopotamia was causing the British Government much anxiety. Intense discontent and agitation had finally led to a serious rebellion against the British authorities. The story of that rebellion does not fall within the scope of this work, but it is important to note that the revolt had not only been encouraged by the Iraqi ex-officers in the Turkish army, who had joined the Arab Revolt and were now the trusted advisers of Faiṣal in Damascus, but was actually organized and led by them. While Faiṣal himself cannot be accused of having directly participated in the events which convulsed Iraq, his indirect responsibility cannot be entirely denied. He could not resist the pressure of senior Iraqi officers for at least some help, lest he should completely lose their confidence if not altogether their support.[38]

"Monsieur le Président,

"La Délégation Libanaise, venue à Paris dûment mandatée par toutes les populations du Grand-Liban pour la défense des intérêtes de son pays apprend avec une vive émotion la Parodie du Congrès tenu à Damas, tendant à englober le Liban dans les convoitises de l'Emir Fayçal . . . .

"S'appuyant sur les traditions de mutuel dévouement et sur les siècles d'amitié qui lient le Liban à la France, et aussi sur les solennelles et récentes assurances du Gouvernement de la République, la Délégation Libanaise a le ferme espoir que la France prendra toutes les mesures pour sauvegarder les intérêts du Liban si étroitement solidaires de ceux de la France."

Ḥarfūsh, pp. 623-624.

37. See p. 112 above, and appendix H.

38. One of these leading Iraqi officers, Ali Jawdat, related to the author in April 1955, in Baghdad, the following story: "One day, towards the end of March, a fellow officer and myself went to see Faiṣal. We told him: 'Before we joined the Arab Revolt in the Ḥejāz, we were Ottoman officers in the Turkish army. We did not fight with you to save anything called "Syria" or called "Palestine." We fought for the liberation of all the Arab lands. Then you came here and have now proclaimed yourself King of an independent Syria. But we are Iraqis and Iraq is under British occupation. Did we fight to get rid of the Turks in our country, only to replace them by the British? Some of our brother

There were also those who strongly advised Faiṣal to make common cause with Mustafa Kemal Pasha and let the Arabs and the Turks fight once more side by side and thus prevent the French from establishing themselves anywhere in the Middle East.[39] Disappointed at the lack of success which Faiṣal had in Paris during his second trip to obtain the full independence of Syria, this group convinced the Emīr Zaid of the necessity of getting in touch with the Turks and sounding their attitude towards Arab aspirations. Indeed, on 10 February 1920, the India Office transmitted a copy of an Intelligence Report, to the Foreign office in London, concerning the "alleged intrigues of Faisul with the Bolsheviks" and his desire to make common cause with the Turks against whom "all hatred had been dispelled." According to this Intelligence Report which had come from Switzerland, the Emīr Shakīb Arslān was at St. Moritz. This distinguished Druze leader, writer and political adviser to Faiṣal, had sent a letter to Maksim Litvinov, the Soviet diplomat who was then at Copenhagen. The letter which was "in the name of, and on behalf of the Emir Faisul" assured Litvinov that "Faisul has learnt a bitter lesson in France" and that "he felt no manner of resentment against Litvinov; all hatred against the Turk had been

officers tried to return to their country recently but the British authorities forced them back, having threatened to send them as prisoners to India. We have now decided to fight the British and liberate Iraq.' Faiṣal replied that the question of Iraq concerned his brother 'Abdallah. We said: 'Give us arms and money and send with us your brother Zaid. We shall then organize guerrilla bands in the north of Iraq.' But Faiṣal refused. 'If I were to send my brother with you,' he told us, 'it would mean that I was against the British but that is neither in my interest nor in yours." However, we firmly insisted to get some help and finally Faiṣal gave us five thousand Egyptian Pounds (the currency in use at the time). One night, we arranged to force the door of one of the army stores in Damascus. With the arms thus obtained we left for Aleppo. There, we converted our Egyptian money into Turkish gold sovereigns (much more popular than paper currency!) We then proceeded to Dair-ez-Zor, organized our bands and eventually made a successful attack on Tel-'Afar, west of Mosul." Some years later, in 1967, Ali Jawdat included the above-mentioned interview with Faiṣal, in his published *Dhikrayāt* [Memories], pp. 90-96.

39. In Damascus, the Correspondent of an Arabic newspaper reported that the Government had decided to engage the service of experienced and eminent Turks who had served in high positions in the Ottoman Empire. *See Lisān al-Ḥāl* (Beirut), no. 364/8014, 22 March 1920, p. 2, col. 3. Faiṣal had expressed more than once, both privately and publicly, his sympathy and admiration for the Kemalist movement in Turkey. See al-Ḥuṣrī, pp. 161-162.

dispelled and all that was now wanted was mutual trust and combination in support of the common cause."[40]

As far as we know, nothing definite and practical transpired from this contact with Litvinov. However, two prominent Syrians did actually travel to Turkey, sometime in January, and met secretly the representatives of Mustapha Kemal Pasha in Istanbul. A tentative agreement as a basis of cooperation was drawn up. But when the emissaries returned, in April, the situation had already changed in Syria. King Faiṣal refused to enter into negotiations with the Turks.[41] When Faiṣal did change his mind some time in

40. F.O. 371/5032. Political, Eastern Turkey, E 21/2/44. From India Office to Foreign Office, London.

41. The principal emissary to Turkey was Sa'īd Ḥaidar, a prominent member of *Hizb al-Istiqlāl* of the General Syrian Congress and one of the founders of the famous secret Arab society, *al-Fatāt*. Sa'īd Ḥaidar related to the author the following account of his visit to Turkey: "While Faiṣal was still in Paris, during his second trip, we learned with much regret and disappointment that the British had insisted that he should come to an understanding with the French. The Emīr Sa'īd was at that time Faiṣal's deputy in Damascus and the Head of the Government." Sa'īd Bey was confidentially asked by the Syrian Government to go on a special mission of Turkey and get in touch with the leader of the Turkish nationalists, Mustafa Kemal Pasha. He was to be accompanied by Badī' Bekdāsh, a high ranking officer of Syrian origin who had served in the Turkish army and who had, through marriage connections, close contacts with influential Turks. (He had married the daughter of Rif'at Bey, the President of the Turkish Senate and his sister was the wife of the Turkish Ambassador in Paris.) Sa'īd Bey and Badī' Bekdāsh were in Beirut getting ready to leave when Faiṣal arrived from Paris on 7 January, 1920. When the Emīr learned of their mission, he called Sa'īd Ḥaidar and asked him to give up the whole idea and return with him to Damascus. Sa'īd Ḥaidar who was determined to go, as he greatly feared that Syria might become a French colony, told Faiṣal that he was under Government orders which he had to obey. The Emīr finally acquiesced. The two emissaries left on an Italian boat, ostensibly for Egypt. In Port Sa'īd, they changed boats and proceeded to Constantinople. Once in the Turkish capital, they were secretly introduced to the members of a Committee representing Mustafa Kemal who was himself in Samsun. After much negotiation, a four-point agreement was drafted for the approval of the Syrian Government, as follows: (1) Certain modifications to be introduced in the northern boundary of Syria, particularly in the region of Mosul; (2) a united front to be organized against the Western Powers, "from Ma'ān to the Black Sea"; (3) The Turkish and Arab armies to be placed under a unified command; (4) In the event of the successful outcome of their efforts against the West, the Arabs and Turks will live side by side in two independent States but their relations will be nearly on the same lines as the relations of Austria and Hungary in the pre-War Austro-Hungarian Empire. This relationship will be governed by a Treaty to last for fifty years. Such was the outline of the

July 1920; it was then too late. Not only in Syria, but in Iraq also, the idea of joining forces with the Turks was being seriously considered by some of the Iraqi nationalists. No wonder then that when Churchill, as Minister of Colonies, spoke in the House of Commons on the situation in the Middle East, on 22 March 1920, he said, referring to the cause of anxiety in Mesopotamia: "There are the Arabs who have been disturbed by the occupation of Syria, and who are inclined now, for the first time, in many ways to make common cause with the Turkish Nationalists, thus uniting two forces by whose division our policy has hitherto prospered."[42] Concerning the recognition of the validity of Syrian independence as proclaimed in Damascus, which was brought up in the House on the same day and to which Mr. David Ormsby-Gore referred as "the recent proceedings in Syria," the Prime Minister gave the following answer: "The Emir Feisal was informed that the situation of Syria would shortly be examined by the Peace Conference, with a view to arriving at a settlement in accord with the declarations that have been exchanged between the British, French and Arab Governments."[43]

The most important consequence of 8 March was the irreparable loss of strength and standing of Faiṣal on the international plane. He was left with no real friends or supporters. He embarrassed his British ally to such an extent that he lost much sympathy for his cause and he confirmed the French and Lebanese fears and suspicions of his real intention. The Lebanese took matters in their own hands—with the knowledge and support of the French authorities. A great meeting composed of the Administrative Council of Lebanon, of village heads and mayors, of Lebanese notables, of representatives of various Christian communities and of a distinguished group of eminent Druzes, was held in Be'abda, the old administrative capital of Lebanon, on Monday, 22 March, and proclaimed the independence of Lebanon. At three o'clock in the afternoon

basis on which, it was hoped, Arab and Turk might cooperate for the defense of their mutual interests against the West.

42. Great Britain, *Parliamentary Debates, House of Commons*, vol. 127, Fifth Ser., 1920, p. 186.

43. Ibid., p. 142.

and in the midst of an imposing ceremony, the first Lebanese flag was hoisted and unfurled on the Government House at Be'abda, in the presence of contingents of the Lebanese army, who marched past and took the salute.[44] The significance of this event could neither be ignored nor minimized in Damascus.

44. See *Lisān al-Ḥāl* (Beirut), no. 365/8015, 23 March 1920, p. 2. The Lebanese flag was the French flag: blue, white, and red, with a green Cedar tree, the symbol of the Lebanon, in the middle of the white stripe. See also F.O. 371/5034, telegram of 23 March 1920.

CHAPTER EIGHT

SYRIA FALLS UNDER FRENCH MANDATE

"The mandate is a provisional system designed to enable populations which, politically speaking, are still minors to educate themselves so as arrive one day at full self-government. This presupposes that the mandatory Power will gradually create native organizations in the mandated territory such as may, when complete, be able to ensure entirely the government of the country and such as may, if they carry out their duties in a proper manner, render the intervention of the Mandatory unnecessary. It appears from this that there should not be any intervention on the part of the organization of the mandatory Power in the internal affairs of the native governments."

Permanent Mandates Commission,
Minutes of the Eighth Session (Extraordinary).

MEANWHILE, Great Britain and France were working out their own plans for the future of the Arab Near East. The Allied Supreme Council met at San Remo from 19 to 26 April. Millerand and Lloyd George were present in person. The main purpose of this meeting was to draft the Turkish Treaty. In six sessions from the 19th to the 24th, the Treaty of Sèvres was constructed. Article 94 of this Treaty read: "The High Contracting Parties agree that Syria and Mesopotamia shall, in accordance with the fourth paragraph of Article 22, Part I (Covenant of the League of Nations), be provisionally recognised as independent States subject to the rendering of administrative advice and assistance by a Mandatory until such time as they are able to stand alone...."[1] On 25 April, the assignment of Mandates for Mesopotamia, Palestine and Syria took place. These were the "A" Mandates and the mandatories "chosen by the Principal Allied Powers" were France for Syria (including the Lebanon) and Great Britain for Mesopotamia and Palestine.

This new political system was in accordance with the provisions of Article 22 of the Covenant of the League of Nations. It had ori-

1. *Papers Relating to the Foreign Relations of the United States*, vol. 8, p. 95.

ginally been propounded in connection with the disposal of the German Colonies on the agreed principle that "not a single captured colony should be restored to Germany" and "on the absence of any real desire on the part of the representatives of Great Britain (the British Ministers who composed the Imperial War Cabinet) to add any more territory to the vast areas of undeveloped land now under the flag." [2] The well-being and development of the peoples of the colonies needed the tutelage of "advanced nations who by reason of their resources, their experience or their geographical position can best undertake this responsibility, and who are willing to accept it, and that this tutelage should be exercised by them as Mandatories on behalf of the League...." (Article 22). When it was also decided to apply the Mandatory system to the Near East, the final draft of Article 22, which was approved on 28 April 1919, included the now famous paragraph 4, without specifically stating, however, to which precise territories that paragraph applied, for it only said: "Certain communities formerly belonging to the Turkish Empire have reached a stage of development where their existence as independent nations can be provisionally recognized subject to the rendering of administrative advice and assistance by a Mandatory until such time as they are able to stand alone. The wishes of these communities must be a principal consideration in the selection of the Mandatory...." It was left to the Conference of San Remo, almost exactly a year later, to define the precise territories. Even then, the actual boundary lines were not agreed upon until the Franco-British Convention of 23 December 1920 was signed, "to settle completely the problems raised by the attribution to France of the Mandate over Syria and the Lebanon... conferred by the Supreme Council at San Remo...." [3]

To emphasize once more the importance of oil in the affairs of the Middle East, it should be stated that on the day the Mandates were assigned at San Remo, Lloyd George and Millerand confirmed with their signature a Memorandum of Agreement on oil which had been drawn up and initialled the previous day by M. Philippe Berthelot, "Directeur des Affaires politiques et com-

2. Lloyd George, vol. 1, pp. 114-115.
3. Cmd. 1195, Miscellaneous No. 4 (1921).

merciales" at the French Ministry of Foreign Affairs and Professor Sir John Cadman, Director in Charge of His Majesty's Petroleum Department. In Mesopotamia, the British Government undertook "to grant to the French Government or its nominee 25 per cent of the net output of crude oil ... or in the event of a private petroleum company being used to develop the Mesopotamian oilfields, the British Government will place at the disposal of the French Government a share of 25 per cent in such company...." The French Government, in turn, agreed to give every facility for the passage of two separate pipelines in "territory within a French sphere of influence" (obviously Syria and the Lebanon, in this case), "for the transport of oil from Mesopotamia and Persia through French spheres of influence to a port or ports on the Eastern Mediterranean.[4]

In substance, the Mandate System was, by the admission of Lloyd George himself, "a substitute for old Imperialism."[5] Gen. Smuts had written that the peoples left behind by the decomposition of Russia, Austria and Turkey were mostly untrained politically; "many of them are either incapable of or deficient in power of self-government; they are mostly destitute, and will require much nursing towards economic and political independence."[6] It was also, together with another modification — the above-mentioned Franco-British Convention of 23 December 1920 — the last form in which the Sykes-Picot Agreement was finally carried out.[7]

4. Cmd. 675, Miscellaneous No. 11 (1920).

5. Lloyd George, 1:622. In the Chamber of Deputies on 25 June, M. Daladier, referring to the Mandate on Syria which France had obtained at San Remo, said that it was a grave error for France to lay its hands on Syria and try to dominate it: "On parlait autrefois de pénétration pacifique; maintenant, vous parlez de mandat. En réalité, vous leur offrez un mandat à la pointe de nos baïonnettes." *Journal Officiel, Débats Parlementaires*, vol. 4, 25 June 1920, p. 2431.

6. J.C. Smuts, *The League of Nations : A Practical Suggestion*(London,1918), p. 11.

7. M. Robert de Caix, who was in the early days of the Mandate Secretary General of the French High Commissioner in Syria and the Lebanon, wrote in *L'Europe Nouvelle* of 16 March 1929: "Le Mandat syrien et libanais fut dévolu à la France pai les principales puissances alliées au cours de la conférence de San-Rémo, au commencement de 1920. C'est sous sa forme que devaient prendre effet les accords anglo-russes de mai 1916 qui, entre autres stipulations, avaient reconnu la Mésopotamie zone d'influence britannique et la Syrie zone d'influence française."

On 27 April, Lord Allenby sent a telegram to Faiṣal, from Cairo, informing him on behalf on His Majesty's Government, of the decision taken at San Remo to place Syria under the Mandate of France, Mesopotamia and Palestine under the Mandate of Great Britain. But like a doctor who tries to break gently and tactfully the bad news to a patient's father by starting with the assurance that the patient is not actually in danger of death, Lord Allenby's telegram began with the news that as a result of the decisions taken at San Remo, Syria and Iraq have been recognized — as "two independent countries" — but it added immediately "on condition that they receive help and assistance from the Mandatory Power, until such time when they would be able to stand alone," His Majesty's Government was also ready to recognize Faiṣal, *en principe*, as the Head of an Independent Syrian State, but it believed strongly that the question of his "kingship" was a matter which only the Peace Conference had the right to consider. Consequently, Faiṣal was strongly urged to return to Europe without delay to present his case in detail before the Members of that Conference at its next session in Paris towards the end of May.[8]

Another telegram came from the French Prime Minister, M. Millerand, on 1 May. It was in the form of a "Declaration" and was published on 3 May, in *Al-'Aṣimah.* This telegram, too, started by saying that the French Government recognized that the peoples who spoke the Arabic language and belonged to different religious denominations — all of whom lived in the province of Syria— had the right to rule themselves by themselves as independent peoples (a reference, undoubtedly, to the right of the Lebanese to live in an independent Lebanon). This was in line with the previous proclamations of the French Government and with the general principles for the liberation of people announced by the Peace Conference. Meanwhile, Millerand's cable continued, it was the duty of the French Government to accept the task which the Peace Conference had assigned to it — that of giving advice and assistance to those people so that they may fulfil their legal aspirations. But their independence will be guaranteed against any attack on the national boundaries which will be fixed by the said Confe-

8. Al-Ḥuṣrī, pp. 275-276.

rence.[9] The reader will have already noticed that in this official proclamation, there is not a single mention of the word "Mandate".

The announcement of the French Mandate for Syria was a great blow to the Syrian national aspirations. There were strikes and violent demonstrations in all the Syrian towns by angry crowds protesting against the Mandate and asking the Government to take immediate steps to effectively protect the independence of their country. The Syrian Cabinet of Rikābī Pasha fell and Faiṣal appointed Hāshim al-Atāsī, the President of the Syrian Congress, as his new Prime Minister. A new Cabinet was formed on 3 May and appeared, the same day, before the Syrian Congress which ever since 8 March, had been acting like an "*Assemblée Nationale*," bringing to mind the turbulent days of the French Revolution. In an outline of its program as presented to that Congress, the Cabinet pledged itself to carry out three outstanding aims: (1) to support fully the complete independence of the country with the right of diplomatic representation abroad; (2) to stand for the unity of Syria within "its natural boundaries" — rejecting the claim of the Zionists to transform a part of "southern Syria," i.e., Palestine, into a Jewish national home and (3) to oppose any foreign intervention which might affect Syrian national sovereignty. The Cabinet welcomed the decision of the San Remo Conference as far as the recognition of Syria's independence was concerned, but it promised to do everything in its power not to be shackled by a Mandatory Power. There was a veiled threat in one of the concluding lines of that Program, that Syria was prepared to meet force with force. It said that if the Peace Conference, at its next meeting in Paris, ignored the promises of the Allies and did not act justly towards the Syrian demands, then "the greatest guarantee" of the rights of Syria resided in "the power of its people and their firm determination" to defend those rights.[10]

The determination of the Syrian nationalists, supported by the ex-Iraqi officers in the Turkish army, to revolt and fight against France, came to a head as soon as the San Remo decisions were announced. These decisions brushed aside any hesitations that Faiṣal

9. Ibid., p. 274.
10. For the original Arabic text, see al-Ḥuṣrī, pp. 242-244.

might still have had and swept him in the torrent of emotional nationalism which was whirling around him. Indeed, Faiṣal himself, in his letter to Hāshim al-Atāsī, on 3 May asking him to form the new Cabinet, had specifically accused the French Government of having caused the Government crisis in Damascus by Millerand's telegram of 1 May and had directed his Prime Minister to form a Cabinet whose first aim would be to defend the rights of Syria and its "sacred independence."[11]

The new Ministry considered the allocation of the Mandate for Syria to France as a provocation and a challenge to Syrian nationalism. One of its first acts was to issue a decree making compulsory military service universal in its application to all the Syrians. Various national organizations redoubled their activities to prepare the people for the defense of their country, "in case a war should break out with France." At the same time, guerrilla attacks against the French positions between Syria and the Lebanon were intensified. The Syrian intransigence towards the French had received much encouragement earlier during the year when the French forces in Cilicia, and particularly in Marash, had been seriously defeated by a formidable striking force which Mustapha Kemal Pasha had organized. Faced with the decision of either losing Cilicia to the Turks or Syria to the Arabs—and partly also because of their grudge against Great Britain for the difficulties which they alleged the latter had created for them in Syria, the French Government decided to come to terms with Mustapha Kemal.[12] This enabled General Gouraud to withdraw his troops from the Turkish front and mass them on the western borders of Syria. The writer was

11. Al-Ḥuṣrī, p. 240.

12. Lloyd George condemned this French action in no uncertain terms as "treachery." He wrote: "During the whole of this wretched business (the routing of Greek forces in Asia Minor) some of the Allied Powers played a treacherous part. The Italians sold arms to Mustapha Kemal to fight the Greeks, and were paid out of money supplied by Moscow. The French Government negotiated a secret Treaty with Kemal behind the backs of the British Ministry." Lloyd George, 2: 1349.

For an account of the disastrous consequences of French action to the Armenian population of Cilicia, see Stanley Elphinstone Kerr, *The Lions of Marash: Personal Experiences with American Near East Relief, 1920-1922* (Albany: State University of New York Press, 1973).

assured by one of the former members of the Syrian Congress that they could not believe in those days that Great Britain would really ever allow France to make a direct military attack on Syria. He was also told by a former Minister in Faiṣal's Cabinet that Faiṣal counted very much on a vague and oral promise which had been given to him by President Wilson in Paris, to the effect that if the Syrian people really succeded in establishing their independence, he (President Wilson) would never allow it to be destroyed by force of arms. But in March 1920, President Wilson was already a sick man, suffering from physical debility, and on the 19th of that month, his Peace policy was repudiated. The American Senate voted against the Covenant of the League of Nations — The President having refused, to the bitter end, to accept certain reservations urged by the Republicans. As a result America withdrew from the Supreme Council of the Allies.

The Lebanese Delegation, at this time, continued to be actively at work in Paris to prevent any amalgamation of the Lebanon with Syria.[13] When, early in May, its members learned of the decisions of the San Remo Conference, they were filled with dismay at the absence of any reference to the Lebanon in that document. They wrote, on 13 May, to M. Millerand expressing their great anxiety and disappointment and trusting to receive some assurance that the complete independence of the Lebanon would be preserved by the French, in whom the Lebanese had placed their full confidence. On the 19th, Millerand answered assuring the Delegation that France, upon whom a Mandate over Syria had been conferred by the Supreme Council of the Allied Powers, had never changed its intention of establishing the independence of the Lebanon under the French Mandate.[14]

On 27 May, Faiṣal delivered his longest speech since his entry into Damascus, at a great banquet given by himself in Damascus on the occasion of the "Ifṭār" (the breaking of the Muslim

13. Al-Raiḥānī, *Mulūk al-'Arab*, 1: 311.

14. "...En vertu d'une décision du Conseil Suprême, les Puissances Alliées ont conféré le mandat sur la Syrie à la France qui n'a jamais varié dans son intention d'appeler le Liban à l'indépendance sous le mandat français." See the Private Archives of the Maronite Patriarchate at Bkerkī for the full text of this letter.

Fast). The speech seems to have been primarily intended to cheer the downhearted: those who after the first flush of enthusiasm thought now that all was lost and all efforts would remain fruitless, and those also, who, in their despair, had concluded that there was nothing more to do but to fight and die honorably for their country. To Faiṣal, both those ways of thinking were not based on reality. All that had happened, he told his audience, was a recognition of their independence under a Mandate. But they had already declared their own independence and as to the Mandate, which was an elastic term and had no precise meaning, they had categorically rejected it, as its acceptance was humiliating to any nation that loved freedom without fetters. Independence, however, was not a gift: it had to be won and certain means were required to attain it. The nation needed an army, first, to preserve internal order and then to defend its existence when necessary. An army could not come into being without money. Consequently, the Government had issued a loan and Faiṣal expected the nation to subscribe to it generously and thus to prove to the civilized world that Syria was not in need of any outside help, not even money. The two principal objectives to be achieved were thus money and an army.

Meanwhile, there was no reason for despair and no reason to think of dying. "I assure you," said Faiṣal, "that no sentence of death has been passed upon us and such a sentence will never be passed." It was their duty, however, to be ready, and also to be patient and wise. Their thoughts and deeds should not be based on vain imaginings, but on material and tangible realities. The question of Syria, concluded Faiṣal, was one of the greatest problems of the world. No final settlement could be reached through the words of a newspaper or the speech of an orator whether he was a responsible or an irresponsible person. The nation had to stand firmly united and courageous to the end.[15]

We have already seen how, ever since 8 March, the British Government had urged Faiṣal to come back to Europe and state his claims with a view to coming to an understanding with the French and British Governments. But the members of his Government and the Syrian Congress opposed Faiṣal's return to Europe

15. The text of this speech is found in al-Ḥuṣrī, pp. 223-227.

as long as the Powers had not recognized the full independence of Syria.[16] They preferred to send a delegation to enter into negotiation with the Allies. Actually, such a delegation was appointed in June under the chairmanship of Nūrī Pasha al-Sa'īd, but while its members were deliberating and laying plans for the best way of presenting their case before the Peace Conference, French military preparations in the Lebanon appeared so unusual and ominous that Faiṣal decided, in spite of the opposition of his advisors, to go in person to the Peace Conference.[17] He sent Nūrī Pasha to Beirut to make the necessary arrangements with General Gouraud for the journey to France. The French General is reported to have told Faiṣal's emissary on 9 July, the day they met: "We cannot permit the Emīr to proceed to France before he accepts our demands. These demands will be sent to him in a few days." He added a further threat by saying: "And should the Emīr travel to Europe

16. Another reason, according to 'Abdu'l-Raḥman Shahbandar, Minister of Foreign Affairs in Faiṣal's last Cabinet, was the pernicious propaganda, in certain quarters in Syria, sowing suspicion against Faiṣal's return to Europe. According to this propaganda, Faiṣal would, by a secret agreement, "sell" Syria to France. See article by 'Abdu'l-Raḥman Shahbandar on "Faisal ben al-Ḥusain," in *Al-Muqtaṭaf* (Cairo), vol. 83, pt. 3 (1933), pp. 257-267. See also al-Raiḥānī, *Faiṣal al-Awwal* [Faiṣal I], p. 27.

17. The correspondent of the *Gazette de Lausanne* reported from Paris the following item of news concerning Syria:

"*Chambre des Députés — Les Questions Orientales.* Paris, 26 juin.

"On continue la discussion du budget des affaires étrangères....

"M. Millerand déclare ensuite que la France ne peut abandonner la Syrie, car ce serait compromettre sa situation de puissance méditerranéenne et renier toutes les traditions l'unissant à la Syrie. Nous irons en Syrie, ajoute-t-il, pour apporter aux populations syriennes qui le demandent, l'aide et l'appui sur lesquels elles ont le droit de compter.... Voilà le rôle de civilisation que la France assume en Syrie. Si vous ne l'acceptez pas, votez que la France, désertant ses intérêts en Syrie, manque à ses intérêts les plus clairs et à son devoir le plus sacré (Appl.)." *Gazette de Lausanne,* 27 June 1920, no. 177, p. 4, col. 1.

On 21 June, a cipher telegram was sent from the Foreign Office to Lord Curzon, Minister of Foreign Affairs, who was in France. The telegram said, in part:

"In view of Faiṣal's reported visit to Aleppo to meet Mustapha Kemal's emissaries, and the obvious distrust of French intentions, there appears to be some danger of his joining hands with Turkish nationalists unless he is reassured without delay.

"Would it be possible to obtain assurances from the French Minister for Foreign Affairs to show Faiṣal that he need not fear unprovoked attack by the French?" (F.O. 371/5035).

by some other way, the French Government would categorically refuse to recognise him or to negotiate with him. . . ."[18] Then General Gouraud proceeded to enumerate to Nūrī Pasha the following principal terms which his "demands" would include:[19]

(1) The Rayak-Aleppo railway to be placed under the control of the French army.

(2) Acceptance of the French Mandate.

(3) Abolishing compulsory military service and demobilizing those who had already been conscripted.

(4) Acceptance of the paper currency issued by the "Banque de Syrie."

(5) Punishment of the "criminals" who had committed hostile acts against France.

The crisis came to a head in Syria on 11 July when the news of the French ultimatum spread like wildfire with the return of Nūrī Pasha to Damascus. A wave of anger and commotion ran through all the towns of Syria, accompanied by emotional outbursts and anti-French demonstrations. On that same day, Faiṣal sent a telegram to the Consuls of all the Foreign Powers in Damascus, informing them of the unofficial "ultimatum" he had received from General Gouraud, appealing to the sense of justice of the Allies and begging them and the League of Nations to intervene, in order to prevent bloodshed and save the independence of Syria from destruction by force. He finally urged the Consuls to appoint an Arbitration Committee, composed of representatives of the Allied Governments, to study the demands of General Gouraud, promising in advance that he, Faiṣal, and his people would accept and carry out the decisions of that Committee. The telegram was followed by an explanatory letter to the *Doyen* of the Consular Corps in Damascus, the Marquis de Paterno, Consul General of Italy.[20] Faiṣal enumerated in this letter the above-mentioned conditions of General Gouraud, complained of having been prevented by the

18. Al-Ḥuṣrī, p. 89.

19. Ibid., p. 104; Lloyd-George, 2: 1111-1112.

20. In this connection, see the documents in the archives of the Italian Ministry of Foreign Affairs, in Rome, folder N° 7154 marked "Siria 1920". See also Catroux, *Deux Missions en Moyen-Orient*, pp. 218-219.

General from proceeding to Europe, and expressed great anxiety at the concentration of French troops all along the Syrian border. He suspected that Gouraud had hostile intentions, his troops having already occupied Rayak and an important bridge (Jisr al-Shoghūr) on the road to Aleppo. The Syrian cause was a just cause and Syria wanted to live in peace. He made a personal appeal to the *Doyen* of the Consular Corps to use his influence and prevent the outbreak of a war which would bring nothing but destruction and ruin upon Syria.[21]

A third message was sent out by Faiṣal in the form of a general telegram to Great Britain, Italy, Belgium, the United States, and the League of Nations, asking them to hear "the cry of Syria," and repeating his appeal to stop the overwhelming French forces from entering his country. He asserted that he and his people were "ready to come to an understanding" with the French, on condition that their national honor was preserved and the resolutions of the San Remo Conference were observed. He asked to be allowed to travel to Europe, in answer to the invitation of the Peace Conference and the British Cabinet.[22]

On 13 July, the Government read a statement before the General Syrian Congress, recapitulating the recent developments, particularly the conditions of General Gouraud, protesting against them and asking for international arbitration. The statement ended with the following four points:

"(1) We want peace and the preservation of our independence and honour.

"(2) We reject as unfounded all the accusations against us, intended to embroil our relations with our Allies.

"(3) We do not refuse to enter into negotiations and we are indeed ready to do so. Our Delegation headed by His Majesty the King is ready to leave (for Europe). We accept any solution provided it is not against our independence and our honour....

"(4) We are fully prepared and fully resolved to defend our honour and our rights with all the force that God has given us."[23]

21. For the original Arabic texts of the above-mentioned messages, see al-Ḥuṣrī, pp. 277-280.
22. Ibid., p. 280.
23. Ibid., pp. 282-283.

The next day, 14 July, the great National Holiday of France commemorating the Fall of the Bastille in the name of "Liberté, Égalité and Fraternité," General Gouraud's ultimatum was sent to "His Highness, the Emīr Faiṣal." Before discussing the ultimatum, it will be necessary to relate a significant incident which took place in the Lebanon, between 10 and 12 July. This incident not only infuriated General Gouraud, but it may have influenced his decision to occupy Syria and put an end to Faiṣal's Government within the shortest possible time.[24]

The Lebanese had for sometime been groaning under the military administration of the French and had made representations to General Gouraud pleading to employ the Lebanese themselves in the civil administration of their country. But they received no satisfactory answer and the military spirit of the High Commissioner continued to permeate all Government offices in the Lebanon.[25] In his Report to Earl Curzon on "Recent events in Syria," Col. Meinertzhagen had written earlier in the year, on 13 January 1920: "In the Lebanon, the French Administration have caused considerable discontent by directly controlling the affairs of the Lebanese Administration and depriving them of the independent nature of their Government which they have enjoyed during the old *status quo*."[26] Consequently, the Administrative Council of the Lebanon met secretly on 10 July and, ignoring its own resolution of May 1919 putting the Lebanon under the protection of France, asked now for the complete independence and sovereignty

24. It is of great interest to note that at this time, the General Syrian Congress was busy with the second reading of a Constitution which it had already drawn up for Syria, composed of 148 articles. According to this Constitution, considered to be the first of its kind in the Arab world, Syria was to be a Constitutional Monarchy with a Chamber of Deputies and a Senate. The first seven articles were discussed and approved at their second reading on 12 July. But the proceedings had to stop indefinitely, never to be resumed again, owing to the ultimatum of Gouraud and the events which followed. See *Al-'Aṣimah*, no. 140, of 14 July 1920, pp. 2-3; al-Ḥuṣrī, p. 245; Najīb al-Armanāzī, *Muḥāḍarāt 'an Sūriyya* [Lectures on Syria], pp. 3-4; Rémusat, pp. 11-12, and al-'Umarī, 3: 205-210. For the full Arabic text of this Constitution, see also *Dasātīr fi'l-Bilād al-'Arabiyyah* [Constitutions of Arab countries], published by the Arab League's Institute for Arab Higher Studies (Cairo, 1956), pp. 3-22.

25. Ḥarfūsh, pp. 635-636.

26. *Documents*, 1:4, p. 614.

of the Lebanon, for its absolute neutrality, for an agreement with Syria on the Lebanon's territorial claims, and for cooperation between the Parliaments of the two countries on economic matters. The two Governments, according to the resolutions of the Administrative Council, will work together in trying to get the Powers to approve of those resolutions, as the latter expressed the wishes of the people of the Lebanon and were in the best interests of the country. The resolutions contained also a decision that the signatories would travel in person (to Europe) to bring to the attention of the "Official Circles," the wishes of the Lebanese people. [27] Eight out of twelve members of the Administrative Council voted approvingly on the resolution and set out that same evening for Damascus to join the Syrian Delegation,which they believed was getting ready to leave for Europe. [28] But they had failed to keep their resolutions and their journey secret from the French authorities. They were soon arrested when on their way to Zaḥleh. [29]

On 12 July, General Gouraud wrote an indignant letter to the Maronite Patriarch. He accused the eight members of the Council of having been "bought" with money provided by Faiṣal. He had learned a few days earlier that the Emīr had sent to Beirut the sum of "40,000 *Livres*" to "buy some Lebanese" ("*pour acheter des Libanais*"). The arrested men, Gouraud's letter alleged, had admitted that they had received as advanced payment the sum of "1,500 *Livres*." This was an act of treason which would bring dishonor on Lebanon. Gouraud went on to say that it was profoundly painful for him to inform the Patriarch that among the arrested men was his own brother Sa'dallah. As this event, continued the General, was going to have, in France and in Europe, most unfortunate repercussions it was necessary to separate immediately the true interests of the

27. For a photostatic copy of this document, see the Arabic newspaper *Al-Ḥayāt* (Beirut), no. 2009, 23 November 1952, p. 1. See also Yūsuf Mezhir, *Ta'rīkh Lubnān al-'Am* [General History of Lebanon], 2: 920-925.

28. They were Fuād 'Abd al-Malak, Maḥmūd Jonblāṭ, Sulaimān Kan'ān, Khalīl 'Akl, Sa'dallah al-Ḥuwayyik, Muḥammad al-Ḥāj Muḥsin and Elias al-Shuwairī. The eighth member, Yūsuf al-Brīdī, could not accompany them to Damascus because of ill-health. Ibid., pp. 921-922.

29. They were first exiled to the island of Ruād (Arwād), then to Corsica and finally to Paris. They were released and allowed to return to Lebanon in 1923. Ibid., p. 927.

Lebanon from the interests of those "who wanted to sell it," for it was not fair that a few should dishonor the entire country. Consequently, Gouraud proposed that the Patriarch should send a personal telegram to M. Millerand similar to the one sent by Bishop Mubarak.[30]

Conflicting views have been expressed on the real motives of the eight members of the Lebanese Administrative Council. They have been accused of corruption and of being in collusion with the Government of Damascus. Faiṣal certainly knew about their intentions and had suggested financial help for their journey abroad, knowing how limited their personal means were. But there seems to be no definite evidence of the official French accusation, voiced by General Gouraud, that they were "bought" by Faiṣal.[31]

30. Bkerkī Archives.

Ignace Mubārak, "Archevêque Maronite de Beyrouth," had drafted the text of a telegram to Premier Millerand, in the name of the Patriarch and almost certainly at the request of General Gouraud himself. This telegram was enclosed in Gouraud's letter to the Patriarch. It expressed the fidelity of "tout le peuple et le clergé Maronite à la France" and their indignation "contre un acte de folie qu'ils renient et flétrissent unanimement."

31. The Emīr 'Adil Arslān who was interviewed by the author — and who was in 1920 one of the advisors of Faiṣal — denied categorically the charge of corruption against the "Young Turks" of the Administrative Council. In *Al-Ḥayāt* (Beirut) of 19 and 20 November 1952, the Emīr 'Adil wrote a detailed account of what actually happened in the days immediately preceding the arrest of those eight members. But Amīn al-Raiḥānī, writing in 1924, stated that the money came actually from King Faiṣal through Nūrī Pasha al-Sa'īd as intermediary, although the receipt was written in the name of 'Arif al-Na'mānī, a well-known pro-Faiṣal notable of Beirut. The money was needed for the travel expenses of the "Lebanese Delegation" which intended to go to Europe via Haifa in Palestine and if necessary even to the United States. Al-Raiḥānī, *Mulūk al-'Arab* [Kings of the Arabs], 1: 322.

See also Iskandar Riyāshī, *Qabl wa Ba'd* [Before and After], p. 26, who asserts that there was a "purchase" of ten of the twelve members, the money having been provided by 'Aref al-Na'mānī.

But al-Na'mānī himself has given the final answer to the question of "where did the money come from." Early in 1955, he told Muḥammad Qarah Ali to whom he was dictating his Memoirs that he "paid everything." "I paid," he said, "ten thousand and five hundred gold pounds" to be distributed among the members of the Administrative Council. See *Al-Ḥayāt* (Beirut), no. 2093, March 1953, p. 7.

Al-Na'mānī's memoirs were published serially in *Al-Ḥayāt* (Beirut) in 1953 by Muḥammad Qarah Ali. See nos. 2083-2110 of 20 February to 24 March 1953.

General Gouraud's letter was followed by the immediate dissolution of the Lebanese Administrative Council.[32] On 14 July, the Patriarch wrote to the General expressing his profound surprise at the strange decision which some members of that Council had taken. But what they had done was simply an "incident fâcheux" for it was not necessary to assure the General that the entire country held to its independence under the French Mandate. The Patriarch took the opportunity to express the great confidence the Lebanese had in the French who, as they had already proclaimed, wished sincerely to grant the Lebanon real independence and to guide its steps towards progress and prosperity. The traditional hope of the mass of the people in the goodness of France had not changed, though circumstances had pushed some of them to act with impatience. Knowing the severity with which Gouraud acted on such occasions, the Patriarch appealed to "le Grand Général" to use his wisdom and generosity to put an end to this sad affair, as the Patriarch's sole anxiety was to reconcile the love of his country with the love of France which he had always loved.[33]

Al-Naʻmānī (1883-1955) was a very rich merchant of Beirut. He was a generous benefactor and helped many poor and needy families in Lebanon during the First World War. He was also a personal friend of King Faiṣal, the Hashemite family and many Arab leaders. He became a staunch supporter of Arab independence and unity and spent generously on the Arab cause. He, too, was exiled to Corsica for nearly a year and a half. Released, he returned to Beirut and was given a royal reception at the Beirut harbor by his many friends and admirers. In 1924, when the Wahhabis attacked the Ḥejāz King Ḥusain abdicated in favor of his son Ali, King Ali, desperately in need of money, turned to ʻArif al-Naʻmānī and personally borrowed from him the sum of twenty-two thousand and three hundred gold Pounds to defray the expenses of the "Arab Government" and of the "Arab forces stationed near Mecca." But soon afterwards, in December 1925, King Ali was defeated and abdicated, withdrawing to Iraq where he died in 1934. The above-mentioned sum was, of course, never refunded and all that remained of it in 1959 was the receipt. The author is grateful to ʻArif al-Naʻmānī's family for their kindness in showing him the document of this financial transaction which bears the signature of King Ali.

See also *Al-Ḥayāt* (Beirut), nos. 2815-2818 of 5-8 July, 1955.

32. Arrêté No. 273, Beirut, 12 July 1920: "Art. 1. — Le Conseil administratif du Liban, dans l'impossibilité d'exercer son mandat, est dissous." *Recueil des Actes Administratifs du Haut-Commissariat de la République Française en Syrie et au Liban, Année 1919-1920*, 1: 105.

33. For the French text of this letter see Ḥarfūsh, pp. 638-639.

CHAPTER NINE

THE END OF FAISAL'S GOVERNMENT IN SYRIA

"So fell the Emir Faisal's independent Syrian State — a State created and fostered by Great Britain in fulfilment, or partial fulfilment, of her pledges to the Arabs. It fell because its existence was in direct conflict with French ambitions, in circumstances which prevented British influence being made effective for its preservation — it fell because its own armed strength was insufficient to ensure its survival."

H. W. V. Temperley

A History of the Peace Conference of Paris, Vol. 6.

As we have already learned, on the day the Maronite Patriarch wrote to General Gouraud, i.e., on 14 July, the latter sent his official ultimatum to Faiṣal. The text of the ultimatum began by calling the attention of Faiṣal to the disturbances which had taken place in Syria following the withdrawal of the British forces and their replacement by French troops. Gouraud, in the name of the French Government, wanted "for the last time" to bring to the attention of "his royal highness," the attitude of his Government towards the behaviour of the Syrian Government since the beginning of the current year. These disturbances had affected adversely the progress of Syria and the maintenance, internally, of its political, administrative and economic order. The Syrian Government bore all responsibility towards the people of Syria, which the Peace Conference had entrusted to France to enjoy the benefits of independence, order, tolerance and prosperity. France had already expressed her support for the rights of the Arabic-speaking population living in Syria to self-government, and Faiṣa himself had recognized that it was in the great interest of the Syrian peoples to seek the counsel and help of a great Power, in order to achieve their unity and to organize their national life and had actually, according to Gouraud, invited France to carry out this mission in the name of the Syrian nation.

Gouraud then quoted the text of a telegram which he had received from Clemenceau, in January, at the time when Faiṣal was negotiating with the French Government. According to this telegram, Clemenceau had stated that when he had learned of the attacks of the Bedouins in southern and northern Syria, he had told Faiṣal that he would keep his word with regard to the principles he had temporarily agreed upon with Faiṣal, provided the latter fulfilled meticulously two conditions. These conditions were the sincerity of his intentions and the necessity of making his authority respected by his followers. If these two conditions were not carefully carried out, the French Government would feel free to use force to impose that which had been entrusted to it by the Conference, i.e. law and order and the respect for the rights of the inhabitants. General Gouraud then accused the Damascus Government of not having ceased to follow a hostile attitude towards France, contrary to the policy of cooperation agreed upon with the French Premier. To substantiate this point, General Gouraud listed the following six instances showing the hostility of the Damascus Government towards France under the following headings:

(1) The railway line from Rayak to Aleppo was absolutely necessary for the transport of supplies to the French troops fighting the Turks in the north. By obstinately refusing to allow the French authorities to use that line, the Government of Damascus had committed an act which was definitely hostile. Moreover, it was the Damascus Government which had laid down the principle of guerrilla warfare against the occupying French forces. Its doctrine had been proclaimed by the commander of the Third Division in Aleppo on 13 April: "Since we cannot officially declare war on the French, we must overrun the country with bands which will destroy it little by little. Our officers will command these bands and if any of them is killed, the Government will provide for the maintenance of his family." In support of the above principle, Gouraud enumerated nine "cases" with the names of the responsible leaders. These cases included serious disturbances in the Shīʿite districts, south of Lebanon, particularly in Marjʿayūn, ʿAin-Ibel and Qulayʿah, leading to the massacre of a number of Christians and the pillage and destruction of much Christian property.[1]

1. See al-Raiḥānī, *Mulūk al-ʿArab* [Kings of the Arabs] 1: 314-318, who accuses the French of having deliberately refrained from restoring law and order during the disturbances.

(2) The aggressive policy of the Damascus Government. Faiṣal had introduced into the Damascus Government men well known for their enmity towards France. The program of these men was an insult not only to France for having refused its help, but also to the Supreme Council which had conferred the Syrian Mandate upon France. The rejection of the French Mandate, stated Gouraud may have disastrous consequences for Syria.

(3) Administrative measures taken against France. The Syrian Government's refusal to accept the new Syrian paper currency issued by the Banque de Syrie and backed by the French Government was a new proof of hostility the result of which would be detrimental to the interests of the country. The refusal, in March, to allow grains and cereals to be brought into the French zone, first from Ḥama, then from Damascus and Aleppo would also have the same effect. The Sharifian forces had also expanded their eastern frontier into the Western zone with the intention of pushing France out.

(4) Hostile acts directed against France. Whoever was a friend or a supporter of France in the eastern zone was suspected by the Syrian Government and often ill treated, but whoever was France's enemy in that area was respected, welcomed and protected. Gouraud mentioned a number of specific names. The Damascus Government had also been spreading anti-French propaganda of a sinister type in the Western zone, the latest instance of it being the "purchase" of most of the members of the Lebanese Administrative Council for "forty-two thousand Egyptian pounds."[2]

The Damascus press also attacked continuously everything that was French, and rejected all offers of help from France.

(5) Breaking the Law of Nations. The Commander of the Ḥijazian army had occupied Syria which, however, must continue

2. After the occupation of Syria and the Lebanon by the Allied Forces in October 1918, the money in circulation was Egyptian pound notes and gold sovereigns, both Turkish and English. The French administration itself had to run on Egyptian currency which in turn was based on the Pound Sterling. In 1919, the French Government allowed the establishment of "La Banque de Syrie." Agreement was reached with the French Treasury on 8 and 28 April 1919, whereby this bank was to issue Syrian bank notes based on the French franc. The "Syrian Pound" was divided into one hundred piasters and every five piasters were to be the equivalent of one French franc. See *Recueil des Actes Administratifs du Haut-Commissariat*, Arrêté No. 120, p. 24.

according to International Law, to be considered as Ottoman territory until the Peace Treaty decided otherwise. He must thus preserve the status quo and be its protector. But he had behaved contrary to this law and had assumed the status of supreme sovereignty. Even compulsory military service had been introduced since December 1919, although the country remained still a foreign country. The Syrian Congress itself was an "illegal assembly." It ruled in the name of a Government and a State, the existence of which had not been recognized. It offered the Emīr the royal title without any right and any power of representation.

Capitulations and diplomatic conventions also were not respected in any way.

(6) Losses suffered by France and Syria. France had not yet been able to organize the country as expected because she had been obliged to use her forces to quell the continuous disturbances and to waste her efforts on futile negotiations with the Damascus Government. Consequently, she had to bear a heavy military and financial burden which would no doubt affect the Syrian budget. "The state of anarchy," wrote Gouraud, "into which the trouble fomentors have plunged the country, has reached such proportions that it has been necessary to bring in large forces, considerably more than should have been required for the simple replacement of the British troops, under peaceful conditions."

All these cases were said to constitute sufficient proof that henceforth France could not rely much longer on a Government which had openly shown its hostility towards her and its helplessness to organize and administer its own country. Consequently, France found herself obliged to undertake certain "guarantees" which would insure the safety of her troops and the security of the populations over whom she had received a Mandate from the Peace Conference. The "guarantees" were the following:

1. The Rayak-Aleppo railway should be at the absolute disposal of the French authorities. French military Commissions will control entirely traffic at the stations of Rayak, Baalbek, Ḥoms, Ḥama and Aleppo. It was also necessary to occupy the town of Aleppo, since it was an important junction of communication and could not be allowed to fall into the hands of Turkish troops.

2. Abolishing compulsory military service. The Sharifian army should be reduced to the numbers it possessed on 1 December 1919.

3. Acceptance of the French Mandate. This Mandate would respect the independence of the peoples of Syria. It was in no way incompatible with the principle of government by Syrian authorities whose power was derived from the will of the people. The Mandate implied only collaboration in the form of assistance by the Mandatory Power. It would not assume under my circumstances the form of colonialism, annexation or direct administration.

4. Acceptance of the Syrian paper currency as the national currency of Syria.

5. Punishment of those most guilty for their acts of hostility towards France.

These conditions were presented *en bloc* and had to be accepted *en bloc* within four days, beginning at midnight, 14 July, and ending at midnight the 18th. If these demands were accepted officially and with proper official implementation, their full execution had to take place by the 31st at midnight. If Faiṣal failed to notify General Gouraud within the time indicated, of his acceptance of those conditions, then the General "had the honor" to inform Faiṣal ("j'ai l'honneur de vous faire connaître") that the French Government would take her full freedom of action. [3] And Gouraud was not sure whether the French Government would then be satisfied only with the above-mentioned moderate guarantees. France had always shown tolerance and understanding. She could not be responsible now for the afflictions which might befall Syria. General Gouraud concluded with the following words: "It is the

3. In a personal letter ("lettre personnelle") accompanying this ultimatum, Général Gouraud appealed to Faiṣal ("Son Altesse Royale l'émir Faïçal") to listen to the voice of wisdom and dissociate himself from his government which represented only the extreme sections of the population. Gouraud concluded: "Je ne pense pas pouvoir compter sur l'exécution des garanties dont j'ai l'honneur de soumettre l'acceptation à Votre Altesse Royale, si le gouvernement qui en sera chargé reste celui qui, en marquant tant d'hostilité à l'égard de la France, a tout fait pour attirer sur votre pays les malheurs de la guerre.

"La décision de Votre Altesse Royale peut seule désormais les écarter." Pichon, *Sur la Route des Indes*, p. 362. In the text of the ultimatum, General Gourand always addresses King Faiṣal as "V.A.R." ("Votre Altesse Royale").

Damascus Government which will bear the whole weight of responsibility for the extreme measures which I envisage with regret which I am prepared to enforce with the most resolute firmness." [4]

After the receipt of the ultimatum, Faiṣal had a telegram sent to the representatives of the Powers informing them of the contents of the ultimatum and appealing to them to request their Govern-

4. F.O. 371/5038. Allenby to Curzon. Allenby forwarded a copy of General Gouraud's ultimatum to Earl Curzon of Kedleston who was then the secretary of State for Foreign Affairs. Allenby was at that time the British High Commissioner in Egypt. He accompanied the copy of the ultimatum with the following brief note, dated 30 July 1920:

"My Lord,

"With reference to my telegram N° 730 of July 18th, in which I transmitted to your Lordship the terms of the Ultimatum sent by General Gouraud to the Syrian Government at Damascus, I now beg to forward a copy of the whole document."

It may be of some interest to notice the title of General Gouraud's ultimatum which is as follows: "Note adressée le 14 Juillet 1920 par le Général Gouraud Haut Commissaire de la République Française en Syrie et en Cilicie et Commandant en Chef de l'Armée du Levant à son Altesse Royale l'Émir Feisal." For the Arabic translation of the ultimatum, see al-Ḥuṣrī, pp. 284-292. Lloyd George in *The Truth About the Peace Treaties*, 2: 1111-1112, cites certain excerpts. See also al-Raiḥānī, *Mulūk al-'Arab* [Kings of the Arabs] 1: 322-324, and Wahbah, pp. 206-208.

The *Gazette de Lausanne*, no. 203, of Friday, 23 July 1920, p. 4, col. 4, contains a remarkable assertion by its Paris Correspondent concerning General Gouraud's ultimatum. The correspondent wrote that based on absolutely unimpeachable information which he had received ("*Des renseignements que je tiens d'une source absolument sûre*"), the General sent his ultimatum to the Emīr without first notifying the French Government ("*Le général Gouraud a adressé son ultimatum à l'émir sans en informer le gouvernement français*"). The Correspondent wondered whether Gouraud was afraid that certain Ministers in the French Cabinet would prevail upon him to moderate ("*adoucir*") his terms or whether he wanted to avoid long discussions with Paris in order to preserve secrecy and insure the success of his campaign.

To what extent was General Gouraud's own personal ambition responsible for his ultimatum, if one may believe in the following analysis of his motive? "Le Général Gouraud hanté par l'évocation du passé, voulant qu'une réplique des Pyramides terminât sa carrière, aurait délibérément, pour le seul plaisir d'une victoire orientale traité un allié en ennemi; il aurait persécuté un gouvernement national et populaire et se serait acquis la gloire facile d'entrer dans la ville ouverte de Damas sur un cheval blanc, entouré des tanks, survolé d'avions." Paul de Rémusat, "Les Cent-Jours du Roi de Syrie," *Revue des Études Historiques*, April-June 1924, p. 1.

The official documents keep their secrets in silence.

ments to arbitrate between Syria and France in order to prevent bloodshed in a country which had suffered so much since the beginning of the War.[5]

Meanwhile, in Damascus the popular enthusiasm for "war and victory" was an emotional outburst which was utterly out of touch with the stark and shocking reality of the actual military situation in Syria. Not only the people were completely ignorant of the weakness of the Arab army, but even the responsible leaders, including Cabinet Ministers, had no knowledge of how weak their Government was and how strong and well-equipped was the modern French army. Sāṭi' al-Ḥuṣrī has recorded with great candor and truth the shock which he had when an old and experienced soldier, Yāsīn al-Hāshimī, recently appointed as Chief-of-Staff of the Arab Army which was to defend Syria if attacked by the French, told him that in a serious war his army did not have enough ammunition to last more than two hours.[6] It should be remembered that al-Ḥuṣrī was a personal friend and advisor of Faiṣal and was at this time the Minister of Education in the Syrian Cabinet, Other responsible military men, included Yūsuf al-'Aẓmah, who, when confronted with the stark reality of a war with France, confessed to the same sad and bitter truth. Faiṣal himself and the majority of the members of his Government became now convinced of the absolute necessity of accepting General Gouraud's conditions.[7] But

5. Al-Ḥuṣrī, pp. 292-293.

6. Al-Ḥuṣrī, p. 108. One of the high-ranking officers in Faiṣal's army told the writer that at a meeting with Faiṣal at this time when the critical shortage of ammunition was being discussed, one of the notables present, known as an extremist among the Syrian nationalists, left the room and returned after about half an hour with his handkerchief full of an assortment of bullets and cartridges of various calibres. He placed the handkerchief before Faiṣal and said: "I bought this ammunition from one of the shops in town! How is it that your officers complain that they have no ammunition?" So tragically ignorant of military realities were many of the extreme nationalists who were bringing pressure on Faiṣal to resist the French demands! See also al-Ḥakīm, *Sūriyya wa'l 'Ahd al-Faiṣalī* (Syria and the Period of Faiṣal), pp. 180-182.

7. Sāṭi' al-Ḥuṣrī has stated that the British themselves advised Faiṣal not to reject the French terms. See *Yawm Maisalūn* [the Day of Maisalūn], p. 111. Faiṣal sought the advice of General Allenby. The General suggested the acceptance of Gouraud's ultimatum without hesitation. See F.O. 371/5037, Telegram from Lord Allenby (Cairo) to the Foreign Office in London, dated 16 July 1920. See the Arabic paper *Al-'Amal*, no. 2501, 13 June 1954, p. 6. According to

the Syrian Congress was in a different mood. It launched a vehement attack against Faiṣal and his Council of Ministers. At its meeting of 19 July, a proclamation was issued openly threatening the Government. The Congress declared, in this proclamation to the Syrian people, that if the Government went back on its previous decision of maintaining and defending the independence of the country, and decided to accept any conditions which did not agree with that decision, the Congress would consider that Government as illegal and its action null and void. Syria was a completely independent country. Any foreign intervention was unlawful and the Syrian nation had the right to reject it at any time.[8] When the Congress assembled the next day, the Government ordered its "suspension" for two months.[9] It never met again.

Meanwhile, on 19 July, Mr. Bonar Law, Leader of the House, made the following statement in the House of Commons, concerning General Gouraud's ultimatum: "I understand that the French Government, owing to the attacks made on their forces by Arab troops, and, as they believe, the generally hostile attitude of the Syrian Government, issued an ultimatum on the 14th July demanding, by the 18th July, the control of the Rayak-Aleppo Railway, unconditional acceptance of the French Mandate, the introduction of French Syrian currency, and the surrender for punishment of the Arabs who fought against them. The ultimatum was not submitted to the Supreme Council. The terms of the Mandate for Syria have not yet been submitted to the Allied Powers."[10]

In the afternoon of 20 July, the Syrian Cabinet reached its final decision to accept General Gouraud's conditions and accordingly a telegram of acceptance was forwarded to Gouraud. All the necessary measures were also taken to execute that decision, includ-

reliable information obtained by the author, Faiṣal asked for British intervention when he received Gouraud's ultimatum. He was advised that as the Mandate for Syria had been conferred upon the French Government, he should communicate with that Government. It is also significant of much that the French Government did not inform the British Government that they were delivering an ultimatum to Faiṣal.

8. For the text of the Proclamation, see al-Ḥuṣrī, pp. 259-260.

9. Al-Armanāzī, pp. 4 and 12.

10. *Parliamentary Debates*, House of Commons, Fifth Ser., vol. 132, col. 39.

ing demobilization of the army.[11] But no sooner the news of the acceptance of the ultimatum became known in Damascus than there were immediate and violent demonstrations against the ministry asking it to resign and inciting the population to rise and defend the country. Some demonstrators were accusing even Faiṣal of cowardice and treason. It was with great difficulty that the demonstrators were prevented from approaching Faiṣal's residence.[12]

The next day, Faiṣal received the news in the morning that French troops advancing from Shtūrah and Zaḥleh towards Majdal 'Anjar had entered Wādī al-Ḥarīr on their way to Damascus. Colonel Cousse was asked to investigate the reason for this surprising move. He returned in the afternoon to report that General Gouraud had not received on time Faiṣal's telegram of the day before. The delay was due, according to Colonel Cousse, to the fact that the telegraph lines had been cut near Sirghāya. Therefore the General had ordered his troops to begin their advance. Cousse suggested sending an envoy on behalf of Faiṣal to come to an understanding

11. The Syrian Cabinet did not know at the time that Faiṣal had already sent two telegrams to General Gouraud; the first was through Colonel Toulat, on 18 July, "accepting personally and in principle" the General's conditions. Gouraud answered on the 19th saying that what he wanted was not only an acceptance of his conditions but their execution. He was granting Faiṣal's request to extend the time limit to the 21st. "Consequently," Gouraud wrote, "I have decided that my troops shall not move before 21st July, midnight." The second telegram was through Lieutenant Colonel Cousse, the French liaison officer in Damascus. Its contents are not known but from the reply of Cousse, on behalf of Gouraud, one gathers that the latter was pleased with it. Cousse repeated the assurance that the French troops would not start towards Aleppo before the 21st at midnight and that they would reach it three days later. Faiṣal would be informed about the date of the occupation of other towns. Meanwhile Gouraud was expecting the execution, officially, of the contents of Faiṣal's reply. Cousse ended by giving Faiṣal General Gouraud's assurance that Syria would receive every consideration, kind treatment and justice. There was no reason to fear the Mandate and it was to the best interest of Faiṣal to accept the conditions set forth in Gouraud's ultimatum. Al-Ḥuṣrī, pp. 293-294.

Faiṣal has stated in the Memorandum which he sent to Lloyd George on 11 September 1920 that he received from Lord Curzon, three days before the French occupied Damascus, a letter urging him not to take any hostile attitude towards the French, under any circumstances. See al-'Ayyāshī, *Al-Iḍāḥāt al-Siyāsiyyah* [Political Elucidations], p. 143.

12. See As'ad Ḍāhir, *Mudhakkarātī* [My Memoirs], pp. 139-141., and Yūsuf al-Ḥakīm, *Sūriyya wa'l-'Aḥd al-Faiṣalī* [Syria and the Faisal Period], p. 184.

with Gouraud. The Ministers and Faiṣal agreed unanimously to have Sāṭi' al-Ḥuṣrī, the Minister of Education, undertake this mission.[13]

Sāṭi' al-Ḥuṣrī left Damascus in the afternoon of 21 July, accompanied by Jamīl al-Alshī as "military attaché" and by Colonel Toulat. They reached General Gouraud's headquarters at the well-known Lebanese village and summer resort of 'Aley in the morning of the 22nd.[14] The momentous meeting which followed with General Gouraud has been fully described by King Faiṣal's special envoy himself.[15] The General said that Faiṣal's last telegram, accepting the

13. According to Ronald Storrs, Faiṣal gave him the following translation of the telegram which he sent to General Gouraud:

"July 21st, 1920.

"Monsieur le Général Gouraud,

"Having accepted all the conditions stated in your note of the 14th inst., and finding in spite of that the French troops advancing towards Damascus, and desirous, on the other hand, to avoid till the last moment a useless effusion of blood, I ask for an arrest of operations of the troops which would enable us to discuss affairs as indicated by your telegram received to-day. A member of the Government is proceeding to see you with a commission to discuss affairs in the name of the Government. Faiṣal." (Storrs, p. 430.)

In the Foreign Office archives, (F.O. 371/5037) there is a curious cipher telegram, "secret," from G.H.Q. Egypt to War Office, dated 24 July 1920, stating that "Feisal's acceptance of ultimatum" was "held up" by the "Postmaster General at Damascus, until French crossed frontier."

The telegram continues: "Ultimately, Feisul got into communication with General Gouraud and said he would accept ultimatum but French had advanced by that time and Feisul's irregulars who were joined by Bedouins had got out of hand...."

If this serious accusation could be proved to be correct, it would suggest that there was collussion between certain Syrian elements and the French, to bring about the end of Faiṣal's regime in Damascus.

14. On their way to the Lebanon, al-Ḥuṣrī and Toulat noticed that the Syrian army was taking precautionary defensive measures near Khān Maisalūn about 20 miles south west of Damascus, on the hills overlooking Wadī Zarzūr. Yūsuf al-'Aẓmah himself had chosen that site for the concentration of his troops. The party saw also French troops and tanks and stopped for a while at the field headquarters of General Goybet, the commander-in-chief of the French forces advancing on Syria. Al-Ḥuṣrī succeeded in obtaining from General Goybet an "armistice of 24 hours," so that he may have time to see General Gouraud and settle "the misunderstanding" with him. Al-Ḥuṣrī, p. 119.

15. Al-Ḥuṣrī, pp. 121-137. This is the only authentic account which we have in Arabic on this subject. For the text of an anonymous account in French found in Widener Library, Harvard University, see William Ernest Hocking, *The Spirit of World Politics*, Appendix I, pp. 533-540. It seems that this account was written by al-Ḥuṣrī himself.

conditions of the ultimatum, had arrived half an hour after he had given his order for the troops to advance on the chosen objectives. When it was pointed out to him that the said telegram had been handed to Colonel Cousse in Damascus *six hours before* the appointed time, Gouraud replied that the Damascus Government was responsible for his not receiving that message in time, alleging that Syrian rebel bands had cut the telegraph lines between Zabadānī and Sirghāyā.[16] As to the previous personal telegrams of Faiṣal, they, according to Gouraud, said nothing about the execution of his conditions. Their acceptance of those conditions was not enough. But now that the intentions of Faiṣal and his Government were made quite clear to the General, why could he not order his troops to stop where they had camped and to return to their base? This request seemed to have upset the General visibly. "Ah, Ça non!" he is reported to have exclaimed, adding: "We have no confidence in you anymore.... We have therefore to ask you for new guarantees...." Whereupon, he took out from one of the drawers of his desk a prepared statement and started reading to Sāṭiʿ al-Ḥuṣrī eight "new guarantees." They included the staying of the French troops at the point of their farthest advance in Syrian territory, the withdrawal of Syrian forces from their positions and their removal nearer to Damascus, the complete control over the Rayak railway junction by the French military expedition, and the presence of a French Mission in Damascus, with the purpose of applying the French Mandate by cooperating with the Government to reorganize its administration and its services in line with the requirements of that Mandate. It was now evident beyond the silghtest doubt — to Faiṣal's personal envoy — that the French were absolutely determined to occupy Damascus and establish the French Mandate in Syria. Further prolonged and heated discussion produced only one result, the postponement of the final advance of the French forces on Damascus until the following morning, so that Faiṣal's envoy could have time to return to Damascus and present to Faiṣal

16. "According to Feisal's statement with regard to his account of the Syrian Rising, he despatched on July 20 at 5:30 p.m., six and a half hours before the expiry of the time allowed, a detailed answer to the French political officer in Damascus." See "Feisal Explains," *The Morning Post*, October 1920. See also Wahbah, p. 209.

and to the Council of Ministers the new demands of General Gouraud. A special personal letter was also written by the General to Faiṣal. "Please hand his letter to His Royal Highness the Emir," were the last words of General Gouraud to Sāṭi' al-Ḥuṣrī; "I appeal in it to his partriotism and to his great wisdom."

Further delays on the way and the impossibility of reaching Damascus on time obliged al-Ḥuṣrī to visit again General Goybet at his headquarters and appeal to him to extend the "zero-hour" to midnight, 23 July. The request was granted with the approval of General Gouraud. Late at night, al-Ḥuṣrī arrived in Damascus and reported immediately to King Faiṣal, handing him General Gouraud's letter.[17] The Council of Ministers met the next morning, in the presence of Faiṣal and was fully informed of the "new guarantees" demanded by Gouraud. In the midst of the great astonishment and consternation of the Ministers, Colonel Cousse arrived with a new telegram from General Gouraud announcing that owing to scarcity of water and the bad condition of the road, it had been found necessary for the French troops to move forward and camp at Khān Maisalūn.[18] It was quite evident by now that there was no way of accepting General Gouraud's conditions. The Council of Ministers decided, as a last resort, to send once more telegrams of appeal to the Allied Governments and to call a meeting of all the representatives of Foreign Powers to inform them in detail of the gravity of the situation. Sāṭi' al-Ḥuṣrī was again delegated for the latter task.[19]

17. Gouraud's letter appealed to Faiṣal to rid himself of "*les extrémistes*" around him, to assure the establishment of friendly relations between Syria and France and to apply the Mandate in an atmosphere permeated with the spirit of understanding and sincerity. The General repeated his previous assurances that the Mandate was not against the independence of the country. Al-Ḥuṣrī, p. 138. See also Pichon, *Sur la Route des Indes*, p. 362.

18. Al-Ḥuṣrī, pp. 139-140, who gives the Arabic translation of this text of the telegram.

19. When Lawrence learned about the events in Syria at this time, he wrote a letter to *The Times*, dated All Souls College, July 22, in which he said, in part: "The Arabs rebelled against the Turks during the war not because the Turk Government was notably bad, but because they wanted independence. They did not risk their lives in battle to change masters, to become British subjects or French citizens, but to win a show of their own. . . ." *The Times* (London), 23 July 1920, p. 15, col. 5.

The Foreign Consuls met at the Italian Consulate in Damascus. The Syrian Government had learned that the new Foreign Minister of Italy, Count Sforza, was paying much attention to Middle Eastern affairs. The Marquis de Paterno since his arrival in Damascus had shown great sympathy for the Arab cause in general and for the Syrian case in particular. On this particular occasion, he voiced openly his regrets and his condemnation of the contemplated action against Syria.[20]

But when Sāṭi' al-Ḥuṣrī returned to Faiṣal's residence, "the Order for Defense" had already spread among the population and the emotional excitement was reaching its highest pitch among the "demonstrators" in the streets and bazaars of the city. When Colonel Cousse came at sunset to receive Faiṣal's final reply, none had been written yet. He went away with a note addressed to General Gouraud, which said in part: "We do not want war. But accepting the conditions set forth in your last Communication exposes us, inevitably, to a civil war. We are ready to execute the conditions stated in your ultimatum of 14th July, four of which have already been executed... on condition that the French forces withdraw from the areas occupied lately".[21]

On 24 July, at dawn, the battle of Maisalūn began.[22] Before the noon hour of that same day, all resistance on the part of Faiṣal's

20. Al-Ḥuṣrī, pp. 141 and 143. It is interesting to note that the American Consul told al-Ḥuṣrī at the beginning of the meeting that his Government had decided some time ago not to interfere in European politics.

21. Ibid., p. 144. See also Storrs, p. 430.

22. See Testis, "L'Œuvre de la France en Syrie — 1. Le Général Gouraud Pacificateur," *Revue des Deux Mondes* 61 (1921): 824-825.

The engagement has been dramatically described by Pierre Lyautey: "Position redoutable, aux teintes brutales, d'une aube de juillet... quand à 8 h 30, les bataillons s'élancent à l'assaut du rédan. De l'ouest accourent les Africains, grands diables de Sénégalais qui poussent des cris de triomphe; du nord, aux accents de la nouba, des Algériens prêts à danser une sarabande; du centre, des Parisiens qui entonnent la Madelon; et, au sud galopant sur leurs chevaux, des spahis du Maroc qui hurlent le chant de guerre des bleddards. Incroyable mêlée que celle de toutes ces races unies sous un même drapeau, le nôtre, le 24 juillet 1920, sur le chemin de Damas." Pierre Lyautey, *Le Drame Oriental de la France* (Paris, 1923), p. 169.

On 24 July, Faiṣal sent a very brief telegram to his father, King Ḥusain, informing him that the fighting had begun, adding "victory comes from God" (*al-naṣr min Allāh*). This telegram followed two previous telegrams sent to King

army had come to an end. The Minister of War, Yūsuf al-'Aẓmah was lying among the dead.[23] Algerian troops, Senegalese, Moroccans, Africans and French, supported by tanks, armored cars, heavy artillery and airplanes were now advancing on Damascus.[24]

Ḥusain on 21 and 23 July. In these messages, Faiṣal beseeched his father for immediate help. In his cable of the 21st he told his father that General Gouraud's forces were advancing towards Damascus in spite of the fact that he had accepted the General's ultimatum. He called the attention of the "civilized world" to this "crime" and appealed for justice and equity. King Ḥusain forwarded copies of this telegram to the representatives of the Foreign Powers in Jeddah requesting them to "do the necessary" and adding that he feared the Arab '*Umma* would rise to defend itself. The text of Faiṣal's telegram was also sent to the Foreign Ministers of Great Britain, Italy, the United States of America, Japan and Belgium, accompanied by a written protest from King Ḥusain. See *Al-Qibla*, no. 403, 26 July 1920, pp. 1-2.

23. On 27 July 1920, the Italian Consul-General in Damascus, Marquis de Paterno sent a telegram, N° 690, to the Ministry of Foreign Affairs, via Beirut, giving news of the death of the War Minister, "at the head of his battalion," and adding: "After he was killed by a cannon shell, the battery passed over his body. This useless despicable act against a hero has suscitated general disgust ...." (Rome, *Ministry of Foreign Affairs*, Folio 1367/1567/Siria 1920/7151). The traveller today, going between Beirut and Damascus can see beside the main road near Khān Maisalūn the tomb of Yūsuf al-'Aẓmah.

24. It is difficult to call the clash of arms between the Third Division of the French "Armée du Levant" with all its modern equipment and modern training and a motley crowd of ill-equipped and untrained Arab irregulars composed of townspeople and Bedouins as a "Battle" in the modern sense of the word.

In the *Revue des Troupes du Levant*, no. 5, of January 1937, General Goybet, Commander-in-Chief of the French forces advancing on Damascus, has given the total number of French casualties as fifty-two killed and 200 wounded. The exact figure of the Arab "army" at Maisalūn will probably never be known, in the absence of official records. There were probably not more than 600 regulars, part of the old Arab army, many of whom had been demobilized, and between two thousand and four thousand irregulars composed of townspeople, who at a moment of great national enthusiasm had joined in as "Mujāhidīn" (going for a "Jihād)" and of Bedouins — most of them volunteers. See al-Ḥuṣrī, p. 343; Amīn Raiḥānī, 1: 328; Pichon, *Sur la Route des Indes*, p. 330; and the Arabic paper *Al-'Amal* (Beirut), no. 2507, 20 June 1954, p. 6, col. 2. See also Dāghir, pp. 144-145.

Faiṣal himself, in an interview with the Special Correspondent of *The Morning Post*, which took place at the Palace Hotel in Milan on 1 September 1920, is reported to have said (referring to Maisalūn): "I disbanded my troops, leaving only 350 regulars with a thousand or two thousand Damascus volunteers.... Hostilities occurred, and a regular massacre of my Arabs began ...." See "Syria's Future: Feisal Interviewed—His Mission to Europe," in *The Morning Post* of 6 September 1920. Two of the surviving "irregulars" who fought at Maisalūn told the writer that not only had they "very little ammunition," but that when the

On the afternoon of the same day, Faiṣal and his Council of Ministers moved out to the village of Kisweh, a railway junction on the way to Amman, about 12 miles southeast of Damascus.[25] The Ministers left by train and the King followed by car. Faiṣal seems to have been at this time under a deep psychological strain: should he throw in his lot with the French and come to an agreement with them at the eleventh hour, or should he remain aloof and insist on the independence of Syria? Apparently, he was seeking a compromise, for he sent Nūrī Pasha al-Sa'īd to Damascus to find out if any understanding was possible with the French. The next day, after the city was occupied by an imposing French force, a telegram was received from Nūrī Pasha saying that a "temporary agreement" had been reached, that the French were allowing the old Government to stay in power and that it was necessary for Faiṣal to remain close to Damascus.[26] This message and the oral reports which Faiṣal

engagement started, they discovered that the bullets and cartridges which had been distributed to them were of a different calibre to the rifle which they carried! It is, then, not a little surprising to read in the official French Communiqué, released in Beirut on 24 July, in the evening, that the engagement which had taken place that morning near Khān Maisalūn was comparable with "the greatest battles of the Great War" and that the defeat of the "Sharīfian army" was "the greatest victory for the French forces in Syria." Al-Ḥuṣrī, p. 324.

In the light of the above-mentioned facts, it is regrettable that Professor Temperley seems to convey the impression that it was the Arabs who gave the *casus belli* for General Gouraud's attack on Syria, when he writes: "On the 22nd July an attack was made on a French outpost by Arab horsemen; and on the 23rd July [*sic*!] the French replied with an offensive against the positions held by Syrian troops. . . . " Temperley, 6: 158. On the other hand, Lloyd George, writing fourteen years after Temperley, in 1938, says: "Gouraud's violent attack was prompted no doubt by the encouragement received from those in Paris whose aim at that time was undoubtedly to convert Syria into a French province, like Algeria, Tunis, or Morocco." Lloyd George, 2: 1113. Four years earlier, in 1934, Liddell Hart had written: "In Syria, Feisal paid the penalty of French haste, when the possessors of the newly awarded mandate seized the first chance of repudiating the agreement that Clemenceau had made, and of installing themselves in Damascus. Even by the admission of the French High Commissioner's staff, Feisal had striven to moderate the bellicosity of the Arab extremists. . . . . The French forces had been set in motion by Gouraud, whose soldierly simplicity made him an easy lever for political schemers to handle." Basil Liddell Hart, "*T.E. Lawrence — In Arabia and After*," pp. 396-397.

25. See *Al-Muqtaṭaf*, (Cairo), pt. 3, vol. 83, (1933) p. 265. See also al-Ḥakīm, p. 199.

26. For the Arabic text of this telegram, see al-Ḥuṣrī, p. 149.

received from Damascus gave him enough hope to take the grave decision of appointing 'Alā'-ud-Dīn al-Drūbī to form a new Government. Faiṣal was under the impression that with al-Drūbī as Prime Minister, agreement with the French was guaranteed. This new Council of Ministers was almost immediately formed.[27] But on the same day, he received indirectly from the Marquis de Paterno, the alarming news that the French had decided to put an end to the "Faiṣal Regime," specially as he, Faiṣal, had already "fled from the capital." De Paterno's own advice was that Faiṣal should immediately return to Damascus. That same evening Faiṣal was back in the city. But events began to move now with bewildering rapidity. On the following day, 26 July, General Goybet called for a meeting of the members of the new Government and read to them a statement to the effect that the Emir Faiṣal had dragged the country to within "a distance of two fingers" from destruction and ruin. His responsibility was great for all the sanguine disturbances which had taken place on the Syrian stage during the last few months. It was evident that he could not be allowed to continue ruling the country. The new Council, which had accepted to function under the French Mandate, had the confidence of the French authorities, but it could not wash its hands of the failures of the past and reject its responsibility for the serious destruction of property and for much blood which had been spilled. Consequently, its first task was to collect a reparations fine of "200,000 gold Dinars" which would be distributed to the Syrian families that had suffered loss of life and property.[28] When Faiṣal learned what Goybet had said, he protested telegraphically to Gouraud. The French reply was a letter which Colonel Toulat brought to Faiṣal asking him, in compliance with "the decision taken by the Government of the French Republic," to leave Damascus with his family and retinue,

27. The members included three Ministers of the previous Cabinet: Fāris al-Khūrī, Jalal-ud-Dīn, Yūsuf al-Ḥakīm and four new Ministers: Jamīl al-Alshī, 'Aṭā al-Ayyūbī, 'Abdu'l-Raḥman al-Yūsuf, Badī' al-Mu'ayyad. See al-Ḥuṣrī, p. 150.

28. "L'émir Faiṣal a conduit son pays à deux doigts de sa perte." For the text of General Goybet's address to the Council of Ministers, see *Al-'Aṣimah* of 29 July 1920. See also Pichon, *Sur la Route des Indes*, pp. 367-368, and al-Ḥakīm, p. 209.

with the shortest possible delay. Faiṣal's departure was fixed for the next day, 28 July, at 5:00 o'clock in the morning, on a special train leaving from the Ḥejāz Station for Der'a.[29] Before leaving, Faiṣal sent an indignant and strongly worded protest to General Gouraud in which he said that he did not recognize that the French Government had any right to divest him of the authority which had been granted to him officially by the Peace Conference for the purpose of governing the Eastern zone. The entrance of French troops in Damascus was a violation of the decisions taken by the Peace Conference and was against the principles of the League of Nations. This protest was the last act of Faiṣal as "King of Syria" asserting his "sovereign power" while still on the Syrian soil.

Faiṣal arrived in Der'ā on the 28th. But two very urgent telegrams from 'Alā' ud-Dīn al-Drūbī dated 29 and 31 July, requested the King of behalf of the French authorities to leave Der'ā, without further delay and by the same train, for Ḥejāz via Ma'an or Haifa. At the same time, a French airplane on 29 July dropped leaflets on Der'ā giving "ten hours" to the inhabitants of that town and of the surrounding region to ask Faiṣal to leave their country otherwise his train was to be sent back to Damascus and they would be exposing themselves to bombardment from the air.[30]

The Emīr 'Ādil Arslān had already gone to Palestine and got in touch with the British High Commissioner, Sir Herbert Samuel with regard to Faiṣal's arrival in Haifa and his departure for England. On 1 August, Faiṣal left Syria for Haifa, twenty-two months after his triumphant entry into Damascus on 1 October 1918.[31]

29. "July 27th, 1920. From Colonel Toulat, Chief of the French Mission. To H.R.H. Amir Faisal. Damascus.

"I have the honour to communicate to Y.R.H. a decision of the French Government requesting you to leave Damascus as soon as possible by way of the Hejaz Railways, with Y.R.H.'s Family and Suite.

"A special train will be at the disposal of Y.R.H. and Suite. This train will leave the Hejaz Station at 5 hours to-morrow July 28th, 1920.

"I beg Y.R.H. to accept the expression of my high consideration. Toulat." Storrs, p. 430. See also al-Ḥuṣrī, p. 152, and al-Ḥakīm, p. 209.

30. Al-Ḥuṣrī, pp. 154-156.

31. A brief item of news in *The Times* (London) of 3 August 1920 (p. 10, col. 3) from "Our Correspondent" in Haifa and dated 1 August said: "The Emir

"I went with Sir Herbert to greet Faiṣal and Zaid", wrote Sir Ronald Storrs, "when the train of exile passed through Ludd, where we mounted him a guard of honour a hundred strong. He carried himself with dignity and the noble resignation of Islam:

Nor called the gods with angry spite
To vindicate his helpless right

though the tears stood in his eyes and he was wounded to the soul." [32]

In the following two chapters, the writer will attempt to give an interpretation of the events which led to the inevitable downfall of Faiṣal and the end of the first phase of Arab struggle for political independence. As a conclusion to this chapter, however, it is fitting to quote two very significant opinions, one by an eminent Professor and the other by a great Statesman. Professor Temperley wrote — and it is worth repeating it here again: [33]

"So fell the Emīr Faiṣal's independent Syrian State — a State created and fostered by Great Britain in fulfilment, or partial fulfilment, of her pledges to the Arabs. It fell because its existence was in direct conflict with French ambitions, in circumstances which prevented British influence being made effective for its preservation — it fell because its own armed strength was insufficient to ensure its survival."

Winston Churchill, as Secretary of State for the Colonies, explained the situation to the Imperial Conference in 1921 thus:

Feisal arrived in Haifa today from Der'a where his safety was imperilled. He was received with a guard of honour and is the guest of the District Governor."

32. Storrs, p. 431. Lord Samuel has written in his *Memoirs*: "I decided that he (Faiṣal) should be received on Palestine territory, not as a defeated fugitive, but as a respected friend; ordered a guard of honour to parade when his train arrived; went, with Storrs, to meet him at a stopping place on his way through.... I was told afterwards that when the Emīr saw the soldiers drawn up on the platform on his arrival he did not know whether they were not there to arrest him; and, after the emotional strain of the previous days, almost broke down when he found that they were a guard of honour." Viscount Samuel, *Memoirs* (London, 1945), pp. 158-159.

33. Temperley, 6: 158. This passage has already been quoted at the beginning of his chapter.

"...General Gouraud marched an army against Damascus, routed the Arabs, seized the city, and is now in occupation of the four towns I have mentioned (Damascus, Aleppo, Homs, and Hama) as well as the whole of Syria. The operations had been conducted very largely by black African troops, and it was extremely painful to British opinion, and to British officers particularly who had served the Arabs, to see those who had been our comrades such a little time before and our Allies, and who looked to us for protection and to see their wrongs righted, to look on while they were thrashed and trampled down and their cities taken against the spirit of the treaties, if not against the letter, by the French; and that has been a deep source of pain to politicians and to the military men who have been concerned. However, *we have these strong ties with the French and they have to prevail and we were not able to do anything to help the Arabs in the matter....*" [34]

34. Cited by Lloyd George, 2: 1113-1114. Author's Italics.

CHAPTER TEN

AN INTERPRETATION OF THE ALLIED "PROMISES"

"... *The secret Agreements relating to the Near and Middle East to which various Allies subscribed during the war (should be placed) in their proper perspective and ... in the setting to which they inseparably belong — the gigantic struggle for national survival, which required of the nations involved in it the use of every expedient permissible in diplomacy and war. Unless considered in their true historical setting the secret Treaties and Agreements bear a distorted and entirely misleading aspect, and possess little relationship with reality.*"

H. W. V. Temperley, ed., *A History of the Peace Conference of Paris,* 6:2.

FOR MORE THAN FIVE DECADES, Arab and non-Arab critics have execrated the wartime undertakings and agreements as not only ambiguous and mutually incompatible but also as dishonest betrayals of the East by the West. It is of course easy enough in peacetime to criticize actions hastily taken in the atmosphere of war. In the previous chapters the author has recorded as many as possible of the known facts, and he is tempted to say: "Let the facts speak for themselves." He believes, nevertheless, that some attempt should be made to interpret them and the story as a whole.

In the first place, it should be pointed out that these pledges and agreements were made under psychological conditions created by the anxiety bred by war and the fear of its consequences. Every Power involved in a war wishes to win; and "for victory everything material and moral might be pawned." As Lawrence put it very clearly, "Some Englishmen, of whom Kitchener was chief, believed that a rebellion of Arabs against Turks would enable England, while fighting Germany, simultaneously to defeat her ally Turkey".[1] "On ne fait la guerre que pour ses résultats," were Marshal Foch's words.[2] Sir Edward Grey wrote to Professor Gilbert Murray on 19 March 1919 that the agreements which Great Britain signed

1. Lawrence, *Seven Pillars of Wisdom*, p. 7.
2. Cited by House and Seymour in *What really Happened at Paris*, p. 13.

during the war with her Allies could "only be justified by the pressure of war,"[3] while D.G. Hogarth held that the British involved themselves with the Arabs, only owing to "the exigencies of the life-and-death struggle."[4] Any number of "promises" were therefore made solely with the aim of winning the war at any cost and many of the decisions were influenced by day to day considerations. Promises so made, therefore, reflect as a rule only the passing state of mind of those who make them. But they constitute valuable pointers to the importance of the immediate issues that occasion them. The Allies, moreover, had to consider, not only the wishes of one people or of one government, but the wishes of many peoples and many governments; and these wishes, though they might each possess individual merits, were often conflicting. Thus, as many promises could be given as there were parties concerned, with additional "Statements," "Declarations," and "Proclamations," as the fortunes of war swayed in one direction or another, with the result that in the end the British Government found itself involved in a number of commitments not always compatible with one another.[5] "Old Nūrī Sha'alān wriggling his wise nose, returned

3. Cited by Trevelyan in *Grey of Fallodon*, p. 350.

4. D.G. Hogarth, "Present Discontent in the Near and Middle East," *The Quarterly Review* 464 (October 1920), p. 423.

5. At the opening of the Peace Conference, a British Memorandum dated 8 February 1919 outlined the British policy concerning the Near and Middle East. Towards the end of this Memorandum, the British experts listed the following nineteen "previous commitments" of the British Government concerning the future of the Ottoman Empire: "(1) Règlement Organique of the Lebanon Vilayet, June 9, 1861; (2) Règlement Organique of the Lebanon Vilayet, September 6, 1864; (3) Treaty of Berlin, July 13, 1878, Article 61, relative to ameliorations and reforms in the Ottoman provinces inhabited by Armenians; (4) Agreement, January 23, 1890, with the Sheikh of Kuweit; (5) Agreement, October 15, 1907, with the Sheikh of Kuweit; (6) Proclamation of the Government of India, November 2, 1914, regarding the Moslem Holy Places; (7) Assurance, November 3, 1914, given by the British Resident in the Persian Gulf to the Sheikh of Kuweit; (8) Assurance, November 22, 1914, given by the British Resident in the Persian Gulf to the Sheikh of the Mohamerra; (9) Assurance, February 3, 1915, given in speech by the Viceroy of India to the notables of Basra; (10) Treaty with Italy, April 26, 1915; (11) Treaty, April 30, 1915, ratified November 6, 1915, with the Idrisi Sayyid of Sabia (Northern Tihama district of Yemen); (12) Correspondence, beginning in July 1915, with Hussein Bin Ali, Grand Sherif of Mecca; (13) Treaty, December 26, 1915, ratified July 18, 1916, with Abdul-Aziz Ibn Saud, Amir of Nejd

to me with his file of documents, asking in puzzlement which of them all he might believe. As before, I glibly repeated, 'The last in date', and the Emir's sense of the honour of his word made him see the humour."[6]

In the second place, such promises, by their very nature and the nature of the circumstances, had to be rather vague and indefinite. They were not in any sense, according to Mr. Balfour, "sealed agreements." With a situation changing all the time and an uncertain future, the British could not obviously commit themselves to any precise areas and boundaries in Syria and Lower Mesopotamia in their Correspondence with the Sharīf Ḥusain. Apart from the traditional opportunism of most political negotiators, those responsible for British policy have what appears to be an almost instinctive dislike to committing themselves in advance to any precise course of action. The English language also seems to lend itself admirably to vagueness of expression and lack of precision — at least when skilfully handled by politicians.[7] Sir Reader

and Al-Hasa; (14) Agreement, May 16, 1916, with France; (15) Supplementary Agreement, January 22, 1917, with the Idrisi Sayyid; (16) Agreement, August 18, 1917, with Italy; (17) Letter, November 2, 1917, from Mr. Balfour to Lord Rothschild, regarding Jewish Zionist aspirations; (18) Statement, June 11, 1917, issued by His Majesty's Foreign Office, in answer to a memorial from seven Syrians, and subsequently communicated to King Hussein; (19) Joint Declaration, dated November 9, 1918, by His Majesty's Government and the French Government regarding the future of Syria and Mesopotamia." Quoted from Chapter 3 of an unpublished work by Dr. Harry N. Howard, entitled "The Question of Turkey and the Straits at the Paris Peace Conference (1919)" — by kind permission of its author.

6. Lawrence, *Seven Pillars of Wisdom*, p. 555.

7. The "language" of "Agreements" about the Middle East continues to be "not as clear" as one "seems to think." During the course of the debate on "Surplus War Material (Export)" in the House of Commons, on Tuesday, 24 January 1956, Mr. Hugh Gaitskell, the Leader of the Opposition, said that there was "no possible shadow of doubt" that the Tripartite Agreement of 1950 guaranteed the Arab-Israeli frontiers, and to support his conviction, read the following last sentence of that Agreement: "The three Governments, should they find any of these States was preparing to violate frontiers or armistice lines would, consistently with their obligations as members of the United Nations, immediately take action, both within and outside the United Nations, to prevent such violation." Whereupon, Sir Anthony Eden, the Prime Minister, rose to say: "...I do not want to criticise the 1950 Agreement... but I am bound to say that *the language in respect of the frontier is not as clear as the right hon. Gentleman seems to think.*" (Author's italics). See Great Britain, *Parliamentary Debates, House of Commons*, Official Report, Tuesday, 24 January 1956, vol. 548, No. 81, pp. 66-67.

Bullard has called the McMahon Letters "a monument of ambiguity."[8] The British negotiators, according to Sir Ronald Storrs, complained that the Arabic language was a great stumbling block to understanding between them and the Sharīf Ḥusain.

A telegram (Nº 188) sent from the High Commissioner for Egypt to the Foreign Office and dated 14 May 1915, states:

"The term 'independent sovereign state' has been interpreted in a generic sense because idea of an Arabia united under one ruler recognized as supreme by other Arab Chiefs is as yet inconceivable to the Arab mind."[9] This was followed by an explanatory note in Sir Ronald Storrs' handwriting which said:

"The expression 'Arab Empire', 'Kingdom', 'Government', 'Possessions', etc., is used throughout the Sherifial Correspondence, on both sides, in a general and undefined sense, and is variously rendered by the words Ḥukūma (Government), Mamlaka (Possessions) and Dawla (Power, Dynasty, Kingdom).

"Neither from these terms, nor from any phrase employed by H.M.G. throughout the negotiations, is it possible to elaborate any theory as to the precise nature of this vaguely adumbrated body...."[10]

The mathematical axiom that the shortest distance between two points is a straight line has never or rarely been applied in politics. All the promises and pledges with their ambiguities and contradictions were apparently designed to avoid drawing the straight line. Hence, the real intentions were often camouflaged or obscured by verbiage.[11] It seems also that a democratic Government cannot often afford to be definite and precise, since it is obliged to account

8. Bullard, p. 69.

9. F.O. 141/461 File No. 1198/1.

10. Ibid.

11. Rarely have politicians been as particular as Harry Boyle, the Oriental Secretary of Lord Cromer, in the use of precise words. Sir Thomas Hohler has reported the following reply of Boyle to a journalist who inquired about a rumored Royal engagement: "Young man, I regret to find that you are ignorant of the very alphabet of your calling. Members of the Royal houses are *not* engaged. They are betrothed. In similar manner we speak of the conjunction of elephants and the copulation of mice." Clara Boyle, *A Servant of the Empire: A Memoir of Harry Boyle* (London, 1938), p. xix.

for its actions, especially when they go wrong. Only a Dictator can be precise.

Thirdly, the pledges were given to people about whom little was known. Though there existed a small group of British "experts," not much was known by responsible statesmen in Great Britain about the Arabs or the Arab lands.[12] Foremost amongst these experts was Sir Mark Sykes, whose advice at times guided Lloyd George in Arab affairs. But there is little evidence that even these experts — though they might know the "facts" of the immediate situation — had any deep knowledge of Arab psychology, of the power of Islam in Arab lands and on Arab minds, and of the nascent but explosive force of the Arab national awakening. Almost all of them did not know the Arabic language. Even Sykes, with his "deep and wide range of knowledge" of the Arab world, was sufficiently misled by superficial appearances and his own imperfect understanding of the deeper issues to write in a letter to Lloyd George, on 2 September 1918: "Our Arab, Syrian and Palestine policy has not landed us in any great difficulties, and has, on the other hand, given us a considerable return in prestige, booty and enemy casualties. We have friendly populations, native allies, and good material and moral assets for a peace conference should one occur at any time...."[13] In Lawrence's view, Mark Sykes "was the imaginative advocate of unconvincing world-movements, also a bundle of prejudice, intuitions, half-sciences...."[14] Lawrence himself was not any better with his contradictory nature, insatiable

12. If, at the time of the Munich Agreement in 1938, Czechoslovakia was, according to Mr. Neville Chamberlain, that "far away land about which we know very little," how much more far away was Syria and how much less was the knowledge of the Secretary of State for Foreign Affairs about it when he signed the Sykes-Picot Agreement in 1916! Lloyd George, who himself did not know much about Syria except that Palestine was the Holy Land and its Biblical boundaries were from "Dan to Beersheba," wrote of Viscount Grey of Fallodon, in his *War Memoirs*: "He was the most insular of our statesmen.... He had no real understanding of foreigners... (and) he lacked the knowledge of foreign countries." Lloyd George, *War Memoirs* 1:60.

13. Shane Leslie, p. 283.

14. Lawrence, *Seven Pillars of Wisdom*, p. 58.

For a study and appreciation of Sir Mark Sykes, see Christopher Sykes, *Two Studies In Virtue* (London, 1953), pp. 173-177 and 230-232.

ego and confusing paradoxes. Moreover, the word "Arab" was at the time only a generic name. Therefore, when the British Government gave their "promises" to the "Arabs," it is not clear what Arabs they had in mind. Only once, there was a specific reference to the "Arabs of Hedjaz."[15]

As to Sharīf Ḥusain, he insisted that he spoke for all the Arabs; but the British, though they never told him so, could not admit his claim.[16] It must also be remembered that the British Government believed, as a result of its own experience with the Muslims of India,[17] that the vast majority of Muslims throughout the world ("90 per cent of the Muslim world" is Storrs' estimate) "must call Husain a renegade and traitor to the Vicar of God." An extract from "the Proceedings of a meeting of the War Committee, held on Friday, June 30, 1916," marked "*Very Secret*," reads as follows:

"The Prime Minister read to the War Committee a telegram communicated by the Secretary of State for India, describing the profound sensation caused in India by the news of the Arab revolt, which appears to be generally condemned by Mohammedan opinion in that country, and the bad effect produced on the North-west frontier by the Shereef's action."[18]

"We could not conceal from ourselves," wrote Sir Ronald Storrs, "(and with difficulty from him) that the Sharīf's pretentions bordered upon the tragi-comic." But the British felt it necessary under the circumstances to raise and maintain the Sharīf's prestige, and "for this and other reasons we were in the end committed far more deeply in bullion, in munitions of war, and in promises very hard to fulfill, than most of us had dreamed of in September 1914."[19] Nearly five months after the beginning of the Revolt, on 30 October 1916, the Sharīf was proclaimed in Mecca "King of the Arabs"[20]

15. See above, p. 4, the cipher telegram of the Foreign Office to Mr. Cheetham in Cairo (F.O. 371/2139).

16. Al-Raiḥānī, *Ta'rīkh Najd al-Ḥadīth* [History of modern Najd], pp. 208 and 311-316.

17. For the attitude of the Muslims of India towards Turkey and Islam, see Mantoux, pp. 98-104.

18. Great Britain, CAB. 37/150, War Committee (W.C. 52).

19. Storrs, p. 153.

20. See 'Abdallah, *Mudhakkarātī* [My Memoirs], pp. 129-131, and Antonius, p. 213.

But the Allies rejected this title and finally recognized him as "King of the Hejaz."

In this connection, Arnold Toynbee has written that, from the beginning of his negotiations with Great Britain in 1915, Sharīf Ḥusain "presented a claim for the independence not only of the Ḥijāz but of all the Arab countries in Asia, and... the Arab area for which Husayn claimed independence included the entire Arab Peninsula except the British Aden Protectorate, and here he had no title whatever to speak on behalf of his fellow-rulers of their subjects, either in the Ottoman or in the British Zone." Toynbee adds: "The Arab rulers in the British Zone, for example the Gulf Chiefs, were in direct treaty relations with Great Britain already... Accordingly, the British pledge to recognize and support the independence of the Arabs within the limits proposed by Husayn was not only made subject to certain modifications and conditions on account of French claims on Syria, but was given expressly without prejudice to existing British treaties with Arab chiefs; and, even apart from these specific limitations, there was no implication that, in other portions of the area, Arab independence should be interpreted as the rule of the Amir Husayn." [21]

A telegram sent by the Foreign Office to the High Commissioner in Egypt, General Sir Edmund Allenby, dated 21 March 1919, and marked "Secret, No. 362," read, in part: "With reference to your despatch Nº 81. Until the future of Syria and the selection of its mandate or mandates is finally settled by the Peace Conference, harm may be done by such language as King Hussein used in his communications with the Syrian Union Party. It would be better that he should adhere to his original role as the spokesman rather than the sovereign by right of the Arab peoples of the Turkish Empire." [22]

21. Toynbee, *Survey of International Affairs*, 1, pp. 286-287.

22. Great Britain, F.O. 141/776. About four months later, on 8 July 1919, Col. Wilson ("Wilson Pasha") wrote from The British Agency in Jeddah to General Allenby in Cairo: "Sir, I have frequently urged that King Hussein should be informed that his interpretation of the original agreements is not accepted by His Majesty's Government." Great Britain, F.O. 141/776. Secret, No. 20/19/1919.

Not only were the Arabs not united at the time when the British were negotiating with the Sharīf Ḥusain, but the British could not see any prospect of Arab union in the foreseeable future. The promises which the British made to the Sharīf, and the territorial arrangements which were agreed upon in the Sykes-Picot Agreement were not, in their understanding, about any independent Arab nations.[23] In the remarkably frank Memorandum which Mr. Balfour wrote from Paris to the British Cabinet on 11 August 1919, "respecting Syria, Palestine and Mesopotamia," he asks, "Where and what are these 'independent nations'?[24] Are they by any chance identical with Syria, Mesopotamia and Palestine?" But Mr. Balfour asserts that no such idea was present to the minds of those who framed the Sykes-Picot Agreement. "They never supposed themselves," says Mr. Balfour, "to be dealing with three nations already in existence, ready for 'provisional recognition,' only requiring the removal of the Turk, the advice of a mandatory, and a little time to enable them to 'stand alone'.... With the Arab race, Arab culture and Arab social and religious organisation (to say nothing of Jews, Maronites, Druzes and Kurds) they knew they had to deal. But this is a very different thing." The Allies had liberated territories occupied by the Turks and emancipated the Arabs "so long oppressed by the Turks." The "grateful inhabitants" of these areas freed from "the yoke of Turkish tyranny" should now welcome their saviours as "mandatory powers." This line of Western reasoning was a grievous error; it was based on utter ignorance of the role of Islam in Arab-Turkish relations in the Ottoman Empire.[25]

To many devout Muslims in the Arab world, the destruction of the Ottoman Empire by Western Christian nations was a great

23. *The Times* went as far as to say in a leading article on Friday, 30 December 1921 (col. 2, p. 9), that "the wisdom of choosing during the war the Sherif of Mecca, famed throughout the Mahomedan world for his extortions, as the leader of the Arab revolt may well be questioned now."

In a secret Report which Lawrence wrote — on 9 November 1918 — for the British Cabinet, on his return to England, he says: "The Sherif had no idea that we wanted him as a figurehead." Garnett, p. 266.

24. See above, pp. 97-98, and also *Documents* 1:4, p. 340-349.

25. For a study of Arab-Turkish relations, see Zeine, *The Emergence of Arab nationalism, with a Background Study of Arab-Turkish Relations in the Near East*, pp. 1-16 and 46-72.

tragedy for Islam. The most important factor which bound the Arabs to the Turks was Islam. This is the most significant cardinal element in Arab-Turkish relations for nearly four centuries. The Ottoman Turks were Muslims and the Arab lands became, after 1516, part of the powerful Ottoman Empire. The Arabs as Muslims were proud of Turkish power and prestige and proud to belong to it. The Ottoman Empire was their Empire as much as it was the Turks'. It is also safe to say that Ottoman rule protected the Arab world and Islam from foreign encroachments for nearly four hundred years and in general accorded a wide measure of local autonomy to the Arab provinces.

This Muslim concern for the Ottoman Empire has been clearly stated by the late Agha Khan in his Memoirs. The Agha Khan went to London as the leader of a deputation to the Prime Minister, Lloyd George, "representing the views, not only of Muslims but of the whole articulate population of India." He writes:

"The reasons for Muslim concern were profound and historic. Turkey stood almost alone in the world of that time as the sole surviving independent Muslim nation; with all its shortcomings, the imperial regime in Constantinople was a visible and enduring reminder of the temporal greatness of Islam's achievements. In the Caliphate there was, too, for all of the Sunni sect or persuasion, a spiritual link of the utmost significance....

"Muslim opposition to the break-up of the Turkish Empire had a basis — however much misunderstood it may have been — of true statesmanship and of understanding of the absorbing political realities of the Middle East. First, we felt that the separation of the Arabs from the Turks (hailed at the time as emancipation from a tyranny, although within a few years all Arab nationalists were singing a very different tune) would not lead to the emergence of a single strong Arab nation extending from Egypt to Persia and from Alexandretta to Aden and the Indian Ocean. We foresaw in large measure what actually happened: the formation of a number of small Arab nations, for many years of little more than colonial status, under British and French overlordship, We predicted that the Arabs would in fact merely be changing masters, and where these masters had been Muslim Turks they would now be Christians, or (as ultimately happened in a large part of Palestine) Jews....

"Our instinctive Muslim faith in the idea of the continuance of Turkey as a Great Power has wisdom in it, for it would have achieved practical results, in the security and the stability of the Middle East...."[26]

After the collapse of the Ottoman Empire, the Arabs, in the opinion of the Allies, were not only weak and without, politically speaking, any national status, but they were "accustomed" to being ruled by Great Powers. Had not Lawrence written that Syria, as a corridor between sea and desert, joining Africa to Asia, Arabia to Europe, had been a "prize-ring, a vassal, of Anatolia, of Greece, of Rome, of Egypt, of Arabia, of Persia, of Mesopotamia," and, therefore, "Syria was by nature a vassal country"?[27] The Secretary of State for Foreign Affairs, Mr. Balfour himself, from his reading of history, had also concluded that "overlordship is not alien to the immemorial customs and traditions of this portion of the Eastern world".[28] Finally, Sir Mark Sykes, the chief expert on Arabian affairs and one whose views often prevailed at the Foreign Office, had written: "All Syria welcomed Aurelian as it has welcomed Alexander and as it would welcome England, France or Germany today. The Syrian Arab has long had the knack of falling in with the plans of a successful conqueror."[29] The above quotations throw considerable light on the attitude towards the Arabs prevailing among the "experts" on Arab affairs. One cannot help concluding that the Arabs were not taken seriously and, politically, could not be so taken at the time when the promises and pledges were given.

Fourthly, what did the British Government mean by the various "promises," declarations and proclamations to the Arabs? It is not possible to answer this question fully; but it is safe to say that there seems to have been no definite, clear-cut policy about the Arab world. "Promises" were given and "Agreements" were made without any thought at the time of whether or not they were mutually compatible or practicable. They were at best theoretical and fanciful plans, "sacerdotal pronouncements" and "evangelical

26. *The Memoirs of Aga Khan* (London, 1954), pp. 153-156.
27. *Seven Pillars of Wisdom*, p. 336.
28. *Documents*, 1:4, 343.
29. Shane Leslie, p. 248.

hopes," based on an uncertain contingency: the total defeat of Turkey and its elimination from the Near East. Indeed, it appears that the British Government was itself confused at the end of the War about its own commitments to the Arabs and to the French. The author was told by one with first-hand information that he was asked by the Secretary of State for Foreign Affairs, six weeks before the end of the War, to study fully all these pledges, promises, declarations and proclamations, particularly the McMahon-Ḥusain Correspondence and the Sykes-Picot Agreement, in order to discover in what way they conflicted with one another and whether there was any way of reconciling them. When the War came to an end the British Government and the British Peace Delegation wished to know where they stood vis-à-vis those wartime commitments. The verdict of this "research student" of politics was that a *lawyer* might succeed in reconciling the conflicting promises in these documents, but that the *people* to whom those promises were made would never be able to reconcile them. In 1919, Mr. Balfour had to admit that "these documents are not consistent with each other; they represent no clear-cut policy...."[30]

To begin with, the British Government had its own difficulties about its "promises" to the Arabs. Between the India Office and the Foreign Office there was continuous friction and disagreement over the partition of the Near East. The India Office was opposed to the policy of the McMahon Correspondence with the Sharīf Ḥusain. They wanted Mesopotamia as a province of their own for the protection of the Persian Gulf and the defense of India.[31] They were worried about the rise of Arab nationalism and much annoyed that the Foreign Office encouraged it. The advisors of the India Office on Arab affairs were Sir Arnold Wilson and Miss Gertrude Bell, as against the Foreign Office "Arab experts," D.G. Hogarth,

30. *Documents*, 1:4, p. 343.

31. "Before the outbreak of the war in 1914, Asia was divided between the Imperial and Indian War Intelligence Departments... a line was drawn through Arabia from Akaba to Basra, all north of that line belonging to Whitehall, all south to Simla." But there was overlapping and confusion. Mesopotamia was "within the radius of action of India, though outside their sphere of intelligence." It was "no man's child" or rather "the foster-child of both Simla and Whitehall, the acknowledged child of neither." Great Britain, Cd. 8610, Mesopotamia Commission, p. 96. See also Kirk, pp. 127-128.

T.E. Lawrence and Sir Mark Sykes. Two years after the end of the War, Hogarth wrote that King Ḥusain of the Ḥejāz had said to the British representative in Jeddah in 1917: "You speak to me continually of the British Government and British Policy. But I see five Governments where you see one, and the same number of policies. There is a policy, first of your Foreign Office; second of your Army; third of your Navy; fourth of your Protectorate in Egypt; fifth of your Government in India. Each of these British Governments seems to me to act upon an Arab policy of its own. What are the Arabs to do now, and what are they to expect of you after the War?" Hogarth adds that the old man was right enough at the moment from his point of view: "His people were being dealt with by several British authorities on several divergent lines...."[32] This view is confirmed by Sir Ronald Storrs who, when in Cairo in 1916, thought that it seemed to be nobody's business to harmonize the various views and policies of "The Foreign Office, the India Office, the Admiralty, the War Office, the Government of India and the Residency in Egypt."[33]

It has been said that, for all practical purposes, in relation to the Near and Middle East, the Government of India functioned as a thing apart. Sir Arnold Wilson, representing the India Office point of view, complained at a very early date that the Arab Bureau in Cairo was going beyond its function of co-ordinating Arab policy, by adopting a policy which sought "to impose King Ḥusain and his family upon the whole of Arabia, and at no time did its directors show any desire to look at the problems of Iraq from any other angle...." Wilson adds: "Some of the Arab enthusiasts became more fervent believers in the Arabs than the Arabs themselves...."[34] On the other hand, Hogarth has categorically stated that the purpose of the Government of India was "not at all to call the Arabs to freedom and help them to that end."[35] Their major interest was to preserve British-Indian power in the Persian Gulf and it was

32. See D.G. Hogarth, "Present Discontent in the Near and Middle East," p. 411.

33. Storrs, p. 154.

34. Arnold Wilson, *Mesopotamia, 1917-1920*, p. 110.

35. Hogarth, "Present Discontent in the Near and Middle East," p. 414.

they who for this purpose originally organized, manned, and directed the Eastern offensive in Mesopotamia. "Our authorities in India," wrote Hogarth, "civilian and military alike, almost unanimously preferred the Turk. Turk-British friendship had long been a trump-card in their game of government. To take action against an Ottoman Caliph was a very grievous necessity, imperilling an important *arcanum imperii.* Therefore the view was propagated that we were at war not with the Ottoman nation but with the usurpers of its power (the Young Turks)." [36]

In 1915, the British Government promised the Sharīf Ḥusain that the Arabs would be "independent" after the War. Independence was not defined and the promise was not unqualified. The French, whose interests in that area were very definite as far as Syria and the Lebanon were concerned, were not a party to the British commitments to the Sharīf. In 1916, the British and the French agreed secretly among themselves to give the Arabs "independence," without even informing the Arabs about that "independence." It was a very qualified "independence." The British and French marked their own areas on a secret map in which Arab "independence" was to be created, recognized and protected by them, but this independence was qualified by "the obligatory presence of foreign advisers." "Now, by an 'adviser'," wrote Mr. Balfour, "these documents undoubtedly mean — *though they do not say so* [37] — an adviser whose advice must be followed; and assuredly no state can be described as really independent which has habitually and normally to follow foreign advice supported, if the worse comes to the worst, by troops, aeroplanes and tanks." [38] By this "independence," as Mr. Balfour himself has explained, the Arab-speaking population "would live their own life in their own way, but would be under the patronage, and for certain purposes under the control, either of France or of England. . . ." [39] Moreover, around the "Independent Arabs" and adjacent to them were areas marked by two cheerful colors, "blue" and "red," in which France and

36. Ibid., pp. 414-415.
37. Author's italics.
38. *Documents,* 1:4, p. 344.
39. Ibid., p. 343.

Great Britain were given rights "not easily distinguishable from complete sovereignty," for they were free "to establish such direct or in direct administration or control as they desire." It has been suggested that the agreement looked something like one of those Chinese arrangements of boxes. The outside and the biggest box was annexation pure and simple. Inside it there was another box of an "independent Arab State," subject to division into spheres of influence.[40] And, finally, the last box was labeled simply, "Arab independence."

The British pledges to the Arabs cannot be properly appraised without understanding the state of mind of those who were giving them, as has already been referred to at the beginning of this Chapter, and the various motives which prompted them. The Ḥejāz Revolt, as originally conceived by its progenitors, particularly Wingate and Kitchener, had an objective limited to the Ḥejāz itself. As Lawrence himself has admitted, the advance from 'Aqaba, which he called "The Sherifian invasion of Syria," was "a new operation and a new movement" and it was going to affect European rivalry in the Levant (as indeed it very much did).[41] In 1915 and 1916 the British Government had not contemplated the invasion of Palestine, when they were giving their pledges to the Sharīf Ḥusain. The sole function of the British forces in Egypt was the defense of the Suez Canal, i.e., the protection of Egypt and, beyond Egypt, of course, India. Even when the advance across Sinai began, the first and second stages of that advance and the occupation of El-'Arīsh were all considered necessary for the defense of the Canal. It was essential to occupy the Qatiya basin in the Sinai Desert "to deny to an enemy advancing against the Canal the water in that area."[42]

It was not until March 1917, after the first Battle of Gaza had been fought, that the Government informed Sir Archibald Murray that his "immediate objective should be the defeat of Turkish forces south of Jerusalem and the occupation of that town."[43] Hence, while

40. *Palestine*, vol. 5, no. 17, 31 May, 1919, p. 131.
41. Lawrence, *Secret Dispatches*, p. 161.
42. Cyril Falls, p. 629.
43. Ibid.
Was this move prompted by the desire of the British to secure possession of Palestine (hitherto the "Brown Zone" in the Sykes-Picot Agreement) and

the British Government were supporting the rebellion of Sharīf Ḥusain against the Turks, they had other considerations in mind than the independence of the Arabs.[44]

These pledges had also a "propaganda value" which Lloyd George himself has readily admitted: to mobilize "every opinion and force throughout the world which would weaken the enemy and improve the Allied chances".[45]

Again, in November 1918, both Governments published a Declaration which, to the Syrians and the Iraqis, seemed rightly or

by the influence of powerful Jewish circles in England and in the United States, who were preparing the ground in those countries for the historic Balfour Declaration which followed eight months later? As the British forces (the "Egyptian Expeditionary Force") under General Edmund H. Allenby were preparing to execute a great offensive against the Turks in Palestine and capture Jerusalem, a secret mission composed of Henry Morgenthau, Sr., and Felix Frankfurter arrived in Gibraltar early in July 1917. This Mission had been sent by the United States in an attempt to arrange peace between Turkey and the Allies. Waiting for it at Gibraltar were Dr. Chaim Weizmann and his associate Monsieur Weyl, a well-known French Zionist. Weizmann and Weil "were successful in persuading Morgenthau and Frankfurter . . . to abandon the Special Mission confided to them by President Wilson of negotiating a separate peace with Turkey (by going to Palestine via Egypt to open negotiations with Jamal Pasha) . . . at a most inopportune time for both the Zionists and British." — William Yale, *The Near East: A Modern History*, pp. 241 and 260. See also Chaim Weizmann, *Trial and Error*, pp. 246-251.

44. Without wishing to descend from the sublime to the commonplace, the writer is inclined to think that camels were not a small consideration in the minds of some of those who planned the Ḥejāz Revolt. One of the former members of the Arab Bureau in Cairo told the writer in an interview that the Sharīf and the Arab tribes which he commanded controlled a very large supply of camels for sale, in those days. It was very important to ensure that this most valuable kind of Arab transport was denied to the Turkish Fourth Army in Palestine.

"We have heard," wrote Sir Henry McMahon to the Sharīf Ḥusain, in his letter dated 10 March 1916, "that Ibn Rashid has been selling large quantities of camels to the Turks, which are being sent up to Damascus. We hope that you will be able to use your influence with him in order that he may cease from this practice and, if he still persists, that you will be able to arrange for the Arabs who lie between him and Syria to seize the camels as they pass, a procedure which will be to our mutual advantage." Great Britain, Cmd. 5957 p. 18.

From Esar-Haddon, King of Assyria in the seventh century B.C, to Jemal Pasha in the twentieth century A.D., camels have been most essential for the invasion of Egypt through the Sinai Desert.

45. Lloyd George, vol. 2:1118.

wrongly to supersede or at least to qualify the provisions of the Sykes-Picot Agreement. But even this document, when studied carefully, does not reveal any commitments in which Great Britain and France were not involved as guides, executors and guardians. They had now set themselves a part to play in those liberated territories, which among other things was to establish in Syria and Mesopotamia "national governments and administrations which shall derive their authority from the initiative and free will of the peoples themselves". But it is to be noted again that it was "they" who were to establish these governments and the normal workings of these governments could be assured only by "their support and practical aid". This Declaration was paternalistic in language, Wilsonian in spirit and was, no doubt, meant also for consumption in the United States, in order to allay the apprehensions of President Wilson and the American Peace Delegation in Paris, who were against all secret treaties signed by the Allies during the War.[46] But this Declaration and other promises preceding it implied, and indeed their authors took it for granted, that Great Britain and France would act as "mandatory powers". Even when, later, the Covenant of the League of Nations embodied the Mandate principle, but said that the wishes of the communities over which the Mandate was to be exercised must be a principal consideration in the selection of the mandatory, the policy of the Powers involved was not to admit anything of the kind. Quoting again from that historic document, the Memorandum of Mr. Balfour, "Take Syria, first," wrote Balfour, "do we mean, in the case of Syria, to consult principally the wishes of the inhabitants? We mean nothing of the kind. According to the universally accepted view there are only three possible mandatories — England, America and France. Are we going 'chiefly to consider the wishes of the inhabitants' in deciding which of these is to be selected? We are going to do nothing of the kind. England has refused. America will refuse. So that, what-

46. The Anglo-French Declaration of 7 November 1918 began: "Text of declaration agreed to between the British and French Governments and *communicated to the President of the United States.*" No other declaration or commitment concerning the Near East's partition between Britain and France had been communicated to the President of the United States.

ever the inhabitants may wish, it is France they will certainly have. They may freely choose; but it is Hobson's choice, after all."[47]

In other words, by "independence" Great Britain meant independence "under tutelage." Nevertheless these two key words were omitted from all the documents concerning the Arabs. *Even* Lawrence, who is supposed to have been the most staunch exponent of Arab *independence*, wrote to Lord Curzon on 25 September 1919 that his own ambition was that "the Arabs should be Britain's first brown Dominion and not our last brown colony."[48] As Professor Toynbee has pointed out, "the Allies were really arranging among themselves that Great Britain and France between them should exercise varying degrees of political authority over all Arab territories in Asia except the Hijaz itself."[49] M. Pichon, the French Minister of Foreign Affairs, put it very briefly, but frankly, when in speaking of the Sykes-Picot Agreement on 20 March 1919, he said: "This agreement had two objects. First, to detach the Arabs from the Turks; second, to decide the claims of Great Britain and France."[50] During the debate on the Budget in the French Chamber of Deputies on 24 June 1910, M. Aristide Briand maintained that the agreements of 1916 were "des accords de principe," while M. Ernest Lafont attacked them as "la traduction d'une politique nettement impérialiste."[51]

Thus, when Great Britain and France spoke of establishing "national governments and administrations which shall derive their authority from the initiative and free will of the peoples themselves," they did not have in mind "self-determination" as a *right* but as a principle. There is a fundamental difference between a right and a principle. It is in the light of this interpretation that it is possible to understand what Mr. Bonar Law had in mind when he said, in

47. *Documents*, 1:4, p. 345.

48. Ibid., p. 423, Garnett, p. 291.

49. Arnold J. Toynbee, *The Western Question in Greece and Turkey*, p. 49.

50. *Papers Relating to the Foreign Relations of the United States*, vol. 5:1.

Sir Edward Grey put it more bluntly when, hearing rumors of how things were going at Versailles, he said to a friend: "I am glad I am not there. They are out for loot." G.M. Trevelyan, *Grey of Fallodon*, p. 350.

51. France, *Journal Officiel, Débats Parlementaires, Chambre des Députés*, 2d session of 24 June 1920, p. 2404.

the House of Commons on 19 July 1920, during a Debate on Syria, that in his opinion the Mandate which had been granted to France covering that area "was not inconsistent" with the British pledges to the Arabs.[52]

It is further necessary, to understand the difficulties which Great Britain and France had in the Arab areas which they already ruled, to realize how much more serious those difficulties would have become if the Arabs in the Near East were granted their full independence immediately. Great Britain had to consider her position in Egypt and France hers in North Africa. At the outbreak of the war with Turkey, in December 1914, His Majesty's Government deposed the Khedive 'Abbās Ḥilmī, nominated his uncle Ḥusain Kāmil in his place as "Sultan" of Egypt, and declared a British Protectorate over Egypt. The proclamation of a Protectorate created many problems and much discontent among Egyptian nationalists who considered it "the extinction of Egypt's autonomy." After the publication of the Anglo-French Declaration of 8 November 1918, Sa'd Pasha Zaghlūl, the well-known nationalist leader in Egypt, in an interview with Wingate on 13 November "demanded complete autonomy for Egypt, as an ancient and capable race with a glorious past — far more capable of conducting a well-ordered government than the Arabs, Syrians and Mesopotamians to whom self-determination had so recently been promised."[53] A few days later, Egyptian nationalist leaders were shocked to learn that the Foreign Office had not permitted them to leave Egypt and visit London to present the Egyptian side of the question. "Extremist Indians had been given a hearing by Mr. Montagu; the Arab Emir Faisal was allowed to go to Paris. Were Egyptians less loyal? Why not Egypt?"[54]

The French, on the other hand, were apprehensive lest the independence of Syria should have serious repercussions in the territories under their rule in North Africa. M. Robert de Caix told Mr. Eric Forbes Adam, a member of the British Peace

52. *Great Britain, Parliamentary Debates, House of Commons*, Fifth Ser., vol. 132, col. 41.

53. Wingate, p. 229.

54. Ibid., p. 235.

Delegation, early in November 1919, that difficulties might arise for the French Government if Faiṣal had a port such as Tripoli or Latakia with access to the sea. "His Government were very opposed to ships under the Arab flag appearing in the Mediterranean and calling, for instance, at Algerian and Moroccan ports — for obvious reasons."[55]

55. *Documents*, 1:4, p. 528.

CHAPTER ELEVEN

INTERNATIONAL RELATIONS AND THE OLD DIPLOMACY

"The talk about 'old diplomacy' and 'new diplomacy' is little better than useless chatter.... In as far as changes of methods, as openness and frankness, are the outcome and expression of a change of purpose and spirit among nations, they are good and welcome; but if they are this, they will come naturally without forced talk about them. If they are not this, they will be an illusion and deception.... We must look for a new spirit and purpose among nations, not to a change of method, to secure better things."

Viscount Grey of Fallodon, in *Twenty-Five Years, 1892-1916.*

THERE WAS a further complication between Great Britain and France as far as their own secret Sykes-Picot Agreement was concerned. It had a bargaining power which each side could use to its own advantage. M. Ernest Lafont referred to the agreements of 1916 in the Chamber of Deputies on 24 June 1920 as "un moyen de se procurer une monnaie d'échange, par ces vastes domaines données à la France et qu'il serait possible plus tard, de retrocéder."[1] M. Briand, the next day, speaking in the Chamber, said that it was a fact that those agreements gave France "une large monnaie d'échange."[2] On 22 May 1919, Lloyd George complained that the British Government was giving nearly the whole of the Cameroons to France, although "the whole of the naval part of the campaign had been undertaken by the British." The same was true also about Togoland, conquered by the British and given up to France. Then he added: "This ought to be taken into account in considering the Syrian question."[3] About three months later, on 14 August, Sir G. Grahame wrote from Paris to the Eastern Department of the Foreign Office: "It seems to me that if, as I understand they do, His Majes-

1. See pp. 14-15 above.

2. France, *Journal Officiel, Débats Parlementaires, Chambre des Départés*, 2d session of 24 June 1920, p. 2434.

3. *Papers Relating to the Foreign Relations of the United States*, 5:812.

ty's Government feel the importance to us of preventing a French 'main mise' on Tangiers, we should be in a better diplomatic position were we to forestall the French by giving them to understand that if they want our continued support in Syria, the price will be an abatement of their pretensions about Tangier and a strict application to that town of plain Treaty rights."[4]

A constant source of irritation to the French was the periodical reminders of Lloyd George that the British effort in overthrowing Turkey had been immensely greater than France's help. It was no use to point out to him that in September and October 1918, when Allenby's forces were defeating the Turks in Syria, France had 103 Divisions on the Western Front and the British 61.[5] Perhaps the height of political cynicism was reached when, at an Anglo-French meeting held at the Foreign Office on 23 December 1919, Lord Curzon, speaking for the Prime Minister, said: "When the Sykes-Picot Agreement was concluded, it was on the hypothesis that France and England would make approximately equal efforts in the matter of men and money in conquering Turkey. Unfortunately, it had turned out that the War in this theatre had had to be fought almost entirely by Great Britain, who had expended some £750,000,000 on all the Turkish operations.... *If the French Government would reimburse His Majesty's Government one half this sum they might have any boundary they liked here and else where.*"[6] But as (Sir) Winston Churchill wrote: "The idea that France, bled white in the Trenches of Flanders, should emerge from the Great War without her share of conquered territories was insupportable to him (Clemenceau) and would never have been tolerated by him."[7]

There was a limit, however, beyond which neither ally could put much pressure on the other without weakening its own position in the Near East and creating more difficulties for itself.

4. *Documents*, 1:4, p. 352.

5. *The Times* (London), 19 December 1918.

6. *Documents*, 1:4, p. 599. Author's italics.

7. Winston S. Churchill, *Great Contemporaries* (London, 1937-42), p. 116. The French, proccupied with the Germans on their soil, had limited their contribution to the War against the Turks in the Near East, but "it is just to recognize that Pisani's single battery in the Arab zone had more military influence than a hundred batteries in France." Liddell Hart, p. 380.

To the "very urgent" telegram N° 716 sent by Lord Allenby from Cairo to the Foreign Office in London on 16 July 1920, stating that Faiṣal had received "ultimatum from French" and that his representatives had arrived in Haifa (Palestine) and "wish to know our attitude," the Foreign Office replied on the same day, at 10:00 p.m., with another "very urgent" telegram, N° 653, saying:

> Your 716 and recent telegrams. I am afraid that it is impossible for us to interfere. Since grant of Mandate for Syria to French at San Remo, they have possessed a prior right with reference to purely Syrian affairs which it would be neither right nor expedient for us to contest. Any attempt on our part to do so would produce greatest possible irritation here and would merely result in old game of one party being played up against out there. French disinterest themselves altogether from Palestine and Mesopotamia, employing same argument as regards our position in those countries. If their present attitude to Feisal lands them in future trouble, the responsibility will be exclusively theirs.[8]

Hence, during the Debate on Syria on 19 July,[9] when Mr. Ormsby-Gore and Lord Winterton rose to the defense of Faiṣal and the Arab cause, Mr. Bonar Law was against condemning the action of the French Government (Gouraud's ultimatum to Faiṣal) before finding out first whether that action was just "improper' or "unfriendly" and he added very significantly: "We have accepted a Mandate for Mesopotamia and can we imagine the French Chamber of Deputies being engaged in such a discussion as we have had here today...?" The Debate led to no tangible results and nothing came out of it: "It being Eleven of the Clock, the Motion for the Adjournment of the House lapsed, without Question put."[10]

The Arab leaders may have been aware that there are mixed motives behind the foreign policy of any great power. This foreign policy, particularly during a war, is largely dependent on circumstances and consequently hampered in the application of any prin-

8. F.O. 371/5037. From Lord Allenby to the Foreign Office.

9. See p. 160, above.

10. Great Britain, *Parliamentary Debates, House of Commons*, Fifth Ser., vol. 132, cols. 168, 170, and 188.

ciple, except the overriding instinct of national self-preservation. On the other hand, if the Arab leaders themselves had had the experience of handling the foreign policy of an independent Arab state, they would not, in all likelihood, have been misled by the expedients, the confusion of ill-defined sentiments, and the conflicting trends evident in the Allied diplomacy of the time. And if those leaders had had any knowledge of traditional British diplomacy, they would have known that, when faced with conflicting and opposing interests, this diplomacy has always struck balances and made compromises between such interests, and always, moreover, in so flexible a way as to admit of changed circumstances.[11]

It should be said, however, in all fairness, that a few weeks before Turkey's entry into the World War, Sharīf Ḥusain wrote a personal letter to Sultan Muḥammad Rashād pleading with him to remain neutral and warning him of the consequences of entering the War on the side of Germany. The Ottoman Empire was in no fit state to enter such a war and had nothing to gain from it. This same advice was given, when requested telegraphically, to the Prime Minister, Sa'īd Ḥalīm Pasha, and to the Minister of War, Enver Pasha. The reply was a telegram thanking the Sharīf. But his advice was not followed and Turkey entered the War soon after.[12] The attitude taken by the Sharīf at this juncture should help, at least partly, to dispel the Western illusion, fostered, it is true, by a few Arab leaders, chiefly Christian, that the Arabs before the War, wished to break away or destroy the Ottoman Empire. It is also true to say that among the other educated Arab leaders and thinkers in Syria, Egypt and Iraq — members of Arab secret societies, men in various professions, such as medicine and the law, Arab army officers who had fallen into British hands during the early months of the War, in southern Iraq — there were quite a few who were well aware of the interests of Great Britain and France in Arab lands and dreaded the consequences of an Arab rebellion against Turkey both

11. According to Jeffries, when Faiṣal came to know the Allied politicians better, he gave his opinion about them one day, in Paris, saying: "They are like impressionist pictures. The effect is excellent from a distance." Of Lloyd George, in particular, he said: "I ask him for independence and he gives me Memorandums!" Jeffries, p. 306. See also al-Ḥakīm, pp. 201-203.

12. See 'Abdallah, pp. 98-100.

if the Turks won, *and* if they lost. When the Sharīf Ḥusain started negotiating with the British in 1915, these Arab leaders knew nothing about it, and when they learned what was afoot they were bewildered by the vagueness of the whole situation.[13] They were not even certain what was meant by "Arab countries" at that time, and still less how the future independence of these countries could be guaranteed. There was also the undisputed fact that no Arab leader in Arabia, in Egypt, in Iraq and in Syria could really speak for all the peoples inhabiting this whole area. As far as Syria in particular was concerned, most of its outstanding political leaders had been hanged by Jemal Pasha in the public squares of Beirut and Damascus, before the Sharīf Ḥusain openly declared his revolt against the Turks. Those who remained lived underground, if they remained in Syria, or went abroad — to Egypt, France and the United States; but none of them, not even "the seven,"[14] could speak for the whole of Syria, although they claimed to do so. In a "Report on the Desires of the Syrians" written by E.H. Byrne on 7 October 1918, one reads:

"The fact is that the Syrians are so divided among themselves that there is no group which truly represents them all. Under these conditions two centres of opinion have developed outside of Syria itself, Cairo and Paris....

"The meetings of the Syrians in Cairo have resulted in the formation of a group of Syrians in Cairo desirous of annexation to France. This party is largely Christian and counts among its members some of the most cultured Syrians. Another group of Syrians in Cairo is opposed to annexation to France, but believes in 'the necessity of a French protectorate as an autonomous state'.

"Then there is the Moslem group who did not want the French and believe in 'the Arab faculty for rapid evolution'. They hoped for Syrian independence. 'They desired to acknowledge the spiritual

13. Faiṣal himself did not know about the exact nature of the British pledges. When he was in London in September 1919, he sent an urgent telegram to his father asking him to forward to him the necessary documents. *Documents*, 1: 4, pp. 411-412.

14. See pp. 22-23 above.

headship of the new King of the Hedjaz and even aspired to economic and political union with the new Kingdom".'[15]

Speaking of this Muslim group, Deedes Bey wrote that their general concern was that the French should not be allowed to go to Syria. "So great is their dislike of the French that it is very questionable that if the French were to reign today in Syria they would not drive the Moslems straight away into the hands of the Turks...."[16]

After the Arab Revolt started, King Ḥusain asked Nūrī Pasha al-Sa'īd, who was then in Cairo, to proceed immediately to Mecca. Before leaving. Nūrī Pasha went to confer with Sa'd Pasha Zaghlūl and to share with him his doubts and his fears. Zaghlūl's argument, with which Nūrī Pasha agreed, was to the effect that the Arab lands in those days had no political or sovereign entity which might perish. There was then no Arab independent State in existence, the very life of which was in jeopardy, as was the case with Turkey. Thus, no gamble was involved. Those who worked for the future independence and national sovereignty of the Arabs were pioneers and might even become martyrs.[17] King Ḥusain took almost the same line of thought when Nūrī Pasha had his first audience with him. He had entered into negotiations with the British and revolted against the Turks, because he had seen in the War an "opportunity" to realize Arab aspirations. He had opened a way towards a goal. It was for the Arab leaders now "to take advantage of the situation" thus created. If the War ended with a victory for the Germans and the Turks, the Arab countries would revert to their former status, without losing anything except the lives of those who had risen to fulfil the hopes of those countries. On the other hand, it must be admitted that he was apprehensive about the future of Arab lands if the Allies won. He did wonder who would protect the Arab lands from the well-known national interests of the great Powers and what

15. U.S., National Archives, and Records service. Department of State, *General Records of the American Commission to Negotiate Peace, Paris 1918-1919*, Records Group 256: Inquiry Document No. 82. See also "Weekly Reports on Matters Relating to Near Eastern Affairs," Department of State, Washington — Confidential No. 8, pp. 40-42, cited in E.H. Byrne's Report.

16. John Presland, p. 244.

17. Al-Sa'īd, *Muḥāḍarāt* [*Lectures*], pp. 7-8.

guarantee the Arabs would seek for their rights.[18] But, in the last resort, the attitude of the various Arab leaders and of King Ḥusain himself was one of optimism and fatalism. Their motto might have been: "Let us go ahead, trusting in God and in the justice of our Cause."

It is a fact, however, that the Arabs accepted the pledges and "the loudly-advertised policy of self-determination" at their face value, came into the War on the side of the Allies and fought the Turks. They could not believe that they were "dismantling their chariot from the Ottoman horses and replacing only those horses by western engines." Unfortunately, Lawrence himself, who should have known better, did much harm, psychologically and morally, to the Arab Cause, without, obviously, meaning to do so. Taking such a deep and personal interest in the Arab Revolt and identifying himself with its purpose and the success of its execution, blinded by his hatred for the French, although knowing full well that Syria and the Lebanon had been promised to them, he threw the full weight of his word and of his prestige into the scales, and, on his own authority, assured Faiṣal during the desert campaigns that "our promises held their face value." It is significant that Colonel Gribbon of the Staff Intelligence of the War Office told Yale that "every promise made by Colonel Lawrence to the Arabs will be brushed aside."[19] Hence, the strong feeling of the Arabs, later, that they had been "deceived" and "betrayed." Faiṣal is reported to have told Mrs. Erskine, in an interview:

"The first deception occurred when Field Marshal Lord Allenby announced that Syria had been divided into three zones under the pretext that this arrangement was purely temporary and administrative. The second blow levelled against the Arab's happiness was the confirmation of the Sykes-Picot treaty, which had been denied in 1917. I have seen with my own eyes the map of the country under three colours, revealing the different fate of the three zones. In this way we had to face the bitter truth."[20]

18. See Antonius, pp. 153-155.
19. Garnett, p. 284.
20. Erskine, p. 96.

"The proposals made by the Sherif for a independent Arab State or Confederation," said a *Memorandum* prepared by the Political Intelligence Department

As long as international relations are based on power politics, and on "the old diplomacy," there will always be something unreal and artificial in the relationship that springs up between a weak country and a strong State. The small and weak Powers are "assessed according to their effect upon the relations between the Great Powers." Their interests, their opinions, still less their voices, seldom affect a policy agreed upon by the Great Powers. [21] The Arabs were essentially weak. They were weak because of their lack of unity and oneness of purpose; because of their ignorance of Western diplomacy and the international situation after the War, because of their meager financial and economic resources, and above all because they were militarily impotent. The Arab Revolt, and later Faiṣal's Arab Government in Damascus, were supported and maintained by British money and British arms. One cannot, obviously, be very independent if one has to depend financially on others. The Arab leaders' zeal and enthusiam, optimism and faith were not enough, in themselves, to transform their hopes and aspirations into solid accomplishments.

A word must be said about the French attitude during those two years under review. As we have already seen in the previous chapters, France's relations with Great Britain were marked by intense suspicion of British motives. Wars and colonial rivalries during the last three centuries had left them, even after the Entente Cordiale of 1904, a legacy of mistrust and "an atmosphere of suspicion of each other's motives," as Mr. Wickham Steed wrote in an article in *The Times* on 11 September 1919.

Long before the War, the British knew of the French desire to obtain Syria in the event of the partition of the Ottoman Empire and they had again and again asserted that they had no political designs on Syria. In 1916, both the British and the Russian governments had consented to the Sykes-Picot Agreement that France's share of the Ottoman Empire would definitely include Syria. The French, however, believed that their presence in the Near East,

of the Foreign Office in 1920," were taken up by his Majesty's Government as conducing to the immediate military prosecution of the war against Turkey rather than as affording a satisfatory political settlement of the Arab countries after the war" (F.O. 371/5036).

21. Harold Nicolson, *The Evolution of Diplomatic Method* (London, 1954), p. 74.

astride the British imperial lines of communication, was only tolerated by Great Britain, but not accepted as a permanent fact. The basic tenet of British policy in the Middle East, according to the French, was the principle that this whole area was primarily the "domain" or the "preserve" of Great Britain.[22] Had Sir Edward Grey, in his letter of 16 May 1916 to M. Cambon, not given the impression that the British Government was accepting the Sykes-Picot arrangement rather grudgingly, as "it will involve the abdication of considerable British interests"?[23] They were also convinced that British officers throughout Syria and the Lebanon were intriguing to alienate the Arabs from them and thus make it, if not impossible, at least very difficult, for them to stay in those two countries. They blamed the British for not having clearly and decisively destroyed all the Sharīf Ḥusain's hopes in Syria and the Lebanon and thus effectually removed all future misunderstanding. For the French themselves had been consistent in claiming Syria and, though they had associated themselves with the Anglo-French Declaration of 8 November 1918, in not giving any promises to the Sharīf Ḥusain. On the contrary, Commandant Catroux who was the French representative in Jeddah in 1919, told the late King 'Abdallah: "In Syria you should rely upon France and not believe that there is anybody else except France."[24]

Nevertheless, the French continued to maintain that their greatest source of trouble in the Near East did not lie in the Arabs but in the anti-French policy of the British. Although the British Government vehemently denied the French allegations, Mr. Balfour himself has admitted that "the British officers in Syria have not always played up to the British Ministers in Paris."[25] M. Pichon summed up the French attitude towards England in the Near East when he wrote: "Elle (l'Angleterre) a voulu que le partage du Proche-Orient s'accomplit à son seul bénéfice."[26] General Catroux

22. Catroux, *Deux Missions en Moyen-Orient,* pp. ii and 15.

23. *Documents,* 1:4, p. 245.

24. 'Abdallah, *Mudhakarātī* [My Memoirs], p. 166. See also Catroux, pp. 221-222 and 234.

25. *Documents,* 1:4, p. 342.

26. Pichon, *Le Partage du Proche-Orient,* p. 367.

writing at the end of the Second World War brings up the same point forcefully.[27]

The French were determined to occupy Syria and they occupied it. It would not have mattered, even if they had realized it, that Syria, a preponderantly Muslim country, had no sympathy for them as had Maronite Lebanon. Consequently, one cannot help asking what good did the American (King-Crane) Commission achieve and what useful purpose did it serve?[28]

27. It is well worth stating a French point of view by quoting General Catroux's words:

"Cette politique (de la Grande-Bretagne)... se fonde sur le postulat que le soin des intérêts majeurs de la Grande-Bretagne exclut l'existence, dans le Moyen-Orient, d'une influence politique et économique autre que la sienne propre. Elle a pris naissance avec la campagne du Général Bonaparte en Egypte et à Saint-Jean-d'Acre.... Plus tard, l'Emir Fayçal et son père, le Roi Hussein, en ont été les instruments. Toujours elle a visé à écarter la France du Levant et si l'accord de San-Remo, en 1920, qui installa cette même France en Syrie et au Liban l'a théoriquement mise en sommeil, l'idée maîtresse qui l'inspira n'a jamais été abandonnée. S'inclinant en apparence, la Grande-Bretagne a attendu, pour reprendre activement ce problème fondamental, qu'une conjoncture de 1920 avait commandé. Elle n'a jamais accepté comme un fait politique durable la présence de la France à Damas, capitale historique et cœur intellectuel des pays arabes...." Catroux, *Dans la Bataille de la Méditerranée: Egypte, Levant, Afrique du Nord, 1940-1944* (Paris, 1949), p. 194.

28. Dr. Harry N. Howard has reported ("An American Experiment in Peacemaking: the King-Crane Commission," *Muslim World* 32, no. 2 (April 1942): 122-146) that while King, Crane, and Lybyer believed that an American group could do some good, "Professor Westermann held that a Commission could do a great deal of harm, without achieving anything constructive or adding to the information already available in Paris itself" (p. 128).

In this connection, the following extract from a personal letter written by Westermann to Dr. Howard Bliss on 9 May 1919 will be read with much interest: "My dear Dr. Bliss:

"I received your letter of April 17th yesterday. Last night, I dined with Dr. Gates, President King, and a number of other men who are going on the Commission to Syria with King on the invitation of Mr. Crane. It was a very interesting crowd and there was much discussion of Turkish affairs in general....

"I am afraid that I must deceive you in regard to my stand upon Syria. When the latter was brought up this last time, I was opposed to its going, because the reports from Syria seemed to indicate that the chances were that the Commission could only make trouble, and that it might lead to outbreaks in Syria itself. You know that I was anxious to have it go any time in January, February, or even March. In April, it seemed to me to be too late to accomplish any good. However, the British received cables from General Allenby stating that the Commission must come because of the fact that it had been announced in Syria, and that he

This Commission spent forty-two days — from 10 June to 21 July — touring Palestine, Syria and the Lebanon, visiting thirty-six different towns and cities, making inquiries in various and opposed communities about their political aspirations. They received a total of 1,863 petitions, 1,157 of which were from Syria proper (O.E.T.E.) one of them being the Program of the Syrian Congress which, in the words of the Commissioners, "is the most substantial document presented to the Commission and deserves to be treated with great respect." [29] The vast majority of the Syrian petitions were unfavorable to France and were against a French Mandate. The petitioners and the delegations which were interviewed asked for complete independence of Syria with the hope that it will be granted to other Arab countries. If a Mandate was to be imposed upon them, then their desire was first for an American and then for a British Mandate. [30] However, the United States was not

could not be responsible for the consequences if it did not appear. There may be some question as to the sincerity of these telegrams, but I have not felt that I had the right to question that. Since this element was injected into the situation, I have not opposed the going of the Commission, although it seems to me that now we have the situation here so well in hand that the Commission is purely a formal matter. According to the plans which Mr. Lybyer has in mind, the Commission shall be gone a long time. It seems to me that the matter should now be settled, and that it would be better to settle it now anyway rather than have the matter delayed further." Bliss Papers.

29. See Harry N. Howard, *The King-Crane Commission* (Beirut, 1963), pp. 142-143. See also Appendix I below.

30. It is interesting to note that "Syrian Americans" in the United States of America (composed mainly of Lebanese *émigrés* to that country) believed that an American mandate was the best solution of the Syrian question. They wished for their former country "the privileges and blessings of American liberty and American principles of national government."

The New Syria National League of New York and The Syrian Moderate Party in Egypt formed in 1919, supported very strongly "an American mandate for a united and undivided Syria." They could not "conceive of a better future for Syria and for the other countries that were included in the former Turkish Empire than to be under America's protection and guidance." The motto of the New Syria National League was "Syria for the Syrians, independent and undivided under American guardianship."

A delegation representing eight "Syrian" societies in the United States was received by the Secretary of State, Mr. Robert Lansing, in Washington, on 5 January 1920. The delegation "impressed upon Secretary Lansing the complete trust and confidence of the Syrians in the good purposes of the government of the United Stated of America and earnestly requested its help and influence to... defend the national unity of Syria...." Bliss Papers.

interested in becoming involved in Near Eastern affairs or in getting entangled in Franco-British policies in this area. Basing his studies on American Consular despatches from Damascus, Aleppo, and Beirut, Laurence Evans observes that

"When the independence of Syria was proclaimed, Faiṣal and his government made great efforts to secure American approval and to place their action before the United States in as favorable a light as possible. The Department of State, however, remained aloof....

"The United States took no official notice of Syrian independence and did not recognize Faisal as King.... On March 28, Faisal cabled to President Wilson, informing him of the reasons for declaring his independence and asking for his support.... The Arabs sought only their rights, said Faisal, and would fulfill all their obligations; he concluded by asking for Wilson's influence in obtaining the acceptance by the Allies of the independence of Syria. No answer was returned by the United States to any of these communications from Damascus."[31]

The findings and recommendations of the Commission were embodied in a Report and submitted to the American Commission to Negotiate Peace, in Paris, under the date of 28 August 1919,[32] the Commissioners having completed their work earlier, in Constantinople on 21 August. It is a lengthly document running to upwards of forty thousand words, with a special confidential part at the end, marked "For the use of Americans only," in which the Commissioners "set forth with still greater frankness what they found."

Aside from increasing the bitterness of the French Government and strengthening its intransigence, deepening the line of division between the various opposed communities, stirring the feelings of the people and raising false hopes; aside from "appearing to reopen to appeal a *chose jugée* and so restarting the general settlement,"[33] the Commission achieved no positive and practical results. "By the time

31. Evans, *United States Policy*, pp. 253-54.

32. "Two days later, Mr. Crane advised President Wilson by cable of the essence of the Official recommendations of the Commission." — Howard, "An American Experiment in Peace-making," p. 135.

33. Storrs, p. 355; Raiḥānī, 1:311-312.

the Commission had reported . . . ," wrote Lloyd George, "the Treaty of Versailles had been signed and President Wilson had returned to America." According to Dr. Harry N. Howard, "There is no evidence that he (President Wilson) was ever able fully to read the report while still in office."[34] "The Report was so hostile to the French claims in Syria that the President decided not to send it to the Peace Conference on Turkey."[35]

The critics of the post-war events and settlements in Syria and the Lebanon have accused the Western statesmen and politicians of those days of immoral decisions and unethical actions. It is the author's contention that such a criticism is inappropriate and irrelevant to the issues involved. The politician has his own individual morality. But it must be remembered that he is not "a demi-god sitting in the Palace of Truth" or in the Temple of Righteousness distributing justice equitably to all and sundry. He must take into consideration all his commitments and all his obligations and above all keep in mind first and foremost the interests of his own country. He is also under certain pressures and tensions in connection with his own position in the Government, such as his standing in his constituency, his relations with his other colleagues and the coming elections.

Thus, if not considered on a purely moral level, the pledges and promises were plain statements of political facts. Indeed the word "promise" or "pledge" does not occur in the official texts nor do those texts speak of any definitive treaties.[36] The "promises" to the Sharīf Ḥusain are officially referred to a "Correspondence"; the Sykes-Picot arrangement was an "Agreement"; the Hogarth

34. See Howard, "An American Experiment in Peace-making," p. 136.

35. Lloyd George, 2:1078; Jeffries, p. 302. An abbreviated version of the King-Crane Report was first published in *Editor and Publisher*, vol. 55, no. 27, 2 December 1922.

Later, in 1947, the full text was published in *Papers Relating to the Foreign Relations of the United States*, 7:745-863. See also Baker, 2:206-213, and Howard, *The King-Crane Commission*, pp. 311-320.

36. At a meeting held in 10 Downing Street on 23 September 1919 (with Faiṣal present) to discuss the British pledges to the Sharīf Ḥusain, Lord Curzon said that "There never had been any signed agreement between H.M. Government and King Husain. The discussions between the two parties had been carried on by means of correspondence." *Documents*, 1:4, p. 415.

"Message" of January 1918, the "Declaration" to the Seven, and General Allenby's "Assurances" to Faiṣal were officially considered as simply "Statements" made on behalf of His Majesty's Government.[37] In other words, the politicans in their "Statements" did not believe that they were committing themselves to a set of moral principles with a moral obligation to carry them out. But the Arab leaders considered those Statements as if they were "happy leaves" of a "nosegay plucked from the thornless Garden of Concord."[38]

Consequently, when Great Britain failed to carry out what they thought should have been carried out, to them it appeared that Great Britain was "swearing falsely in making covenants."[39]

There is, however, no evidence that there was any deliberate and premeditated intention to deceive the Arabs. The Allies did not desire to create any political and social evils. They believed that their victory in the Near East had insured "the complete and final emancipation of all those peoples so long oppressed by the Turks." They equally believed that, being themselves highly civilized States, their guidance and tutelage of those peoples, who had not progressed under Ottoman misrule, would be highly beneficial to them. France believed in her "mission civilizatrice" and Great Britain in the superiority of her system of "order and good Government." That meant, of course, the continuance of Great Britain's and France's supremacy in the Near East, but the Allies could not see in this situation any breach of faith with the Arabs.

In addition to all the foregoing factors, there remains one most important consideration for an understanding of the post-war settlements in the Near East, i.e., the principle which governed the foreign policy of a nationally independent and sovereign power, particularly a Great Power. It was the principle of "My country, right

37. See Cmd. 5964.

38. The preamble to a treaty signed between Persia and Great Britain in 1812 reads: "These happy leaves are a nosegay plucked from the thornless Garden of Concord, and tied by the hands of the plenipotentiaries in the form of a definitive Treaty, in which the articles of Friendship and Amity are blended" (translation from the Persian original). See Great Britain, Public Record Office, F.O. 94-159/1, *Persia*.

39. Isaiah 10:4.

or wrong," the first requirement of which has always been conquest, power and glory — the search for "a place in the sun," having secured a place on the earth. This principle has expressed itself in the foreign policy of the Great Powers since time immemorial. Then, foreign policy becomes, as Professor Gilbert Murray has so well expressed it, "the relations between so many bands of outlaws.... When I say 'Outlaws', of course, I do not mean criminals. These outlaws are by nature just as honest honourable as other men; they make treaties with one another and mostly keep them, they pledge their word and generally abide by it. But if they do not, there is nobody to make them. If one wrongs his neighbour, there is generally no one but that neighbour to make him suffer for it; if his neighbour wrongs him, he has no protection except his own knife and gun."[40] Among nations, in general, no moral values exist comparable to moral codes existing between the gentlemen and decent citizens of their own countries. But diplomacy endeavours, whenever necessary, to conceal this by rendering eloquent homage to ethical conceptions and moral maxims in its utterances and statements. Harold Nicolson considers this lip service to international morality as hypocrisy.[41] In practice, it is the principle of power politics and *realpolitik* that rule the relations between the nations. The commitments and agreements reached during the First World War were in the best tradition of power politics. "It gives no satisfaction," wrote Sir Reader Bullard, "to write of the Middle East in terms of power politics, but it would be dangerous not to recognize the facts."[42] Towards the end of the War, and especially after the United States joined the Allies, Great Britain and France considered it imperative to introduce an ideological element into their war aims, in deference to the idealism of President Wilson and to the American conception of establishing a "just democracy throughout the world." Moreover, the holocaust of four years of carnage and untold suffering for millions of people throughout the world had given rise to the paramount need of introducing a new

40. Gilbert Murray, *The Foreign Policy of Sir Edward Grey, 1906-1915* (London, 1915), pp. 41-42.

41. Harold G. Nicolson, *Curzon, The Last Phase, 1919-1925*, p. 395.

42. Bullard, p. 167.

spirit in international relations, and the idealistic pronouncements of the Allies themselves had raised great expectations, but acted later as a boomerang at the Peace Conference.

The minds of the Allies, however, were still engrossed in the patterns of international politics which had characterized the imperialistic and militaristic era of the old world. To President Wilson, the "Old World" was struggling "in the mazes of an antiquated system"; but it was very much alive and the peace aims of the "New World" receded into a dim and distant future. The following two quotations are a sad commentary on the state of affairs at the end of the War. The *Manchester Guardian* wrote in its leader on 2 December 1918, in connection with the visit to London of the French and Italian Premiers and Marshal Foch:

"The old Europe is not dead, the Europe of selfish interests of 'imperialist' ambitions, of diplomatic intrigue, of shortsighted views and moral chaos. It is alive among the nations, just as old Adam is alive among us all."

And Mr. Ray Stannard Baker expressed the same idea when he wrote:

"No sooner had the War ended than the high emotional and moral enthusiasm which marked its concluding year began to fade away. The spirit of unity began to disintegrate. The Allies had not, after all, common purposes. Each had its ancient loyalties, necessities, jealousies, ambitions, and these immediately began to reassert themselves. The purposes of the secret treaties were again crowded into the foreground. No miracle had really occurred. Men found themselves back in the old familiar world...."[43]

43. Baker, 1:83.

Referring to the Sykes-Picot Agreement, Pingaud wrote: "C'était là le vice essentiel d'un partage auquel les grandes puissances s'étaient laissées conduire par les traditions de leur politique, la jalousie de leurs rivalités et la poursuite de leur équilibre en Orient...." Pingaud, 3:252.

Furthermore, "If it can be shown that considerations which have since ceased to operate," said a previously quoted *memorandum* prepared by the Political Intelligence Department of the Foreign Office in 1920, "played an important part in the shaping of the agreements, or that new considerations have arisen which could then not have been foreseen, these would be important points in any reconsideration of the agreements, not as legal documents, but as provisional arrangements, to be revised on the basis of equity and common sense...." F.O. 371/5036.

However, the agreements between Great Britain and the Arabs, on the one hand, and Great Britain and the French, on the other, concerning the post-war settlements in Syria and the Lebanon, indicate that although the politician is not "he who sweareth to his own hurt and changeth not,"[44] the evil does not lie in him but in the ascendancy of the modern State, the new Leviathan which, in the last analysis, is a law unto itself. The politician is the high priest and guardian in the Temple of this Leviathan. He must serve it loyally and to the best of his abilities, either by diplomacy or by force. But he cannot serve two masters at the same time. Indeed, would there be any need for diplomacy and war if the motives and actions of all the Powers were ruled by good-will and international justice? The story of the struggle for Arab independence in the years 1918-1920 is a vivid illustration of the fact that the nations did not regulate their relations by a sovereign rule, without fear or favor — the moral law, divine in origin and universal in application. Without this moral law, the peoples of the world will search in vain for justice and lasting peace.

44. Psalms 15:4.

APPENDIX A

No. 4

Translation of a letter from Sir H. McMahon, His Majesty's High Commissioner at Cairo, to the Sherīf of Mecca

October 24, 1915

I have received your letter of the 29th Shawal, 1333, with much pleasure and your expressions of friendliness and sincerity have given me the greatest satisfaction.

I regret that you should have received from my last letter* the impression that I regarded the question of limits and boundaries with coldness and hesitation; such was not the case, but it appeared to me that the time had not yet come when that question could be discussed in a conclusive manner+.

I have realised, however, from your last letter that you regard this question as one of vital and urgent importance. I have, therefore, lost no time in informing the Government of Great Britain of the contents of your letter, and it is with great pleasure that I communicate to you on their behalf the following statement, which I am confident you will receive with satisfaction.

‡ The two districts of Mersina and Alexandretta and portions

* No. 2.

\+ Former reading: "... that the moment had not yet arrived when they could be most profitably discussed."

‡ Former reading: "The district of Mersina and Alexandretta and the portions of Syria lying to the west of the district of Damascus, Homs, Hama and Aleppo cannot be said to be purely Arab, and should be excluded from the proposed limits and boundaries. With the above modification, and without prejudice to our existing treaties with Arab chiefs, we accept these limits and boundaries, and, in regard to those portions of the territories therein in which Great Britain is free to act without detriment to the interests of her ally, France,

of Syria lying to the west of the districts of Damascus, Homs, Hama and Aleppo cannot be said to be purely Arab, and should be excluded from the limits demanded.

With the above modification, and without prejudice to our existing treaties with Arab chiefs, we accept those limits.

As for those regions lying within those frontiers wherein Great Britain is free to act without detriment to the interests of her ally, France, I am empowered in the name of the Government of Great Britain to give the following assurances and make the following reply to your letter:

(1) Subject to the above modifications, Great Britain is prepared to recognise and support the independence of the Arabs in all the regions within the limits demanded by the Sherif of Mecca.

(2) Great Britain will guarantee the Holy Places against all external aggression and will recognise their inviolability.

(3) When the situation admits, Great Britain will give to the Arabs her advice and will assist them to establish what may appear to be the most suitable forms of government in those various territories.

(4) On the other hand, it is understood that the Arabs have decided to seek the advice and guidance of Great Britain only, and that such European advisers and officials as may be required for the formation of a sound form of administration will be British.

(5) With regard to the *vilayets* of Bagdad and Basra, the Arabs will recognise that the established position and interests of Great Britain necessitate special administrative arrangements* in order to secure these territories from foreign aggression to promote the welfare of the local populations and to safeguard our mutual economic interests.

I am convinced that this declaration will assure you beyond all possible doubt of the sympathy of Great Britain towards the

I am empowered, in the name of the Government of Great Britain, to give you the following assurances and make the following reply to your letter:

"Subject to the above modifications, Great Britain is prepared to recognise and support the independence of the Arabs within the territories included in the limits and boundaries proposed by the Sherif of Mecca."

* Former reading: "... special measures of administrative control."

aspirations of her friends* the Arabs and will result in a firm and lasting alliance, the immediate results of which will be the expulsion of the Turks from the Arab countries and the freeing of the Arab peoples from the Turkish yoke, which for so many years has pressed heavily upon them.

I have confined myself in this letter to the more vital and important questions, and if there are any other matters dealt within in your letters which I have omitted to mention, we may discuss them at some convenient date in the future.

It was with very great relief and satisfaction that I heard of the safe arrival of the Holy Carpet and the accompanying offerings which, thanks to the clearness of your directions and the excellence of your arrangements, were landed without trouble or mishap in spite of the dangers and difficulties occasioned by the present sad war. May God soon bring a lasting peace and freedom to all peoples.

I am sending this letter by the hand of your trusted and excellent messenger, Sheikh Mohammed ibn Arif ibn Uraifan, and he will inform you of the various matters of interest, but of less vital importance, which I have not mentioned in this letter.

(Compliments).

(Signed): A. HENRY MCMAHON

* Former reading: "... her traditional friends."

Great Britain, Miscellaneous No. 3 (1939), *Correspondence Between Sir Henry McMahon, G.C.M.C., G.C.V.O., K.C.I.E., C.S.I., His Majesty's High Commissioner at Cairo and The Sherif Hussein of Mecca, July 1915-March 1916* (With a Map); Cmd. 2957.

For the Arabic version of this letter see Plate 1.

APPENDIX B

No. 9

Translation of a letter from the Sherīf of Mecca to Sir H. McMahon, His Majesty's High Commissioner at Cairo

February 18, 1916

(In the name of the Merciful, the Compassionate).

To the most noble His Excellency the High Commissioner. May God protect him. (After compliments and respects).

We received your Excellency's letter dated 25th Rabi El Awal, and its contents filled us with the utmost pleasure and satisfaction at the attainment of the required understanding and the intimacy desired. I ask God to make easy our purposes and prosper our endeavours. Your Excellency will understand the work that is being done, and the reasons for it from the following:

Firstly. We had informed your Excellency that we had sent one of our sons to Syria to command the operations deemed necessary there. We have received a detailed report from him stating that the tyrannies of the Government there have not left of the persons upon whom they could depend, whether of the different ranks of soldiers or of others, save only a few, and those of secondary importance; and that he is awaiting the arrival of the forces announced from different places, especially from the people of the country and the surrounding Arab regions as Aleppo and the south of Mosul, whose total is calculated at not less than 100,000, by their estimate; and he intends, if the majority of the forces mentioned are Arab, to begin the movement by them; and, if otherwise, that is, of the Turks or others, he will observe their advance to the Canal, and when they begin to fight, his movements upon them will be different to what they expect.

Secondly. We purposed sending our eldest son to Medina with sufficient forces to strengthen his brother (who is) in Syria, and with every possibility of occupying the railway line, or carrying out such operations as circumstances may admit. This is the beginning of the principal movement, and we are satisfied in its beginning with what we had levied as guards to keep the interior of the country quiet; they are of the people of Hejaz only, for many reasons which it would take too long to set forth; chiefly the difficulties in the way of providing their necessites with secrecy and speed (although this precaution was not necessary) and to make it easy to bring reinforcements when needed; this is the summary of what you wished to understand. In my opinion it is sufficient, and it is to be taken as a foundation and a standard as to our actions in the face of all changes and unforseen events which the sequence of events may show. It remains for us to state what we need at present:

Firstly. The amount of £50,000 in gold for the monthly pay of the troops levied, and other things the necessity of which needs no explanation. We beg you to send it with all possible haste.

Secondly. 20,000 sacks of rice, 15,000 sacks of flour, 3,000 sacks of barley, 150 sacks of coffee, 150 sacks of sugar, 5,000 rifles of the modern pattern and the necessary ammunition, and 100 boxes of the two sample cartidges (enclosed) and of Martini-Henry cartidges and "Aza", that is those of the rifles of the factory of St. Etienne in France, for the use of those two kinds of rifles of our tribes; it would not be amiss to send 500 boxes of both kinds.

Thirdly. We think it better that the place of deposit of all these things should be Port Sudan.

Fourthly. As the above provisions and munitions are not needed until the beginning of the movement (of which we will inform you officially), they should remain at the above place, and when we need them we will inform the Governor there of the place to which they may be conveyed, and of the intermediaries who will carry orders for receiving them.

Fifthly. The money required should be sent at once to the Governor or Port Sudan, and a confidential agent will be sent by us to receive it, either all at once, or in two instalments, according as he is able, and this (Q̌) is the (secret) sign to be recognised for acccpting thc man.*

Sixthly. Our envoy who will receive the money will be sent to Port Sudan in three weeks' time, that is to say, he will be there on the 5th Jamad Awal (9th March) with a letter from us addressed to Al Khawaga Elias Effendi, saying that he (Elias) will pay him in accordance with the letter, the rent of our properties, and the signature will be clear in our name, but we will instruct him to ask for the Governor of the place, whom you will apprise of this person's arrival. After perusal of the letter, the money should be given to him on condition that no discussion whatever is to be with him of any question concerning us. We beg you most emphatically not to tell him anything, keeping this affair secret, and he should be treated apparently as if he were nothing out of the way.

Let it not be thought that our appointment of another man results from lack of confidence in the bearer; it is only to avoid waste of time, for we are appointing him to a task elsewhere. At the same time we beg you not to embark or send him in a steamer, or officially, the means already arranged being sufficient.

Seventhly. Our representative, bearer of the present letter, has been definitely instructed to ensure the arrival of this, and I think that his mission this time is finished since the condition of things is known both in general and in detail, and there is no need for sending anyone else. In case of need for sending information, it will come from us; yet as our next representative will reach you after three weeks, you may prepare instructions for him to take back. Yet let him be treated simply in appearance.

* The original sign in the Arabic text of this letter, as will be observed, was ˇ

Great Britain, Miscellaneous No. 3 (1939), *Correspondence Between Sir Henry McMahon, G.C.M.C., G.C.V.O., K.C.I.E., C.S.I., His Majesty's High Commissionner at Cairo and The Sherif Hussein of Mecca, July 1915-March 1916* (With a Map); Cmd. 5957.

For the original Arabic text of this letter see Plate 2.

Eighthly. Let the British Government consider this military expenditure in accordance with the books which will be furnished it, explaining how the money has been spent.

To conclude, my best and numberless salutions beyond all increase.

14 Rabīʿ al-Ākhar, 1334

APPENDIX C

Memorandum by the Emīr Faiṣal submitted to the Peace Conference

The country from a line Alexandretta — Persia southward to the Indian Ocean is inhabited by "Arabs" — by which we mean people of closely related Semitic stocks, all speaking the one language, Arabic. The non-Arabic-speaking elements in this area do not, I believe, exceed one per cent of the whole.

The aim of the Arab nationalist movements (of which my father became the leader in war after combined appeals from the Syrian and Mesapotamian branches) is to unite the Arabs eventually into one nation. As an old member of the Syrian Committee I commanded the Syrian revolt, and had under me Syrians, Mesopotamians, and Arabians.

We believe that our ideal of Arab unity in Asia is justified beyond need of argument. If argument is required, we would point to the general principles accepted by the Allies when the United States joined them, to our splendid past, to the tenacity with which our race has for 600 years resisted Turkish attempts to absorb us, and, in a lesser degree, to what we tried our best to do in this war as one of the Allies.

My father has a privileged place among Arabs, as their successful leader, and as the head of their greatest family, and as Sherīf of Mecca. He is convinced of the ultimate triumph of the ideal of unity, if no attempt is made now to force us, by imposing an artificial political unity on the whole, or to hinder it, by dividing the area as spoils of war among great Powers.

The unity of the Arabs in Asia has been made more easy of late years, since the development of railways, telegraphs, and air-roads. In old days the area was too huge, and in parts necessarily too thinly peopled, to communicate common ideas readily.

The various provinces of Arab Asia — Syria, Irak, Jezireh, Hedjaz, Nejd, Yemen — are very different economically and socially, and it is impossible to constrain them into one frame of government.

We believe that Syria, an agricultural and industrial area thickly peopled with sedentary classes, is sufficiently advanced politically to manage her own internal affairs. We feel also that foreign technical advice and help will be a most valuable factor in our national growth. We are willing to pay for this help in cash; we cannot sacrifice for it any part of the freedom we have just won for ourselves by force of arms.

Jezireh and Irak are two huge provinces, made up of three civilised towns, divided by large wastes thinly peopled by semi-nomadic tribes. The world wishes to exploit Mesopotamia rapidly, and we therefore believe that the system of government there will have to be buttressed by the men and material resources of a great foreign Power. We ask, however, that the Government be Arab, in principle and spirit, the selective rather than the elective principle being necessarily followed in the neglected districts, until time makes the broader basis possible. The main duty of the Arab Government there would be to oversee the educational processes which are to advance the tribes to the moral level of the towns.

The Hedjaz is mainly a tribal area, and the government will remain, as in the past, suited to patriarchal conditions. We appreciate these better than Europe, and propose therefore to retain our complete independence there.

The Yemen and Nejd are not likely to submit their cases to the Peace Conference. They look after themselves, and adjust their own relations with the Hedjaz and elsewhere.

In Palestine the enormous majority of the people are Arabs. The Jews are very close to the Arabs in blood, and there is no conflict of character between the two races. In principles we are absolutely at one. Nevertheless, the Arabs cannot risk assuming the responsibility of holding level the scales in the clash of races and religions that have, in this one province so often involved the world in difficulties. They would wish for the effective super-position of a great trustee, so long as a representative local administration commended itself by actively promoting the material prosperity of the country.

* * *

In discussing our provinces in detail I do not lay claim to superior competence. The powers will, I hope, find better means to give fuller effect to the aims of our national movement. I came to Europe, on behalf of my father and the Arabs of Asia, to say that they are expecting the Powers at the Conference not to attach undue importance to superficial differences of condition, and not to consider them only from the low ground of existing European material interests and supposed spheres. They expect the Powers to think of them as one potential people, jealous of their language and liberty, and ask that no steps be taken inconsistent with the prospect of an eventual union of these areas under one sovereign government.

In laying stress on the difference in the social condition of our provinces, I do not wish to give the impression that there exists any real conflict of ideals, material interests, creeds, or character rendering our union impossible. The greatest obstacle we have to overcome is local ignorance, for which the Turkish Government is largely responsible.

In our opinion, if our independence be conceded and our local competence established, the natural influences of race, language, and interest will soon draw us together into one people; but for this the Great Powers will have to ensure us open internal frontiers, common railways and telegraphs, and uniform systems of education. To achieve this they must lay aside the thought of individual profits, and of their old jealousies. In a word, we ask you not to force your whole civilisation upon us, but to help us to pick out what serves us from your experience. In return we can offer you little but gratitude.

January 1st, 1919

Doc. 250 in Miller, *My Diary*, 4: 297-99.

APPENDIX D

"Territorial Claims of the Government of the Hedjaz," presented to the Peace Conference by the Emīr Faiṣal

As representing my father, who, by request of Britain and France, led the Arab rebellion against the Turks, I have come to ask that the Arabic-speaking peoples of Asia, from the line Alexandretta-Diarbekr southward to the Indian Ocean, be recognised as independent sovereign peoples under the guarantee of the League of Nations. The Hedjaz, which is already a sovereign State, and Aden, which is a British dependency, are excluded from the Arab demand.

The confirmation of the States already existing in the area, the adjustment of their boundaries with one another, with the Hedjaz, and with the British at Aden, and the formation of such new States as are required, and their boundaries, are matters for arrangement between us, after the wishes of their respective inhabitants have been ascertained.

Detailed suggestions on these smaller points will be put forward by my Government when the time comes.

I base my request on the principles enunciated by President Wilson (attached), and am confident that the Powers will attach more importance to the bodies and souls of the Arabic-speaking peoples than to their own material interests.

January 29th, 1919

Doc. 251 in Miller, *My Diary*, 4: 300.

APPENDIX E

Extract from an "Outline of Tentative Report and Recommendation Prepared by the Intelligence Section, in Accordance with Instruction, for the President and the Plenipotentiaries, February 21, 1919"

25 Syria

It is recommended:

1) That there be established a Syrian state.

2) That there be applied to the Syrian state the mandatory principle, but no recommendation is made as to the Power to be selected to carry out this principle.

3) That no obstacle be interposed against the final incorporation of the Syrian state in an Arab confederation, if the tendency toward this solution should develop in country.

Discussion

1) It is recommended that there be established a Syrian state. While Syria belongs to the Arab-speaking world, it has an unusually large European population, close commercial and cultural relations with Europe, a strong Christian element and a sedentary mode of life. It should therefore be separated at the outset from the nomad Arab area.

Its eastern boundary has been drawn with these considerations in mind, and runs just beyond the border of the sown land, so as to include all of the grain-growing regions, of which the Hauran below Damascus, is the richest. The northern boundary of Syria, is quite artificial, and indeed this boundary could not be drawn on racial lines.

The new state would have a population of about 400,000 and would about equal in area the state of Bulgaria.

2) It is recommended that there be applied to the Syrian state the mandatory principle, but no recommendation is made as to the Power to be selected to carry out this principle.

3) It is recommended that no obstacle be interposed against the final incorporation of the Syrian state in an Arab confederation, if the tendency toward this solution should develop in the country.

There is a possibility of the future development of an Arab confederation which will include all of the Arab-speaking portions of the former Turkish Empire. The present strength of this Arab movement is hard to gauge. It would be the best solution from the standpoint of the welfare and development of the Arab states.

Doc. 246 in D.H. Miller, *My Diary*, 4: 262.

APPENDIX F

Statement made by President Howard S. Bliss of the Syrian Protestant College, Beirut, Syria, before the Paris Peace Conference (The 'Big Ten') on Thursday afternoon, February 13th at the Quai d'Orsay, Paris

Mr. President,

Gentlemen:

I shall not detain you long. My deep interest in the people of Syria, irrespective of race, creed or condition, bred from a long residence among them (in fact I was born in Mt. Lebanon) is my only excuse for detaining you at all.

First, a preliminary word as to the people themselves: They are intelligent, able, hospitable and lovable, but, together with the sure defects of a long oppressed race — timidity, love of flattery, indirectness — they also have the defects characteristic of a people who are face to face with the results of civilization without having passed through the processes of civilization. They lack balance; they are easily discouraged; they lack political fairness; they do not easily recognize the limitation of their own rights. They must therefore be approached with sympathy, firmness and patience. They are capable of nobly responding to the right appeal and they will grow into capacity for self-determination and independence.

My plea before this body in behalf of the people of Syria is this: that an Inter-Allied or a Neutral Commission be sent at once to Syria in order to give an opportunity to the people of Syria, including the Lebanon, to express in a perfectly untrammelled way their political wishes and aspiration, viz, as to what form of Government they desire and as to what Power, if any, should be their Mandatory Protecting Power.

My plea is based upon the ground that the Twelfth Point of

President Wilson's Fourteen Points and the declaration made by France and Great Britain in November 1918, have committed the Allies and the United States to the granting of such an opportunity to the peoples freed from the Turkish yoke to so express themselves. The declaration referred to is as follows —

"Text of declaration agreed to between the British and French Governments and communicated to the President of the United States of America.

"The aim which France and Great Britain have in view in waging in the East the war let loose on the world by German ambition, is to ensure the complete and final emancipation of all those peoples so long oppressed by the Turks, and to establish national governments and administrations which shall derive their authority from the initiative and free will of the peoples themselves.

"To realize this, France and Great Britain are in agreement to encourage and assist the establishment of native governments in Syria and Mesopotamia, now liberated by the Allies, as also in those territories for whose liberation they are striving and to recognize those governments immediately they are effectively established

"Far from wishing to impose on the peoples of these regions this or that institution, they have no other care than to assure, by their support and practical aid, the normal workings of such governments and administrations as the people shall themselves have adopted; to guarantee impartial and even justice for all, to facilitate the economic development of the country by arousing and encouraging local initiative, to foster the spread of education, to put an end to those factions too long exploited by Turkish policy — such is the part which the two allied governments have set themselves to play in liberated territories."

I maintain that such an opportunity for self-expression has not as yet been given. Up to the time I left Beirut, viz, January 9th, the stringency of the censorship of the Press and of the Post Office, the difficulty of holding public or private meetings for the discussion of political problems, and the great obstacles in travelling, had made it practically impossible for the people (suffering from centuries of intimidation, and hence timid to a degree) to express their political opinions with any kind of freedom.

It is true that a Lebanese delegation has succeeded in reaching Paris and is here today, but there are many other groups beside this particular delegation, including other groups from the Lebanon who would gladly have been here to speak for themselves and others, had they been as fortunate as this group in being able to organize themselves and to find the means of travelling hither.

The point is this: Up to January 9th (the date of my leaving) no notice of any arrangements have been published anywhere in Syria, so far as I know, looking to anything like a general poll of the people of Syria (always including the Lebanon) or even anything like an attempt had been made to secure a widespread knowledge of public sentiment. I did hear, more or less, of lists of names that were being made up attached to various petitions in favor of this or that programme, but although in a position to hear of any official or thorough or systematic general plan to ascertain the wishes of the people, no such report came to my knowledge. To my own knowledge many interested citizens of Beirut and the Lebanon were never approached for the purpose of ascertaining their political desires.

I therefore plead that the above mentioned Commission should be sent out by the Peace Conference as soon as possible, with ample powers given to them, and of course with the wholehearted support granted to them by the French and British authorities now in Syria.

The ascertaining of the desires of the people should proceed either without the presence of any foreign power (and this is impracticable) or in the presence of both French and British authorities under whom Syria has been living for the past four months.

The people are easily frightened and intimidated even when there is nothing to fear from any source, and hence these precautions. The advantage of knowing what the people wish would be a boon to the power eventually becoming the Mandatory Power, as well as to the people of Syria.

One word as to the work of the Commission. Their task will not be an easy one. They must approach it, in my opinion, in the spirit of large sympathy, infinite patience, frankness and goodwill. In the hands of fair and open minded men — resourceful, shrewd and generous — men who can make clear their honest purpose to a timid but intelligent people, very valuable results can be secured.

The result of this inquiry will be, I am convinced, the discovery of a desire for the erection of a State or States looking eventually to complete independence but at present seeking the guardianship of a Mandatory Power.

Both the State or States and the Mandatory Power should be under the control of the League of Nations.

Unless in this State or States there shall be an absolute separation between Religion and the State, most serious results must inevitably arise.

The Government, on the one hand, Religion on the other, can best pursue their majestic tasks apart. Surely Oriental history, if not all history, is making this abundantly clear.

[Some extempore words were added, to the following effect, but the exact phrases cannot now be reproduced]:

One word more: Unless the Mandatory Power, working under the League of Nations, shall pursue its God-given task in Syria in the same lofty spirit in which the Allies and the United States, working together, have striven to maintain, in the recent world-struggle, the noblest ideals, then will be failure.

But on the other hand, given the same desire and purpose to labor distinterestedly and patiently for the uplift of an intelligent, worthy but oppressed people, the result cannot but prove a blessing to Syria and to the whole world.

Private Papers of Howard S. Bliss.

APPENDIX G

Aide-Mémoire in Regard to the Occupation of Syria, Palestine and Mesopotamia Pending the Decision in Regard to Mandates

1. Steps will be taken immediately to prepare for the evacuation by the British Army of Syria and Cilicia including the Taurus tunnel.

2. Notice is given both to the French Government and to their Emir Feisal of our intentions to commence the evacuation of Syria and Cilicia on November 1, 1919.

3. In deciding to whom to hand over responsibility for garrisoning the various districts in the evacuated area, regard will be had to the engagements and declarations of the British and French Governments, not only as between themselves, but as between them and the Arabs.

4. In pursuance of this policy the garrisons in Syria west of the Sykes-Picot line and the garrisons in Cilicia will be replaced by a French force, and the garrisons at Damascus, Homs, Hama, and Aleppo will be replaced by an Arab force.

5. After the withdrawal of their forces neither the British Government nor the British Commander-in-Chief shall have any responsibility within the zones from which the Army has retired.

6. The territories occupied by British troops will then be Palestine, defined in accordance with its ancient boundaries of Dan to Beersheba, and Mesopotamia including Mosul, the occupation thus being in harmony with the arrangements concluded in December 1918, between M. Clemenceau and Mr. Lloyd George.

7. The British Government are prepared at any time to discuss the boundaries between Palestine and Syria and between Mesopotamia and Syria. In the event of disagreement in regard to the above boundaries, the British Government are prepared to

PLATE 1 Arabic version of Letter no. 4, written by Sir Henry McMahon to the Sharīf Ḥusain of Mecca (for translation, see Appendix A).

مستعدة بان تعترف باستقلال العرب وتؤيد ذلك الاستقلال في جميع الاقاليم الداخلة في الحدود التي يطلبها دولة شريف مكة

(٢) ان بريطانيا العظمى تضمن الاماكن المقدسة من كل اعتداء خارجي وتعترف بوجوب منع التعدي عليها

(٣) وعندما تسمح الظروف تمد بريطانيا العظمى العرب بنصائحها وتساعدهم على ايجاد هيئات حاكمة ملائمة لتلك الاقاليم المختلفة

(٤) هذا وان المفهوم ان العرب قد قرروا طلب نصائح وارشادات بريطانيا العظمى وحدها وان المستشارين والموظفين الاوروبيين اللازمين لتشكيل هيئة ادارية قويمة يكونون من الانكليز

(٥) اما من خصوص ولايتي بغداد والبصرة فان العرب تعترف ان مركز ومصالح بريطانيا العظمى الموطدة هناك تستلزم اتخاذ تدابير ادارية مخصوصة لوقاية هذه الاقاليم من الاعتداء الاجنبي وزيادة خير سكانها وحماية مصالحنا الاقتصادية المتبادلة.

واني متيقن ان هذا التصريح يؤكد لدولتكم بدون ادنى ارتياب ميل بريطانيا العظمى نحو رغائب اصحابها العرب وتنتهي بعقد محالفة دائمة ثابتة معهم ويكون من نتائجها المستعجلة طرد الاتراك من بلاد العرب وتحرير الشعوب العربية من نير الاتراك الذي اثقل كاهلهم السنين الطوال.

ولقد اقتصرت في كتابي هذا على المسائل الحيوية ذات الاهمية الكبرى وان كان هناك مسائل في خطاباتكم لم تذكر هنا فسنعود الى البحث فيها في وقت مناسب في المستقبل

ولقد تلقيت بمزيد السرور والرضى خبر وصول الكسوة الشريفة وما معها من الصدقات بالسلامة وانها بفضل ارشاداتكم السامية وتدابيركم المحكمة قد انزلت الى البر بلا تعب ولا ضرر رغما عن الاخطار والمصاعب التي سببتها هذه الحرب المحزنة ونرجو الحق سبحانه وتعالى ان يعجل الصلح الدائم والحرية لاهل العالم

اني مرسل خطابي هذا مع رسولكم النبيل الامين الشيخ محمد بن عارف بن عريفان وسيعرض على مسامعكم

بعض المسائل المفيدة التي هي من الدرجة الثانية من الاهمية ولم اذكرها في كتابي هذا .

وفي الختام ابث دولة الشريف ذا الحسب المنيف والامير الجليل كامل تحيتي وخالص مودتي واعرب عن محبتي له ولجميع افراد اسرته الكريمة راجيا من ذي الجلال ان يوفقنا جميعا لما فيه خير العالم وصالح الشعوب ان بيده مفاتيح الامر والغيب يحركها كيف يشاء، ونسأله تعالى حسن الختام والسلام

تحريرا في يوم الاثنين ١٥ ذي الحجة ١٣٣٣

قيدنا الاكرم الشريف بعاليه بهذا اللون

نائب جلالة الملك
السير ارثر مكماهون

72/16

9

33

بسم الله الرحمن الرحيم

الحضرة ذو الاصالة فخامة نائب جلالة الملك دام مرعيا

[illegible]

١٤ ربيع الآخر ١٣٣٤

PLATE 2 Original Arabic text of Letter no. 9, written by the Sharīf Ḥusain of Mecca to Sir Henry McMahon (for translation, see Appendix B).

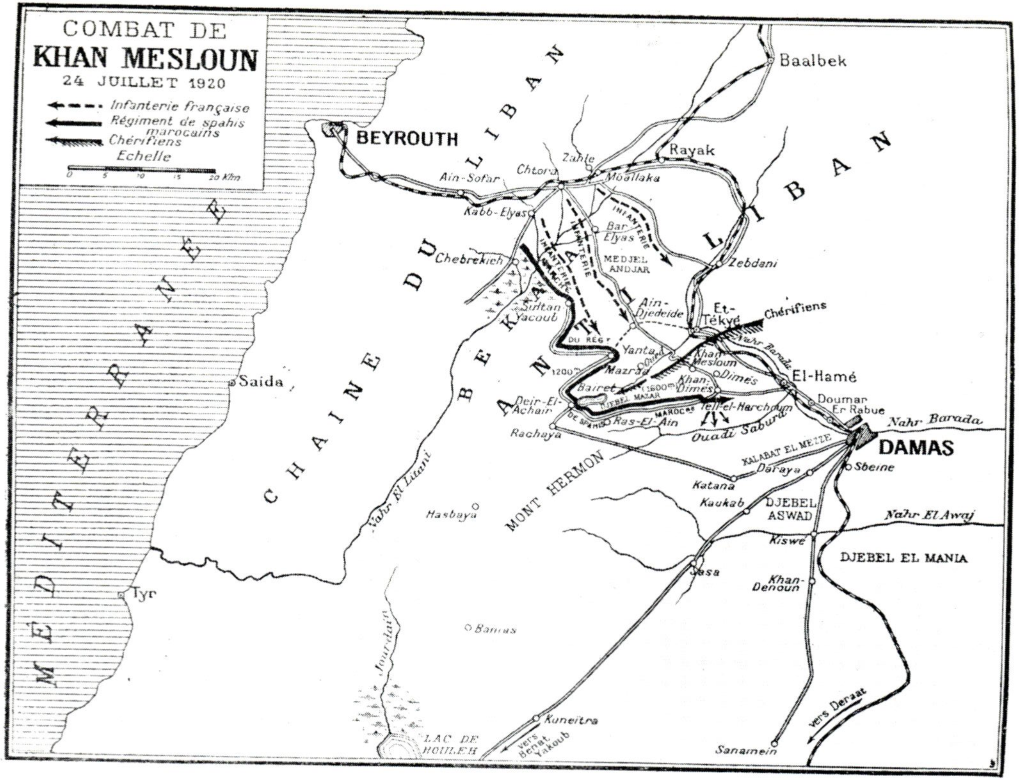

PLATE 3 Map of the battle of Maisalūn, 24 July 1920.
(From *Sur la Route des Indes*, by Jean Pichon, Paris 1932, p. 232).

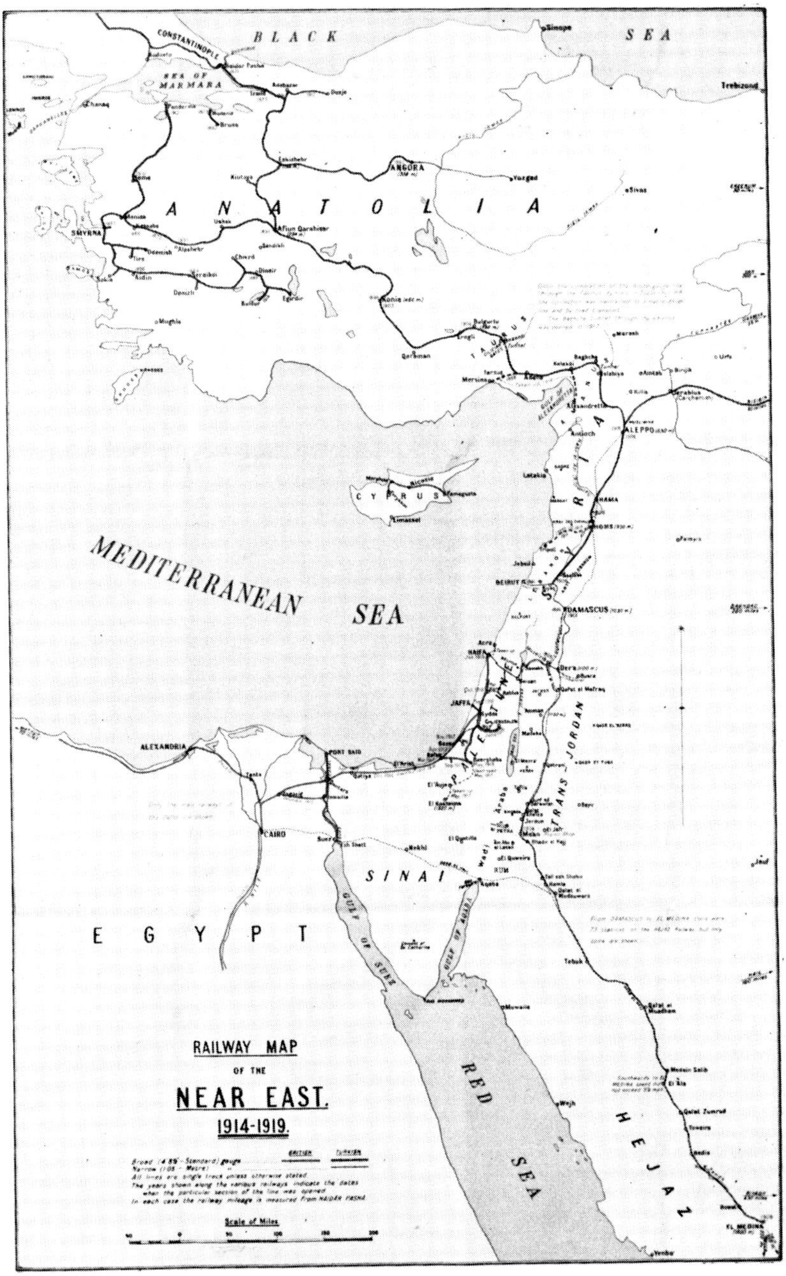

PLATE 4 General map of the battlefield area in the Near East, 1914-1919. (From the map Volume of *Military Operations: Egypt and Palestine*, I. *History of the Great War I* by Cyril Falls and A.F. Becke.) Reproduced by kind permission of the Controller of Her Britannic Majesty's Stationery Office.

No I

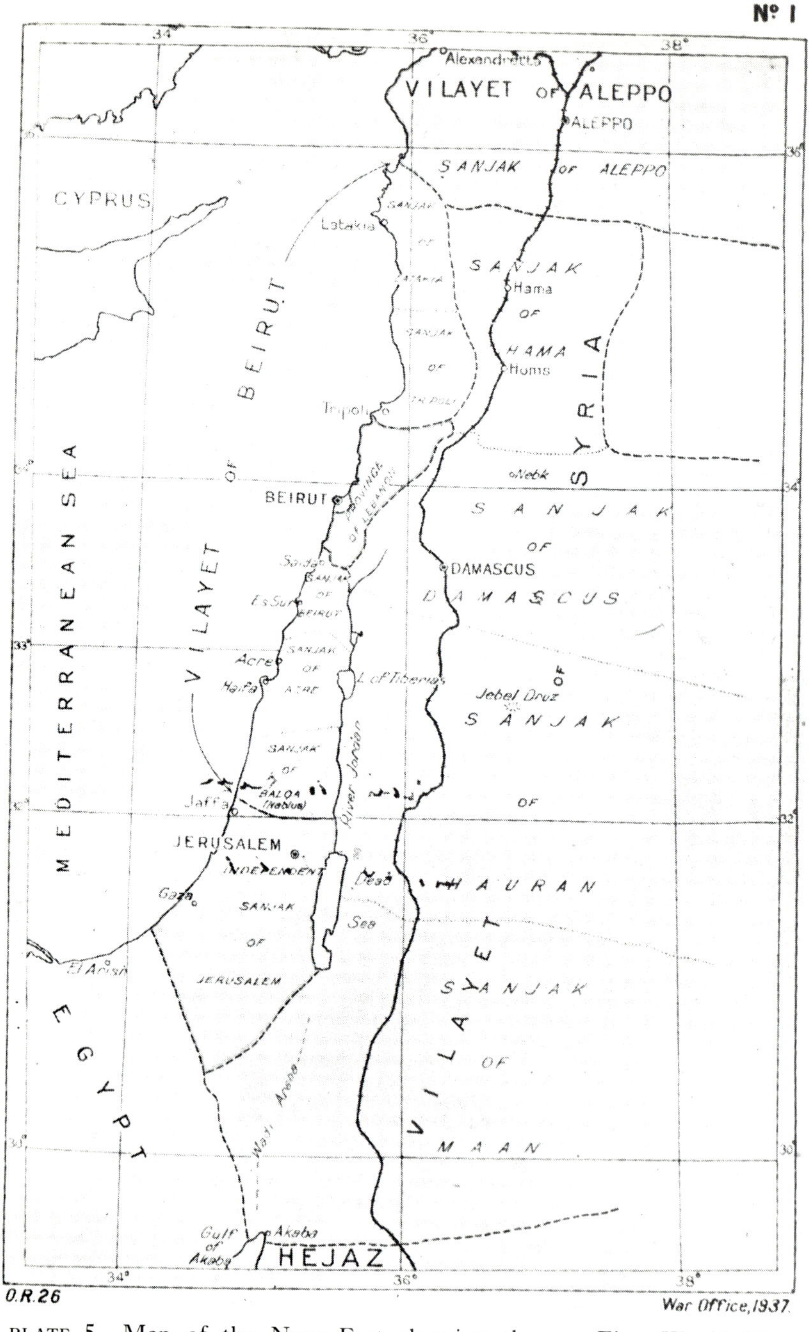

PLATE 5 Map of the Near East showing the pre-First World War Ottoman Vilayets and Sanjaks. (From *Palestine Royal Commission Report*, London 1937, facing p. 19). Reproduced by kind permission of the Controller of Her Britannic Majesty's Stationery Office.

MAP TO ILLUSTRATE THE AGREEMENT OF 1916.

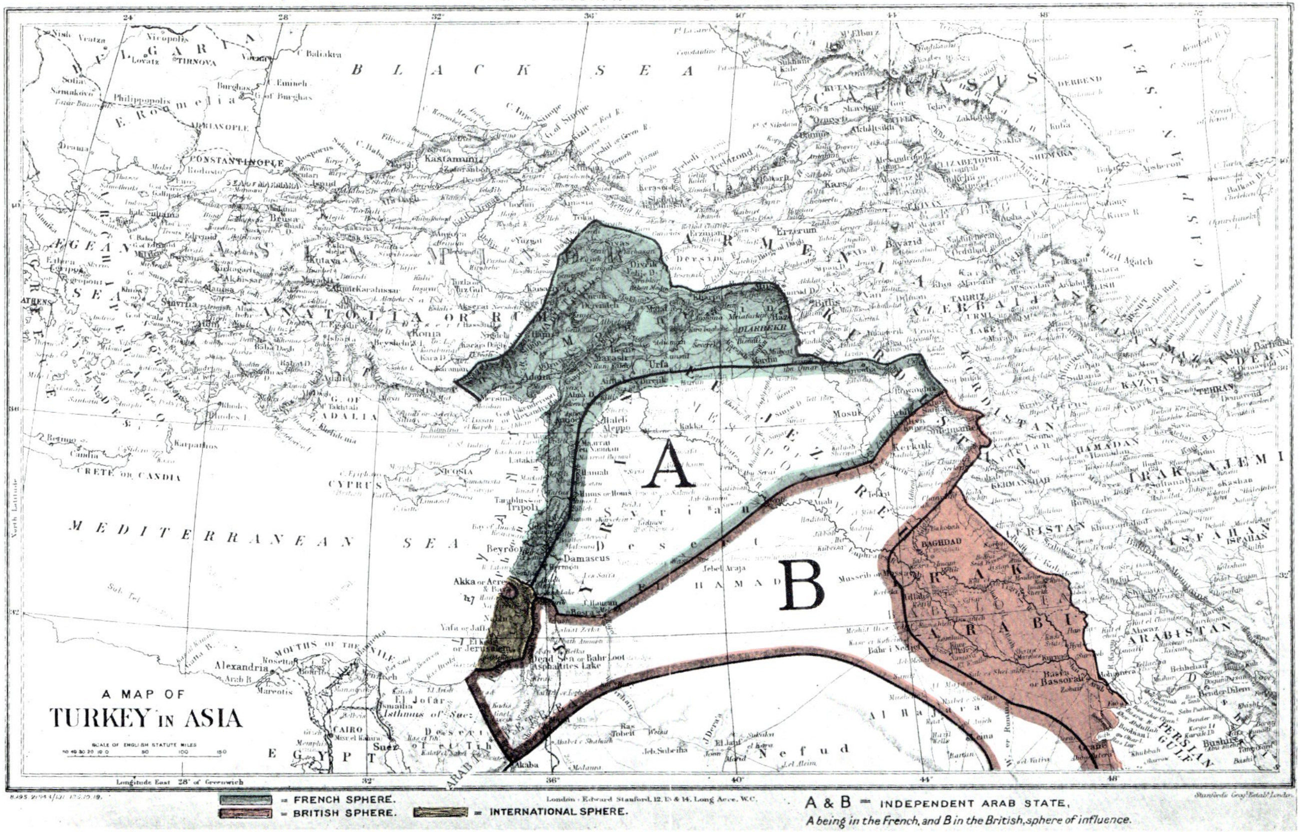

PLATE 6 Map showing the Sykes-Picot Agreement of 1916; reproduced from the colored map attached to the original agreement.

GENERAL HEADQUARTERS,

Egyptian Expeditionary Force,

1st Echelon,

~~[illegible]~~) 4/[illegible]/18.

To His Highness

The Emir Faisal.

After Greetings.

I am taking the opportunity of Lieut. Colonel Dawnay's departure to Akaba to send my greetings and good wishes to Your Highness.

I have discussed with Lieut. Colonel Dawnay your requirements and your plans for the future, and he will communicate my views to Your Highness.

There is one point which I find it necessary to make quite clear to Your Highness in order to avoid any misunderstanding in the future. It is that , in the event of your extending your military operations far in advance of the right flank of my force, you must not reckon upon the support and cooperation of my Army, as you will enter districts which are outside my sphere of operations and to which my forces will be unable to penetrate at present.

I think it wise to inform you of this in order that Your Highness may be under no misapprehension when formulating your plans.

I need not assure Your Highness that you will receive all the support and assistance which I can furnish and I am convinced that the sympathy and spirit of cooperation which is now established between us will help us to defeat our common enemy.

With compliments,

General,
Commanding - in - Chief;
Egyptian Expeditionary Force.

PLATE 7 Letter from General Allenby to the Emīr Faiṣal.

submit the question to the arbitration of a referee appointed by President Wilson.

8. In accordance with the principles of the Sykes-Picot agreement the French Government shall not object to the Arab State granting to the British Government the right to construct, administer, and be the sole proprietor of a railway line connecting Haifa with Mesopotamia on a trace to be decided on after survey anywhere as far north as the latitude of Deir-ez-Zor. The British Government shall have the right to construct oil pipe lines as well as the railway lines. The British Government shall, in addition, have a perpetual right at all times to improve the facilities of these railway and oil pipe lines and to transport troops along the railway, and these rights shall be exercisable even in time of war, without infringement of the neutrality of the French Government or of the Arab State. In the event of disagreement as to the trace of the railway line and oil pipe lines the British Government are prepared to submit this question to the arbitration of a referee appointed by President Wilson.

9. The British Government notify the French Government and the Emir Feisal of their intention immediately to carry out a survey with the object of finding, if practicable, a trace for the railway line and pipe lines entirely within the British mandate, in order to enable them to avoid the necessity of exercising the right of construction referred to above.

10. Until the boundaries of Palestine and Mesopotamia are determined, the British Commander-in-Chief shall have the right to occupy outposts in accordance with the boundary claimed by the British Government.

11. The French Government, having accepted responsibility for the protection of the Armenian people, the British Government will consent to the immediate despatch of French troops via Alexandretta and Mersina for this purpose.

Paris, Sept. 13, 1919

Appendix B to Doc. No. 57: Notes of a Meeting of the Heads of Delegations of the Five Great Powers, held in M. Clemenceau's Room at the War Office, Paris, on Monday, 15 Sept. 1919, at 10.30 a.m., in E.L. Woodward and Rohan Butler, eds., *Documents on British Foreign Policy*, 1919-1939, 1st ser., vol. 1 (1919), pp. 700-701.

APPENDIX H

Letter from President Clemenceau to the Maronite Patriarch

PRÉSIDENCE
DU
CONSEIL

Paris, le 10 Novembre 1919

Monseigneur,

Les entretiens que, depuis votre arrivée à Paris, vous avez eus avec M. le Ministre des Affaires Étrangères et avec moi-même vous auront confirmé dans la conviction que le Gouvernement de la République demeurait invariablement attaché aux traditions de mutuel dévouement, établies depuis des siècles entre la France et le Liban.

Ces entretiens vous auront également donné la certitude que les solutions que nous poursuivons à la Conférence de la Paix sont, dans leur ensemble, conformes, aux aspirations des populations dont vous êtes le Haut Représentant.

Le désir des Libanais de conserver un Gouvernement autonome et un Statut national indépendant s'accorde parfaitement avec les traditions libérales de la France.

Avec le soutien et l'aide de la France, indépendants de tout autre groupement national, les Libanais sont assurés de conserver leurs traditions, de développer leurs institutions politiques et administratives, de hâter eux-mêmes la mise en valeur complète de leur pays, de voir enfin leurs enfants se préparer dans leurs propres écoles aux fonctions publiques du Liban.

Les limites dans lesquelles s'exercera cette indépendance ne peuvent être arrêtées avant que le Mandant sur la Syrie ait été attribué et défini. Mais la France qui a tout fait en 1860 pour assurer au Liban un territoire plus étendu, n'oublie pas que le resserrement des limites actuelles résulte de la longue oppression dont a souffert le Liban. Désireuse de favoriser le plus possible les relations économiques entre tous les pays confiés à son mandat, elle tiendra également le plus grand compte, plus grand compte, dans la délimitation du Liban, de la nécessité de réserver à la "Montagne" des territoires de plaine et l'accès à la mer indispensable à sa prospérité.

Je suis certain, en vous donnant ces assurances, de répondre aux sentiments qui ont déterminé les populations du Liban à demander une fois de plus le mandat de la France pour leur pays et je veux espérer que la solution définitive donnée par la Conférence à la question syrienne permettra au Gouvernement français d'accomplir dans la plus large mesure les vœux de ces vaillantes populations.

Veuillez agréer, Monseigneur, les assurances de ma haute considération.

Signé: CLEMENCEAU

Sa Béatitude
Monseigneur HOYEK,
Patriarche Maronite

Source: Bkerki, Lebanon. Private Archives of the Maronite Patriarchate.

APPENDIX I

The Program of the Syrian Congress
[Extracts from the King-Crane Report]

The Syrian Congress at Damascus — from the time of reaching Jerusalem, the Commission began to be told of a congress that was in preparation, to be held soon at Damascus, which would for a large part of the population determine the question of a mandate. Sessions were held while the Commission was at Damascus, and on the last day there, a deputation presented to the Commission the program that had been prepared.

The Congress was not elected directly by the people, or by a fresh appeal to the people, the reason given being that time was lacking to revise the voting lists and carry through a new scheme. At the last Turkish election, before the war, electors were chosen to select deputies for the Turkish parliament. The survivors of these electors chose the members of the Damascus Congress. Criticisms were made against the plan of choice to the effect that it was unconstitutional and extra-constitutional, that the electors had mostly belonged to the Party of Union and Progress, and that the members of the Congress were not distributed in proportion to population. Sixty nine members attended, and about 20 others from the west and north had been elected, but had not arrived. There were a number of Christians in the Conference, but no Jews, though some Jews among the electors were said to have given their approval.... Much evidence goes to show that the program prepared represents well the wishes of the people of Syria. The program is as follows:

"We, the undersigned, members of the General Syrian Congress, meeting in Damascus on Wednesday, July 2, 1919, made up of representatives from the three Zones, viz., the Southern, Eastern, and Western, provided with credentials, and authorizations by the inhabitants of our various districts, Moslems, Christians, and Jews, have agreed upon the following statement of the desires of the people of the country who have elected us to present them to the American Section of the International Commission; the fifth article was passed by a very large majority; all the other articles were accepted unanimously.

1. We ask absolutely complete political independence for Syria within these boundaries. The Taurus System on the North; Rafeh and a line running from Al-Juf to the south of the Syrian and the Mejazian line to Akaba on the south; the Euphrates and Khabur Rivers and a line extending east of Abu Kamal to the East of Al-Juf on the East; and the Mediterranean on the west.

2. We ask that the Government of this Syrian country should be a democratic civil constitutional Monarchy on broad decentralization principles, safeguarding the rights of minorities, and that the king be the Emir Feisal, who carried on a glorious struggle in the cause of our liberation and merited our full confidence and entire reliance.

3. Considering the fact that the Arabs inhabiting the Syrian area are not naturally less gifted than other more advanced races and that they are by no means less developed than the Bulgarians, Serbians, Greeks, and Roumanians at the beginning of their independence, we protest against Article 22 of the Covenant of the League of Nations, placing us among the nations in their middle stage of development which stand in need of a mandatory power.

4. In the event of the rejection by the Peace Conference of this just protest for certain considerations that we may not understand, we relying on the declarations of President Wilson that his object in waging war was to put an end to the ambition of conquest and colonization, can only regard the mandate mentioned in the Covenant of the League of Nations as equivalent to the rendering of economical and technical assistance that does not prejudice our complete independence. And desiring that our country should not fall a prey to colonization and believing that the American Nation is farthest from any thought of colonization and has no political ambition in our country, we will seek the technical and economic

assistance from the United States of America, provided that such assistance does not exceed twenty years.

5. In the event of America not finding herself in a position to accept our desire for assistance, we will seek this assistance from Great Britain, also provided that such assistance does not infringe the complete independence and unity of our country, and that the duration of such assistance does not exceed that mentioned in the previous article.

6. We do not acknowledge any right claimed by the French Government in any part whatever of our Syrian country and refuse that she should assist us or have a hand in our country under any circumstances and in any place.

7. We oppose the pretensions of the Zionists to create a Jewish commonwealth in the southern part of Syria, known as Palestine, and oppose Zionist migration to any part of our country; for we do not acknowledge their title, but consider them a grave peril to our people from the national, economical, and political points of view. Our Jewish compatriots shall enjoy our common rights and assume the common responsibilities.

8. We ask that there should be no separation of the southern part of Syria, known as Palestine, nor of the littoral western zone, which includes Lebanon, from the Syrian country. We desire that the unity of the country should be guaranteed against partition under whatever circumstances.

9. We ask complete independence for emancipated Mesopotamia and that there should be no economical barriers between the two countries.

10. The fundamental principles laid down by President Wilson in condemnation of secret treaties impel us to protest most emphatically against any treaty that stipulates the partition of our Syrian country, against any private engagement aiming at the establishment of Zionism in the southern part of Syria; therefore we ask the complete annulment of these conventions and agreements.

11. The noble principles enunciated by President Wilson strengthen our confidence that our desires emanating from the depth of our hearts, shall be the decisive factor in determining our

future; and that President Wilson and the free American people will be supporters for the realization of our hopes, thereby proving their sincerity and noble sympathy with aspiration of the weaker nations in general and our Arab people in particular.

We also have the fullest confidence that the Peace Conference will realize that we would not have risen against the Turks, with whom we had participated in all civil, political, and representative privileges, but for their violation of our national rights, and so will grant us our desires in full in order that our political rights may not be less after the war than they were before, since we have shed so much blood in the cause of our liberty and independence.

We request to be allowed to send a delegation to represent us at the Peace Conference to defend our rights and secure the realization of our aspirations."

The program mostly speaks sufficiently for itself. Various points in it are commented upon elsewhere in this report, it is the most substantial document presented to the Commission and deserves to be treated with great respect. The result of an extensive and arduous political process, it affords a basis on which the Syrians can get together, and as firm a foundation for a Syrian national organization as can be obtained. The mandatory power will possess in this program a commitment to liberal government which will be found to be very valuable in starting the new state in the right direction.

See *Papers Relating to the Foreign Relations of the United States*, 12: 780-81.

BIBLIOGRAPHY

I. BOOKS AND OFFICIAL PUBLICATIONS

'ABDALLAH, KING OF JORDAN. *Al-'Amālī al-siyāsiyyah* (My political hopes). Amman, 1939.

———. *Mudhakkarātī* [My memoirs]. Jerusalem, 1945.

———. *Al-Mu'tamar al-'Arabī al-Awwal* (The First Arab Congress). Cairo, 1913.

ABOUSSOUAN, BENOIT. *Le problème politique syrien.* Paris, 1924 or 5.

ALBRECHT-CARRIÉ, RENÉ. *Italy at the Peace Conference.* New York: Carnegie Endowment for World Peace, 1938.

AMERY, L. S. *My Political Life.* Vol. 2, *War and Peace,* 1914-1929. London, 1953.

'AMMOUN, ISKANDAR. *Le Liban après la guerre.* By Iskandar 'Ammoun and Auguste Adib. Cairo, 1919.

ANTONIUS, GEORGE. *The Arab Awakening: The Story of the Arab National Movement.* London: Hamish Hamilton, 1938.

AL-ARMANĀZĪ, NAJĪB. *Muḥāḍarāt 'an Sūriyyā, min al-iḥtilāl ḥattā al-jalā'* [Lectures on Syria from the occupation to the evacuation]. Cairo, 1954.

AL-ASWAD, IBRĀHIM BEY. *Tanwīr al-adhhān fī tārīkh Lubnān* [Enlightening the mind by the history of Lebanon]. 4 vols. Beirut, 1925.

AL-'AYYĀSHĪ, GHĀLIB. *Al-Iḍāḥāt al-Siyāsiyyah wa-asrār al-intidāb al-ifransī fī Sūriyya* [Political classifications and the secrets of the French mandate in Syria]. Beirut, 1955.

'AZOURY, NÉGĪB. *Le réveil de la nation arabe dans l'Asie Turque en présence des intérêts et des rivalités des puissances étrangères, de la Curie romaine et du Patriarcat œcuménique.* Paris: Plon, 1905.

BAKER, RAY STANNARD. *Woodrow Wilson and World Settlement: Written from his Unpublished and Personal Material.* Garden City: Doubleday, Page & Co., 1922. 3 vols.

AL-BANNĀ, ANWAR AL-JUNDĪ. *Qaḍāyā al-Aqṭār al-Islāmiyyah* [Problems of the Muslim Countries]. Cairo, 1946.

BARDOUX, JACQUES. *Lloyd George et la France.* Paris, 1923.

BARRÈS, MAURICE. *Une enquête aux Pays du Levant en 1914.* 2 vols. Paris, 1923.

BELL, GERTRUDE LOWTHIAN. *The Arab War: Confidential Information for General Headquarters from Gertrude Bell, Being Despatches Reprinted from the Arab Bulletin.* London: Golden Cockerel Press, 1940.

———. *The Letters of Gertrude Bell.* London: E. Benn, 1927.

BELLOC, HILAIRE. *The Battleground: Syria and Palestine, the Seed plot of Religion.* Philadelphia: Lippincott, 1936.

BIERSTADT, EDWARD HALE. *The Great Betrayal: A Survey of the Near East Problem.* New York: R. M. McBride & Co., 1924.

AL-BIKASĪNĪ, LUTFALLAH NAṢR. *Nabdhat min Waqā'i' al-ḥarb al-kawniyyah* [A brief account of the events of the (1st) World War]. Beirut, 1922.

BIRDWOOD, LORD. *Nuri as-Said: A Study in Arab Leadership.* London, 1959.

BONARDI, PIERRE. *L'Imbroglio Syrien.* Paris, 1927.

BOURDARIC, PAUL. *France, Syrie, Angleterre: La Question de Syrie, Confidentiel.* Paris, n.d.

BOURGEOIS, ÉMILE. *L'Europe et le Problème Méditerranéen*, 1970-1830. Paris, 1931.

BRÉMOND, ÉDOUARD. *Le Hedjaz dans la guerre mondiale.* Paris: Payot, 1931.

BRUNEAU, ANDRÉ. *Traditions et politique de la France au Levant.* Paris, 1932.

BULLARD, SIR READER WILLIAM. *Britain and the Middle East from Earliest Times to 1963.* London: Hutchinson [1964].

AL-BUWĀRĪ, BISHĀRA G. *Arba' seniy al-ḥarb* [Four years of war]. New York [1926]?

CAMBON, PAUL. *Correspondance*, 1870-1924. 3 vols. Paris: B. Grasset, 1940-46.

CATALUCCIO, FRANCESCO. *Storia del Nazionalismo Arabo per Gli Studi di Politica Internazionale.* Milan, 1939.

CATROUX, GÉNÉRAL. *Deux missions en Moyen Orient* (1919-1922). Paris, 1958.

CATROUX, LT. COL. *Le Mandat Français en Syrie.* Paris, 1922.

CEMAL (Aḥmad) PAŞA. *Kaifa jalat al-quwwāt al-'Uthmāniyyah 'an bilād al-'Arab* [How did the Ottoman forces evacuate the Arab countries]. Translated by Fuad Maidani. Beirut, 1932.

CEMAL (Aḥmad) PAŞA. *Memories of a Turkish Statesman*, 1913-1919. New York: George H. Doran Co., 1922.

———. *La vérité sur la Question Syrienne*. Istanbul, 1916.

CHARLES-ROUX, FRANÇOIS. *La France et les Chrétiens d'Orient*. Paris, 1939.

CHARMETANT, MGR. *Constantinople, Syrie et Palestine : Lettre ouverte à nos hommes d'État*. Paris, 1915.

CHEKRI, GANEM (Comité central syrien). *La Syrie devant la conférence : Mémoire à M. Georges Clemenceau, président du Conseil français, président de la Conférence de la Paix et à MM. les délégués des Puissances alliées et associées à cette conférence*. Paris, 1919.

———. *La Question Syrienne exposée par les Syriens : A LL. Excellences les Plénipotentiaires Alliées et Associées à la Conférence de la Paix*. Paris, 1919.

———. *L'Opinion Syrienne à l'Étranger pendant la guerre*. Paris, 1918.

AL-CHÉRIF, IHSAN. *Le Statut International de la Syrie*. Paris, 1920.

CHIROL, SIR VALENTINE. *Fifty Years in a Changing World*. London, 1927.

COCKS, F. SEYMOUR. *The Secret Treaties and Understandings*. London: National Labour Press, 1918.

CONTENSON, LUDOVIC DE. *Les réformes en Turquie d'Asie : La Question Arménienne, la Question Syrienne*. 2d ed. Paris: Plon, 1913.

CRANE, CHARLES R. *The Row in Syria*. New York, 1922.

CRESSATY, COUNT R. J. M. *Les Intérêts Français en Syrie*. Paris, 1915.

CUMMING, HENRY H. *Franco-British Rivalry in the Post-War Near East : The Decline of French Influence*, 1914-1923. London: Oxford University Press, 1938.

DĀGHIR, AS'AD. *Mudhakkarātī 'alā hāmish al-qaḍiyyah al-'Arabiyyah* [My memoirs around the Arab Question]. Cairo, 1959.

DANE, EDMUND. *British Campaigns in the Near East*, 1914-1918. 2 vols. New York, 1917-19.

DARWAZAH, MUḤAMMAD 'IZZAT. *Ḥawl al-Ḥarakat al-'Arabiyyah al-Ḥadīthah* [Concerning the modern Arab movement]. 2 vols. Sidon, Lebanon, 1956.

DAVID, PHILIPPE. *Un gouvernement arabe à Damas : Le Congrès Syrien*. Paris, 1923.

DICKINSON, G. LOWES. *Documents and Statements Relating to Peace Proposals and War Aims*. London, 1919.

De Haes, Jacob. *History of Palestine: The Last two Thousand Years.* New York: Macmillan Co., 1934.

Doris, J. *La Syrie aux Syriens.* Paris, 1926.

Dupuy, Trevor Nevitt. *The Campaigns on the Turkish Fronts.* By Trevor Nevitt Dupuy and Grace Person Hayes. New York, 1967.

Erskine, Mrs. Steuart. *King Faisal of Iraq.* Plymouth, 1933.

Esco Foundation for Palestine, Inc. *Palestine: A Study of Jewish, Arab, and British Policies.* New Haven: Yale University Press, 1947.

Evans, Laurence. *United States Policy and the Partition of Turkey,* 1914-1924. Baltimore: Johns Hopkins Press, 1965.

Exposé du Conseil Libanais au gouvernement et parlement français. Bibliothèque de Documentation Internationale Contemporaine. Paris: Université de Paris [1920?].

Falls, Cyril Bentham. *Military Operations: Egypt and Palestine, from June 1917 to the End of the War.* 2 pts. History of the Great War Based on Official Documents. London: H.M.S.O., 1930.

Flandin, Étienne. *Rapport sur la Syrie et la Palestine, présenté par M. Etienne Flandin.* Paris, 1915.

Frischwasser-Ra'anan, H. F. *Frontiers of a Nation.* London, 1955.

Gardner, Brian. *Allenby.* London, 1965.

Gautherot, Gustave. *La France en Syrie et en Cilicie.* Courbevoie, Seine, 1920.

Georges-Gaulis, Berthe. *La Question Arabe de l'Arabie du Roi Ibn Saoud à l'indépendance syrienne.* Paris: Berger-Levrault, 1930.

Ghali, Paul. *Les nationalités détachées de l'Empire ottoman à la suite de la guerre.* Paris: Domat-Montchrestiens, 1934.

Ghilini, Hector. *Les Leçons du Siècle.* Paris, 1934.

al-Ghusain, Fā'iz. *Mudhakkarātī 'an al-thawrat al-'Arabiyyah* [My memoirs of the Arab Revolt]. Damascus, 1956.

Gianini, A. *Documenti per la storia della Pace Orientale,* 1915-1932. Rome, 1943.

———. *L'Ultima fase della questione Orientale,* 1913-1932. Rome, 1933.

Gontaut-Biron, Comte R. de. *Comment la France s'est installée en Syrie,* 1918-1919. Paris, 1922.

GOTTLIEB, W. W. *Studies in Secret Diplomacy During the First World War.* London, 1957.

GRAVES, SIR ROBERT WINDHAM. *Lawrence and the Arabian Adventure.* New York, 1928.

GREY, SIR EDWARD. *Twenty-five Years,* 1892-1916. 2 vols. New York, 1925.

GROUSSET, RENÉ. *Le réveil de l'Asie.* Paris, 1924.

AL-ḤAKĪM, YŪSUF. *Sūriyyah wa'l-'Ahd al-Faiṣali* [Syria and the Faiṣal period]. Beirut, 1966.

HANOTAUX, GABRIEL, *Études diplomatiques : La Politique de l'équilibre,* 1907-1911. Paris, 1914 (or 1912).

ḤARFŪSH, IBRĀHIM. *Dalā'il al-'ināyat al-Samadāniyyah* [Proofs of divine protection]. Jounieh, Lebanon, 1935.

HENRY-HAYE et PIERRE VIÉNOT. *Les Relations de la France et de la Syrie.* Paris: Centre d'études de Politique Étrangère, 1939.

HOCKING, WILLIAM ERNEST. *The Spirit of World Politics.* New York, 1932.

HOGARTH, DAVID GEORGE. *Arabia.* Oxford, 1922.

HOURANI, ALBERT HABIB. *Syria and Lebanon : A Political Essay.* London: Oxford University Press for Royal Institute of International Affairs, 1946.

HOUSE, EDWARD MANDELL. *What Really Happened at Paris : The Story of the Peace Conference,* 1918-1919. Edited by C. Seymour. London, 1921.

———. *The Intimate Papers of Colonel House.* 4 vols. London, 1926.

HOWARD, HARRY NICHOLAS. *The Partition of Turkey : A Diplomatic History,* 1913-1923. Norman: University of Oklahoma, Press, 1931.

———. *The King-Crane Commission.* Beirut, 1963.

AL-ḤUṢARĪ, ABŪ KHALDŪN SĀṬI'. *Al-Bilād al-'Arabiyyah wa'l-dawlah al-'Uthmāniyyah* [The Arab countries and the Ottoman Empire]. Cairo, 1957.

———. *Yawm Maisalūn* [The day of Maisalun]. Beirut, 1947-48.

INGRAMS, DOREEN. *Palestine Papers,* 1917-1922: *Seeds of Conflict.* London, 1972.

JAWDAT, 'ALĪ. *Dhikrayāt* [Memoirs], 1900-1958. Beirut, 1967.

JEFFRIES, JOSEPH MARY NAGLE. *Palestine : The Reality.* London: Longmans, Green, and Co., 1939.

Jewish Agency for Palestine. *Documents Relating to the McMahon Letters.* London, 1939.

Joffre, Alphonse. *Le Mandat de la France sur la Syrie et le Grand-Liban.* Lyon, 1924.

Jung, Eugène. *Les puissances devant la révolte arabe.* Paris: Hachette, 1924.

Kahil Bey, Jean, M. N. *Les Aspirations Syriennes : Le vœu de la Syrie.* Cairo, 1916.

———. *Syriens et Arabes.* Cairo, 1919.

Kedourie, Elie. *England and the Middle East : The Destruction of the Ottoman Empire,* 1914-1921. London: Bowes & Bowes, 1956.

———. *The Chatham House Version and Other Middle-Eastern Studies.* London, 1970.

Kerr, Stanley Elphinstone. *The Lions of Marash : Personal Experiences with American Near East Relief,* 1919-1922. Albany: State University of New York Press, 1973.

Khairallah, K. T. *Le problème du Levant ; Les régions arabes libérées, Syrie, Irak, Liban : Lettre Ouverte à la Société des Nations.* Paris, 1919.

Kirk, George Edward. *A Short History of the Middle East, from the Rise of Islam to Modern Times.* London: Methuen, 1948.

Kirkbride, Alec. *An Awakening : The Arab Campaign,* 1917-1918. Tavistock: University Press of Arabia, 1971.

Klieman, Aaron S. *Foundations of British Policy in the Arab World : The Cairo Conference of 1921.* Baltimore, 1970.

Kohn, Hans. *A History of Nationalism in the East.* Translated by Margaret M. Green. New York: Harcourt, Brace, 1929.

———. *Nationalism and Imperialism in the Hither East.* London, 1932.

Kurd-ʿAlī, Muḥammad. *Khiṭaṭ al-Shām* [History and Civilization of Syria]. 6 vols. Damascus, 1925-27.

Laloy, E., ed. *Les Documents Secrets des Archives du Ministère des Affaires Etrangères de Russie.* Paris, 1919.

Lammens, Henri. *La Syrie : Précis Historique.* 2 vols. Beirut: Imprimerie Catholique, 1921.

Lamy, Étienne Marie Victor. *La France du Levant.* Paris, 1900.

Lansing, Robert. *The Big Four, and Others of the Peace Conference.* Boston: Houghton, Mifflin, 1921.

———. *The Peace Negotiations : A Personal Narrative.* Boston: Houghton, Mifflin, 1921.

LAPRADELLE, G. A., ed. *La Paix de Versailles: La Conférence de la Paix et la Société des Nations.* Paris, 1929.

LARCHER, MAURICE. *La Guerre Turque dans la guerre mondiale.* Paris, 1926.

LAURENT-VIBER, R. *Ce que j'ai vu en Orient.* Paris, 1924.

LAWRENCE, THOMAS EDWARD. *The Letters of T. E. Lawrence.* Edited by David Garnett. London, 1921.

———. *Secret Despatches from Arabia.* London: Golden Cockerel Press, 1939.

———. *Seven Pillars of Wisdom: A Triumph.* London: Jonathan Cape, 1935.

LESLIE, SHANE. *Mark Sykes: His Life and Letters.* London, 1923.

LIAUTEY, PIERRE. *Brochure rédigée par M. Pierre Liautey, Chef de Cabinet du général Gouraud en Syrie : La Syrie et le Liban.* Paris: Haut-Commissariat de la République française en Syrie et au Liban, 1922.

LIDDELL HART, BASIL. *T.E. Lawrence in Arabia and After.* London, 1934-45.

LLOYD GEORGE, DAVID. *The Truth About the Peace Treaties.* 2 vols. London, 1938.

LODER, J. DE V. *The Truth About Mesopotamia, Palestine and Syria.* London, 1923.

LOHEAC, LYNE. *Le Liban à la Conférence de la Paix* (1919-1920). Maîtrise d'Histoire présentée à la Faculté de Lettres de Paris X - Nanterre, octobre 1972.

LUQUET, JEAN. *La Politique des Mandats dans le Levant.* Paris, 1924.

MANTOUX, PAUL. *Les Délibérations du Conseil des Quatre* (24 Mars-28 Juin 1919). 2 vols. Paris, 1955.

MANUEL, FRANK EDWARD. *The Realities of American-Palestine Relations.* Washington: Public Affairs Press, 1949.

MAS'AD, SHAIKH BŪLOS. *Lubnān wa Sūriyyah qabl al-intidāb wa ba'dahū* [Lebanon and Syria before and after the mandate]. Héliopolis: Imprimerie Syrienne, 1929.

MASSEY, WILLIAM THOMAS. *Allenby's Final Triumph.* London: Constable and Co., 1920.

McGILVARY, MARGARET. *The Dawn of a New Era in Syria.* New York, 1920.

MEARS, ELIOT GRINNEL. *Modern Turkey: A Politico-Economic Interpretation,* 1908-1923. New York, 1924.

MEINERTZHAGEN, RICHARD. *Middle East Diary*, 1917-1956. London, 1959.

MEZHIR, YŪSUF. *Ta'rīkh Lubnān al-'Ām* [A general history of Lebanon]. 2 vols. Beirut, n.d.

MILLER, DAVID HUNTER. *My Diary at the Conference of Paris*, 1918-1919. 22 vols. New York, 1924.

MONROE, ELIZABETH. *Britain's Moment in the Middle East*, 1914-1956. London, 1963.

MONTAGNE, ROBERT. *L'Évolution moderne des pays arabes*. Paris, 1935.

MOUTRAN, N. *La Syrie de demain*. Paris, 1914.

MURRAY, GILBERT. *The Foreign Policy of Sir Edward Grey*, 1906-1915. London, 1915.

MŪSĀ, SULAIMĀN. *Al-ḥarakat al-'Arabiyyah* [The Arab movement], 1908-1924. Beirut, 1970.

AL-MŪSELI, MUḤAMMAD. *Tārīkh Muqaddarat al-'Irāq al-Siyāsiyyah* [A history of the political destinies of Iraq]. 3 vols. Baghdad, 1925.

The Near East from Within. By a German Diplomatist. London, 1915.

NEVAKIVI, JUKKA. *Britain, France and the Arab Middle East*, 1914-1920. London: Athlone Press, 1969.

NICOLSON, SIR HAROLD GEORGE. *Curzon : The Last Phase*, 1919-1925. New York, 1934.

———. *Peacemaking*, 1919. Boston, 1933.

ORPEN, SIR WILLIAM. *An Onlooker in France*, 1917-1919. London, 1921.

PANARETOFF, STEPHAN. *Near Eastern Affairs and Conditions*. New York, 1922.

PIC, P. *Syrie et Palestine : Mandats français et anglais dans le Proche-Orient*. Paris, 1924.

PICHON, JEAN. *Les origines orientales de la guerre mondiale*. Paris, 1937.

———. *Sur la route des Indes : Un siècle après Bonaparte*. Paris, 1932.

———. *Le partage du Proche-Orient*. Paris: Pegronnet, 1938.

PINGAUD, ALBERT. *Histoire diplomatique de la France pendant la Grande Guerre*. 3 vols. Paris, 1938-40.

POINCARÉ, RAYMOND. *Au service de la France*. 10 vols. Paris, 1926-32.

POLONSKY, J. (transl.). *Les Documents diplomatiques secrets russes*, 1914-1917: *Archives du ministère des Affaires étrangères de Pétrograd*. Paris, 1928.

POWELL, EDWARD ALEXANDER. *The Struggle for Power in Moslem Asia.* New York: Century Co., 1924.

PRESLAND, JOHN [pseud.] (Skelton, Mrs. Gladys). *Deedes Bey: A Study of Sir Wyndham Deedes,* 1883-1923. London: Macmillan, 1942.

QADRĪ, AḤMAD. *Mudhakkarātī 'an al-thawrat al-'Arabiyyah al-kubrā* [My memoirs of the great Arab revolt]. Damascus, 1956.

QAL'AJĪ, QADRĪ. *Jeel al-fidā* [A generation of martyrs]. Beirut, 1967.

RABBATH, E. *L'Évolution politique de la Syrie sous Mandat.* Paris, 1928.

———. *Unité Syrienne et l'Avenir arabe.* Paris, 1937.

RÉMUSAT, PAUL DE. "Les Cent-Jours du Roi de Syrie." In *Revue des Études Historiques* (Paris), April-June 1924.

RIDDEL, GEORGE ALLARDICE, BARON. *Lord Riddel's Intimate Diary of the Peace Conference and After,* 1918-1923. London: V. Gollancz, 1933.

RISTELHUEBER, RENÉ. *Les traditions françaises au Liban.* Paris, 1918.

ROBINSON, EDWARD. *Lawrence the Rebel.* London, 1946.

RONALDSHAY, LAWRENCE JOHN LUMLEY DUNDAS, EARL OF. *The Life of Lord Curzon: Being the Authorized Biography of George Nathaniel, Marques Curzon of Kedleston, K.G.* 3 vols. London: E. Benn, 1928.

ROSSI, ETTORE. *Documenti Sull' Origine E Gli Sviluppi della Questione Arabe,* 1875-1944. Rome, 1944.

SACHAR, HOWARD MORLEY. *The Emergence of the Middle East,* 1914-1924. New York: Knopf, 1969.

SADAKA, NAGIB. *La Question Syrienne pendant la guerre de 1914.* Paris, 1940 or 1941.

AL-SA'ĪD, NURĪ. *Arab Independence and Unity.* Baghdad: Government Press, 1943.

———. *Muḥāḍarāt 'an al-ḥarakat al-'askariyyah li'l jaish al-'arabī fi'l Ḥejāz wa Sūriyyah,* 1916-1918 [Lectures on the military operations of the Arab army in the Hejaz and Syria, 1916-1918]. Baghdad, 1947.

SA'ĪD AMĪN. *Al-Thawrah-al-'Arabiyyah-al-Kubrā* [The great Arab revolt]. 3 vols. Cairo [1934].

SAMNÉ, GEORGES. *L'Effort Syrien pendant la guerre.* Paris: Comité Central Syrien, 1919.

———. *La Syrie.* Paris: Brossard, 1920 or 1921.

SAMUEL, VISCOUNT. *Memoirs.* London, 1945.

SANDERS, OTTO VIKTOR KARL LIMAN VON. *Five Years in Turkey.* Translated by Carl Reichmann. Annapolis: U.S. Naval Institute, 1928.

AL-SA'ŪDE, YŪSUF. *Al-'Arab wa'l-Siyāsah al-Brīṭaniyyah fi'l-ḥarb al-'Alamiyyah al-ūlā* [The Arabs and British policy during the First World War]. By Yusuf al-Saude and Makki Shubaikah. Beirut, [1971.]

SAUVAGET, Jean. *La Culture Française et la Renaissance Arabe.* Paris, 1946.

SAZANOV, SERGE. *Fateful Years,* 1909-1916. London, 1928.

SCOTT, JAMES BROWN. *Official Statements of War Aims and Peace Proposals, December 1916 to November 1918.* Washington, 1921.

———, ed. *The Paris Peace Conference,* 1919: *History and Documents.* Washington: Carnegie Endowment for World Peace, 1934.

SFER, 'ABDULLAH PASHA. *Le Mandat Français et les traditions françaises en Syrie et au Liban.* Paris, 1922.

SHOTWELL, JAMES T. *At the Paris Peace Conference.* New York, 1937.

SOMMERVILLE, S. (edit.). *The Memoirs of Ism'ail Kemal Bey.* London, 1920.

STEED, HENRY WICKHAM. *Through Thirty Years,* 1892-1922: *A Personal Narrative.* 2 vols. London, 1924.

STEIN, LEONARD. *Syria.* London, 1926.

STITT, GEORGE. *A Prince of Arabia: The Emir Shereef Ali Haidar.* London: Allen & Unwin, 1937 or 1948.

STODDARD, LOTHROP. *The New World of Islam.* London, 1921.

STORRS, SIR RONALD. *Orientations.* London, 1937.

TABET, JACQUES-J. *La Syrie.* Paris, 1920.

TARDIEU, ANDRÉ. *The Truth About the Treaty.* Indianapolis, 1921.

TEMPERLEY, HAROLD WILLIAM VAZEILLE, ed. *A History of the Peace Conference of Paris.* 6 vols. London: Oxford University Press, 1920-24.

Thawrat al-'Arab [The revolt of the Arabs]. [By As'ad Dāghir.] Cairo, 1916.

TOYNBEE, ARNOLD JOSEPH. *Survey of International Affairs,* 1925. Vol. 1, *The Islamic World.* Oxford, 1937.

TREVELYAN, GEORGE MACAVLAY. *Grey of Fallodon: The Life and Lettres of Sir Edward Grey, Afterwards Viscount Grey of Fallodon.* Boston: Houghton, Mifflin Co., 1937.

TYAN, FERDINAND PRINCE. *The Entente Cordiale in Lebanon.* London, 1917.

———. *France et Liban, défense des intérêts français en Syrie.* Paris, 1917.

AL-'UMARĪ, MUḤAMMAD ṬĀHIR. *Mulūk al-'Arab* [The kings of the Arabs]. Vol. 1. By Muḥammad Ṭāhir al-'Umarī and Amīn al-Raiḥānī. Beirut, 1924.

———. *Ta'rīkh Najd al-ḥadīth wa mulḥaqātih* [A modern history of Najd and its dependencies]. Beirut, 1928.

———. *Faiṣal al-Awwal* [Faiṣal I]. Beirut, 1934.

VALYI, FÉLIX. *Spiritual and Political Revolutions in Islam.* London, 1925.

VANLANDE, RENÉ. *Le chambardement oriental, Turquie, Liban, Syrie, Palestine, Transjordanie, Iraq.* Paris, 1954.

VÉOU, PAUL DU. *La passion de la Cilicie,* 1919-1922. Paris, 1954.

VILLARS, JEAN BERAUD. *Le Colonel Lawrence ou la recherche de l'Absolu.* Paris, 1955.

WAHBAH, ḤĀFIẒ. *Jazīrat al-'Arab fi'l-qarn al-'ishrīn* [Arabia in the twentieth century]. Cairo, 1935.

WAVELL, ARCHIBALD PERCIVAL WAVELL, 1st EARL of. *Allenby: A Study in Greatness.* London, 1940.

WEIZMANN, CHAIM. *Trial and Error.* London, 1949.

WETTERLÉ, ÉMILE. *En Syrie avec le Général Gouraud.* Paris, 1924.

WHITE, PERCY E. *The Disintegration of the Turkish Empire: The Passing of a Once Great Power.* London, 1920.

WILSON, SIR ARNOLD TALBOT. *Mesopotamia,* 1917-1920: *A Clash of Loyalties.* London, 1931.

WINGATE, SIR RONALD. *Wingate of the Sudan.* London. 1953.

WRIGHT, QUINCY. *Mandates under the League of Nations.* Chicago, 1930.

YALE, WILLIAM. *The Near East: A Modern History.* The University of Michigan History of the Modern World. Ann Arbor: University of Michigan Press, 1958.

YOUNG, SIR HUBERT. *The Independent Arab.* London: J. Murray, 1933.

ZEINE, ZEINE N. *The Emergence of Arab Nationalism with a Background Study of Arab-Turkish Relations in the Near East.* Delmar, N.Y.: Caravan Books, 1973.

II. DOCUMENTS

A. PUBLISHED

France. Ministère des Affaires Etrangères. *Rapport sur la situation de la Syrie et du Liban.* Paris, 1924.

———. Ministère des Affaires Etrangères. Commission des Documents Relatifs aux Origines de la Guerre 1914. *Documents diplomatiques Français,* 1871-1914. 2d ser., 1901-1914. Paris, 1948.

———. Haut-Commissariat en Syrie et au Liban. *Recueil des actes administratifs du Haut-Commissariat de la République Française en Syrie et au Liban: Année* 1919-1920. Vol. 1. Beirut, n.d.

———. Parlement. Chambre des Députés. *Journal Officiel: Annales de la Chambre parlementaires.* Vol. 4. Paris, 1918-20.

Great Britain. Foreign Office. *British Documents on the Origins of the War,* 1898-1914. Edited by G. P. Gooch and Harold W. V. Temperley. Vols. IX and X, London, 1926-38.

———. *Documents on British Foreign Policy,* 1919-1939. Edited by E. L. Woodward and Rohan Butler. First series, vols. 1 and 2, 1919, London, 1947 and vol. 4, 1919, London, 1952.

———. Foreign Office. Handbooks prepared under the Direction of the Historical Section of the Foreign Office. No. 66, "France and the Levant". London, 1920; No. 60, "Syria and Palestine". London, 1920.

———. Parliamentary Debates. Commons. 5th ser. Vols. 100 (1917), 126, 127, 145 (1918), 132 (1920).

———. Admiralty. *A Handbook of Syria (including Palestine).* London, 1919.

———. India Expeditionary Force "D." *A Sketch of the Political History of Persia, Iraq and Arabia, with Special Reference to the Present Campaign.* Calcutta: Government Printing, 1917.

———. Foreign Office. *The Arab Bulletin.* Cairo: Arab Bureau, 1916-19.

———. Foreign Office. Cmd. 5974. "Report of a Committee set up to Consider Certain Correspondence Between Sir Henry McMahon and the Sharif of Mecca in 1915 and 1916".

———. Foreign Office. British State Papers. Cmd. 671. Miscellaneous No. 7. London, 1920. Agreement between France, Russia, Great Britain, and Italy, signed at London, April 26, 1915.

———. Cmd. 1195. London, 1921. Franco-British Convention Concerning the Mandates of Syria, the Lebanon, Palestine, and Mesopotamia.

———. Cmd. 5957. Miscellaneous No. 3. 1939. Correspondence between Sir Henry McMahon, His Majesty's High Commissioner at Cairo, and the Sherif Hussein of Mecca, July 1915-March 1916. London, 1939.

———. Cmd. 5964. Miscellaneous No. 4. 1939. Statements made on behalf of His Majesty's Government during the Year 1918 in regard to the future status of certain parts of the Ottoman Empire. London 1939.

ITALY. Ministero Degli Affari. *I Documenti Diplomatici Italiana.* Sesta set., 1918-1922. Rome.

———. Ministero Degli Affari. Archives. Rome. Folio 1367/1567/ Siria 1920/7151-7154.

U.S. Department of State. *Papers Relating to the Foreign Relations of the United States: The Lansing Papers*, 1914-1920. 2 vols. Washington, 1940.

———. *The World War: Supplement I*, 1917. Washington, 1931.

———. *The World War: Supplement II*, 1917. Washington, 1932.

———. *The Paris Peace Conference*, 1919. Vols. 1, 2, 3, 5, 6, 11, 12, 13. Washington, 1942-47.

B. UNPUBLISHED

The Arab Bulletin. This was the official publication of the Arab Bureau in Cairo, from 1916 to 1919. It contained "Arab Bureau Summaries" which dealt "with any political events in Turkey or elsewhere that affected the Arab Movement." The contents, though printed, were to be treated as "strictly secret."

Khawāṭir [Memoirs] *Ja'far Pasha al-'Askarī*, being an Arabic manuscript of Ja'far Pasha's Memoirs and containing many references to the Arab Revolt and to the situation in Syria in 1918 and 1919.

The Private Papers of Dr. Howard S. Bliss, President of the Syrian Protestant College (now the American University of Beirut), Beirut, Lebanon, during the years 1918-1920. They consist mainly of correspondence and reports on the Syrian Question. (Abbreviation: The Bliss Papers).

The Private Papers of the Maronite Patriarchate, Bkerki, Lebanon.

Washington. U.S. National Archives and Records Service. Department of State. Record Group 59. Department of State. "Report of Syria, Palestine and Mount Lebanon," July 1919, by Capt. William Yale.

———. Record Group 256. General Records of the American Commission to Negotiate Peace, Paris, 1918-1919. Inquiry Documents Nos. 42, 79, 82.

The Wingate Papers: The Private Papers of General Sir Reginald Wingate — Letters, telegrams, despatchs and reports, dealing with the Arab Revolt.

III. PERIODICALS

Asie Française : Bulletin Mensuel du Comité de l'Asie Française
'Aṣimah, Al-
Contemporary Review
Correspondance d'Orient : Etudes
Current History
Daily Telegraph, The (London)
English Review
Figaro, Le (Paris)
Fortune
Intransigeant, L'
Journal des Débats
Journal of International Relations, The
Journal of Modern History, The
Muslim World, The
Near East, The
New Europe, The
Oriente Moderno
North American Review, The
Palestine
Quarterly Review, The
Revue des Deux Mondes
Revue du Monde Musulman
Temps, Le
Times, The (London)
Lisān al-Ḥāl (Beirut)
Manār, Al- (Cairo)
Muqtaṭaf, Al- (Cairo)
Qiblah, Al- (Mecca)

INDEX

'Abdullah, The Emīr, 2, 4, 16; King, 122, 127, 199

'Abdu'l-Majīd, Sultan and Caliph, 18

Acre, 40

Adana, 9

Agamemnon, British battleship, 42

Agha Khan, 180

'Ahd, Al-, 3n8, 10n24, 16n39

Aleppo, 8, 9, 10, 12, 14, 26, 31, 33, 42, 47, 49, 52, 55, 60, 73, 76, 84, 100-101, 116, 147, 154, 156, 171

Alexandretta, 9, 13-14, 40, 55, 73, 85, 180

'Alī, The Emīr, 16

Allenby, General Edmund: Commander-in-Chief of the Egyptian Expeditionary Force, 23-24, 30; Interview with Faiṣal, 30-31; The French protest to, 33; His "assurances" to Faiṣal, 39n36, 44; Supreme authority vested in, 40; His appreciation of Arab help, 74; General Clayton's interview with Faiṣal reported to Lord Curzon by, 81; The situation in Syria reported to Lloyd George by, 86-87; Warning to Faiṣal by, 87n12; Telegram to Faiṣal, 89; His interview with King Ḥusain, 122; Faiṣal's telegram to, 128; Telegram to Faiṣal by, 141; Telegram from Foreign Office, 178; Telegram to the Foreign Office, 193

Anglo-French Declaration, 46-47, 186-187

Aqaba, 17, 21, 23, 31, 59

Arab Bureau, 9, 11, 22, 183

Arab Flag, 25, 38, 104, 190

Arab Government, 28, 36-38, 40-41, 49, 109, 110

Arab independence, 184

Arab Nationalism, 182

Arab Revolt, 5, 15, 16-18, 47, 78, 133, 196-198

Arab Unity, 22, 48, 63, 103, 127

Arabia, 3, 4, 5, 10, 13, 20, 68, 195; Sa'udi, 7

Arabs 1, 2, 3, 4, 5n12, 8-11, 21, 23, 41, 44-45, 47-48; Assistance given to the British forces by, 61; The Allies and the, 65; Independence of the, 74; Their attitude towards France 81; Great Britain and the, 102, 103, 106-107, 177-181, 188, 196-198, 207; Lord Curson's letter concerning France and the, 105-106; King 'Abdullah on history of the, 122; The Turks (Mustafa Kemal Pasha) and the, 134-135, 172, 179; The Sharīf Ḥusain as King of the, 177; The "seven", 23, 195, 204.

Armenia, 20, 93

Armistice, 42, 53

Arslān, The Emīr 'Adil, 38, 151n31, 169

'Askarī, Al-, Ja'far Pasha, 21, 22

Ayyūbī, Al-, Shukrī, Pasha, 28-29, 31, 33, 37-38, 41

Baker, Ray Stannard, 206

Balfour, Arthur J., 20-21, 24n60; His Declaration, 57, 203n2; Allenby's telegram to, 87n12; His views on a "Turkish settlement", 93; His memorandum "respecting Syria, Palestine and Mesopotamia", 97-98, 174, 179, 184-185, 187; The Allied promise and, 179; His views on British officers in Syria, 199

Baghdad, 34, 45, 97

Be'abdā, 34-38, 39, 41, 149

Beirut, 9, 10, 14, 18, 24, 27-29, 33; Vilayat of, 35; Faiṣal in, 49-50; First street sign in 66n11; Winter residence of the French High Commissioner, 117; The Syrian Congress and the Muslims of, 131; Arab leaders hanged in, 195

Bell, Gertrude, 182

Bkerkī, 40

Bliss, Howard S., His statement at the Council of Ten, 65-67; His declaration before the American Commissioners, 70-71; Letter to President Wilson, 88n15; Letter of Westermann to, 200n28

Brémond, General Ed., 12-15, 16, 44, 51-52

Britain, Great, 2, 4, 7, 9-10, 19-20, 22, 24, 45-46, 53-56, 74, 82-83, 89-90; Refuses to become mandatory for Syria, 93, 108; King Ḥusain's criticism of the policy of, 122; The Arab Near East and, 138; Mesopotamia and Palestine under the Mandate of, 141; Faiṣal's Syrian State created by, 170; Memorandum on the Ottoman Empire, 173n5; The defeat of Turkey and the efforts of, 192; The Arabs and 199, 204, 207

Bulfin, General Sir Edward, 39, 50

Bullard, Sir Reader, 205

Byrne, E.H., 19

Cairo, 2, 8, 19, 89, 92

Cambon, Paul, 13, 14, 199

Cheetham, Sir Milne, 3, 4

Christians, 34, 36, 50, 65, 136, 180

Churchill, Sir Winston, 170, 192

Cilicia, 13, 15, 80, 100, 143

Clayton (General) Sir Gilbert, 17, 31-33, 81, 90n19, 91, 92-93

Clemenceau, Georges; Arrival in London, 53; Agrees to transfer Mosul and Palestine to the British, 55-56; Lawrence and, 62; The Council of Ten and, 67-72; Faiṣal and, 76-77; Loyd George and, 80-87, 107-108; He accuses the British of being anti-French in Syria, 95-96; Evacuation of British troops agreed upon by Lloyd George and, 99-100; The Lebanese Delegation received by, 112; His defeat in the French elections, 123; his telegram to Gouraud, 153-154

Commission (Inter-Allied, later: King-Crane or American Peace Commission), Dr. Howard Bliss pleads for an Inter-Allied, 66, 71, 88n15, 90, President Wilson supports the formation of an Inter-Allied, 75; Clemenceau, opposed to, 87-88; The American members (King-Crane) of the Commission leave for Syria, 87, 88n15; 90-91, 94-95, 200-202

Congress, General Syrian, 120, 125-128; Proclaims Faiṣal King of "United Kingdom of Syria", 126; Rejects the French Mandate, 142; Opposes Faiṣal's return to Europe, 145; Draws up a Constitution for Syria 149n24; Attacks Faiṣal and his Council of Ministers, 160; Faiṣal's Government "suspends" the, 160; King-Crane Commission and, 201

Constantinople, 4, 12, 20-21, 54, 93

Cornwallis, Sir Kinahan, 82

Coulondre, M. 33, 40-41

Council, Lebanese Administrative, 150-152, 155

Cousse, Commandant, 50, 161, 163, 165

Crane, Charles R., 88

Curzon, Lord, 81, 89, 90n16, 91, 95, 98-99, 105-106, 108, 114-115, 119, 128, 149, 188, 192, 203n36

Damascus, 8, 10, 11, 14; Allied troops occupy, 25-26, 30; Sykes-Picot Agreement and, 27-28, 84-85, 100; Faiṣal establishes "Arab Military Government" in, 33, 39-40, 109; The General Syrian Congress meeting at, 125; Iraqi Congress meeting at, 127;

Faiṣal proclaimed King in, 126 French troops advancing towards — and occupying, 166-167

Dā'ūq, Al-, 'Umar Bey, 28, 38, 66n11

Deedes, Sir Windham, 11, 196

Declassé, Théophile, 13

Der'a, 169

Dodge, Dr. Bayard, 39n34

Downie, H.F., 8

Drūbī, 'Alā'-ud-Dīn, 168-169

Eastern Question, 12-13

Egypt, 6, 7, 17, 19; Syrian leaders in, 22; Revolt in, 109; British Protectorate over, 189

Enver Pasha, 3

Evans, Lawrence, 129

Faiṣal, The Emīr (later King), 16-17, 21-23; His triumphant entry into Damascus, 29; Interview between Allenby and, 30; Arab Military Government established in Syria by, 33; His speech at Aleppo, 47-48; His visit to Beirut, 49; His visit to France and England, 51-61; At the Peace Conference, 62-65; Daniel Bliss, Howard Bliss and, 66n11; Meeting between Clemenceau and, 76-77; The *draft* of Clemenceau's letter communicated to, 77; And Faiṣal's reply, 76; His address in the Town Hall of Damascus, 78; His policy towards the French, 81-82; A British mandate for Syria and, 89-90; The Arab case summarized by, 99-100; His second visit to London, 103; Correspondence between Lloyd George, Lord Curzon and, 103-106; His stay in Paris, 110-112; Proposed agreement between the French Government and, 116-124; His return to Syria, 118; His speech in Damascus, 120; Proclaimed as King of "United Kingdom of Syria", 126, 131; The Turks and, 134-136; San-Remo decision communicated to, 141; His appeal to the Syrians to stand firm and united, 144-145; The Administrative Council of Lebanon, 149-150; France's accusations against, 154-156; ultimatum from Gouraud, 157; Demonstrations in Damascus against, 161; His telegrams to Gouraud, 162 Battle of Maisalūn and, 165-166; He leaves for the village of Kisweh, 167; Ordered by the French Government to leave Damascus 169; Arrives in Haifa on his way to England, 170; Mrs. Erskine's interview with, 197

Fārūqī, Al-, Muḥammad Sharīf, 16n39

Fayyāḍ, Habīb; Mayor of Be'abdā, 38

Foch, Marshall, 53, 172, 206

France, 4, 8, 10, 12, 13, 14, 46, 56-57; M. Pichon on Syria and 72; Syria and the presence of, 77; Attitude of Arabs towards, 82; Syria, the share of, 84, 98, 138, 194, 198-199

Germany, 4, 5n12

Ghānim, Shukrī, 67-70

Gough-Calthorpe, Sir S.A., 42

Gouraud, General, 51, 114, 128, 143, 146; Ultimatum to Faiṣal from, 147-149, 153-158, 160-164; Letter to the Maronite Patriarch by, 150-153; Letter to Faiṣal by, 164; Faiṣal sends protest to, 169

Grahame, Sir G., 191

Goybet, General, 162n14; 166, 168

Grey, Sir Edward, 5n12 and n13, 172, 199

Gulf Chiefs, 7

Ḥaidar, Sharīf 'Alī, 18

Ḥaidar Sa'īd, 135n41

Haifa 39, 169, 193

Hankey, Sir Maurice (Lord) 70, 72n22, 74, 86

Howard, Harry N., 173n5, 200n28, 203

Hardinge, Lord, 5

Hāshimī, Al-, Yasīn, 159
Hedjaz, 2-5, 16-17, 19, 25, 31, 33, 37, 38, 68, 79, 95, 110, 130
Hogarth, D.G., 22-23, 80, 90, 182-184, 203, 173
Ḥaqqi, Ismā'īl, 38
Ḥusain, The Sharīf (later, King), 2, 3, 4; 25, 29-30-31; McMahon Correspondence and negotiations with, 6-10, 15, 18-23, 50, 73-74, 99, 101, 122, 174, 182-185. The French informed of the British dealings with, 12; Sykes' interview with 19; Picot's interview with 19; The Sykes-Picot Agreement and, 21-23; The British Government's obligations towards, 105; His telegram and letter to Faiṣal, 113; Arab independence and, 122-127; As "King of the Arabs", 177; His letter to Sultan Muḥammad Rashād, 194; The "promises" to, 203
Ḥuṣrī, Al-, Sāṭi', 76, 118, 159; Mission to General Gouraud, 162-168
Huwayik, Eliās Buṭrus (Hoyek), the Maronite Patriarch, 37-40, 112, 131, 133, 150-153

India Office, 46, 182-184
Iraq, 7, 11, 16, 183; The Emīr 'Abdullah declared King of, 127
Islam, 47, 179-180

Jemāl Pasha, Aḥmad, 21, 195
Jazā'erī, Al-, Muḥammad Sa'īd 26, 28, 37
Jeddah, 5, 122, 183, 199
Jerusalem, 24, 35
Jordan, 98

Kemal Pasha, Mustafa (Ataturk) 113, 134, 135, 143, 146n17
Khūrī, 'Abdullah, 131-132
King, Henry Church, 88
King-Crane Commission; See Commission, Inter-Allied and American
Kisweh, Faiṣal in, 167
Kitchener, Lord, 2-5, 172, 185
Kirkbride, Alec, 2

Lansing, Robert, 20, 66n11, 71, 201n30
Latakia, 14, 34, 190
Law, Bonar, 160
Lawrence, Thomas Edward, 17, 21n54, 23, 26-27; Shukri Pasha al-Ayyūbi sent to Beirut by, 29-31; Leave asked from Allenby by, 32; Arrives in Cairo and, later, in London, 32n16; French attitude towards, 51; Anti-French attitude of, 62; The Emīr Faiṣal accompanied by, 62-64; On Mark-Sykes, 176 Syria as viewed by, 181; and the invasion of Palestine, 185; and the "brown" Dominion, 188; The Arab Revolt and, 197
Lloyd George, 1, 2, 12, 46; Meeting between Clemenceau and 53-58, 72; Lebanon and, 71; Secret Conference of the Four Heads of States and, 72, 75; The Council of Four and, 83; Mandate for Syria and 89; Ḥejāzian Delegation in Paris submitting a Memorandum to, 92; *Aide mémoire* of, 101-102; Clemenceau's reply to the Aide-mémoire of, 107; San-Remo and, 138; France and, 191-192
Lebanon, The, (Mount Lebanon), 10, 15, 24, 29, 34-41; The Council of Ten and, 70n16; British troops to be withdrawn from, 100; The Emīr Faiṣal and the independence of, 116; Faiṣal proclaimed as King of, 126-129; The Administrative Council of, 41, 136, 149-152; A Delegation in Paris from, 112, 131; Assurances given by France to, 132; French military preparations in, 146; Disturbances in, 154; King-Crane Commission and, 201
Litvinov, Maksim, 134-135
Longrigg, Stephen H., 102n9

MacDonald, Malcolm, 7

Maisalūn; Khān, 164; Battle of, 165-166

Mallet, Sir Louis, 5n12

Mandate(s), 35, 55, 89, 91-95, 101, 107, 112; The independence of the Lebanon under the French 116; The Druze Chiefs reject the French, 124n14; Faiṣal and the meaning of, 130; The Allied Supreme Council at San-Remo assigns various, 138-141; Syria allocated as a French, 138-139, 143, 147, 189; General Gouraud and the Syrian, 157, 160; Petitions presented to the King-Crane Commission against French, 201-202

Marj-'Ayūn, 121, 154

Maronites, 34-36, 39, 41, 50, 99, 108, 131, 179, 200

Maṣrī Al-, 'Azīz 'Alī, 3n8

McMahon, Sir Arthur Henry, Appointed High Commissioner in Egypt, 6; — Sharīf Ḥusain Correspondence, 7-10, 15n37, 122; Faiṣal and, 61; Sykes-Picot Agreement and, 73; Nominated as a delegate for the Inter-Allied Commission 87n14; The India Offce and the Correspondence of, 182

Mecca, 2, 3, 4, 5, 10, 17

Mercier, Captain, 48

Mersina, 9, 73

Mesopotamia, 10, 18, 42, 46, 54, 84, 92, 107, 129, 133, 138, 140, 174, 179, 182, 187, 193

Miller, David Hunter, 71

Millerand, Etienne-Alexandre, 123, 132 138, 141, 144, 151

Mirghanī, Al-, 'Alī, 6

Morgenthau, Sr., Henry, Secret mission of, 185n43

Morocco, 109

Mosul, 14, 33, 55-57, 72, 80

Mudros, Armistice of, 42,

Murray, Gilbert, 205

Muslims, 4-5, 6, 13, 17-18, 34, 49, 177, 179, 200

Nicolson, Sir Arthur, 12

Na'mānī, Al-'Ārif, 151n31

Occupied Enemy Territory, 40-41

Olden, Major A.C., 25-26

Ottoman Empire, 1, 4, 23, 24, 25, 35, 40, 43, 93, 111, 131, 180-181, 194, 198

Palestine, 7, 15, 18, 24, 32, 34, 40; America in, 54-55; Amendment to the Sykes-Picot Agreement concerning, 53-59, 83-84; The Balfour Declaration and, 57, 142; Zionist opposition to France in, 59; The American Commission arrives in, 90; Mr. Balfour's Memorandum and, 93; Faiṣal as King of 129; Great Britain obtains Mandate, for, 138; The Emīr Faiṣal in, 169; The British Government and the occupation of, 185.

Paterno, Marquis de, 147, 165, 166n 23, 168

Peace Conference; Faiṣal and the, 50, 59, 61, 62, 63, 64, 83, Faiṣal presents Two Memoranda to the, 63-64; Bliss invited to the, 65-66; The American Commission to report to the, 90; King Ḥusain's desire to represent the Arabs at the, 121n1; The question of Syria and, 153

Peace Plan, The British, 54

Pichon, Jean, 60, 65, 67, 69, 72, 73-74, 80-81, 83, 86, 98, 107, 199

Piépape, Colonel de, 39-41

Picot, Georges, 12, 19, 40, 48, 51, 60, 90n19

Poincaré, R. 12n27

Price, Philips, 21

Rayak - Aleppo railway, 147, 154, 156, 163; Occupied by French troops, 148

Rikābī, 'Alī Riḍā Pasha; Military Governor of Damascus, 28; Head of the "Arab Constitutional Government", 34; Forced to resign, 119n4; First Prime Minister of the new Kingdom of Syria, 127; Fall of the Syrian Cabinet of, 142

Russia, 2, 12

Sa'd, Al-, Ḥabīb Pasha, As Governor-General of the Lebanon, 39; As Head of the Lebanese Administrative Council, 38-41

Sa'īd, Al-, Nūrī Pasha, The Arab Flag and 29, Dinner at Victoria Hotel, 33; Pursuing the remnants of the Turkish Fourth Army, 41-42; In Beirut with the Emīr Faiṣal, 49; Memorandum on a united Arab Government by, 92; General Gouraud and, 145-146; 'Ārif al-Na'mānī, King Faiṣal and, 151n31; Sa'd Pasha Zaghlūl and, 196

Samuel, Sir Herbert, 169-170

San-Remo, Allied Supreme Council meeting at, 138; Conference of, 139 148; Mandates conferred at, 141-142, 144

Sa'ūd, Ibn, 11n25, 122

Sazanov, Serge, 14

Sèvres, Treaty of, 138

Sha'alān, Nūrī, 173

Shehāb, Mālik, 38

Shotwell, James T., 69

Sidon, 14, 34

Steed, Wickham, 62, 75-76, 78, 80-81, 198

Storrs, Sir Ronald, 2, 170, 175, 177, 183,

Sudan, 5-6

Suez, Canal, 185

Sykes, Sir Mark, 19, 60, 70, 176, 183

Sykes-Picot Agreement, 13-15, 18-20, 30, 47, 53-54, 56, 72, 84-85, 98, 101, 108, 111, 140, 203; *The Manchester Guardian* published summary of, 20; Jemāl Pasha communicated to the Emīr Faiṣal text of, 21; King Ḥusain, the Arab nationalists and, 32; Ammendment to, 55; Faiṣal and, 59; France and, 61; Interpretation of 191-193; As one of several conflicting documents, 182; The Anglo-French Declaration and, 187; M. Pichon on, 188; The bargaining power of, 191; The war efforts of the Allies and, 192; France's share of the Ottoman Empire and, 197-199

Syria, 9, 10, 19, 20, 24; Traditional interests of France in, 12; Faiṣal's proclamation to the people of, 33-34; Mount Lebanon detached from, 35, 36; As "Occupied Enemy Territory", 40; The Armistice and, 42; The Anglo-French Declaration and, 46; Clemenceau and, 55-56; The Council of Ten and the Question of, 65-66; The Secret Conference of the Heads of States and, 72-75; France's presence in, 77; French mandate for, 81, 103, 110, 138-142; The Council of Four and, 83-93; Great Britain unwilling to accept a mandate for, 89-90, 92-93, 108; American Commission and, 94; British troops to withdraw form, 101, 104; Reinstituting Turkish rule in, 113; The Emīr Faiṣal, King of, 126; Anti-French demonstrations in, 147; Fall of, 170; Winston Churchill on, 170; Mr. Balfour on, 187; King-Crane Commission in, 201-203

Temperley, H. W. V., 153, 170

Toulat, Colonel, 168, 169n29

Toynbee, Arnold, J., I, 178, 188

Tripoli, 14, 49, 207

Trotsky, Leon, 20

Turkey, 1, 2, 4, 5, 7, 12-13, 20, 21; Armistice with, 42, 53; Britain against Turkey, 73, 105; Arabs lands and, 127; Its continuance as a Great Power, 181; Its elimination from the Near East, 182

Turkish Petroleum Company, 57

Turks, 1, 2, 16, 17, 28, 47; Arabs and, 101, 134, 188; Iraqi nationalists and, 136; The French Government and, 143; Arabs against Turks, 172; Territories occupied by, 180, 195-197; Allenby's forces defeating, 192

Tyre, 14

Tyrell, Sir W., 2

United States of America, Secret Diplomacy and, 85; Arab unification to be on the same lines as the, 92; Anglo-French Declaration and, 187; Syrian independence and, 201-202

Varney, Vice-Admiral, 39

Vickery, Lt.-Col. C.E., 122-123

Victoria Hotel, Interview between Allenby and Faiṣal in, 30; Dinner incident at, 33

Vilayet, Ottoman, 33-34

War Office, 6

War, First World, 43, 127, 205

Wavell, Sir Archibald, 30

Weizmann, Chaim, 59, 185n43

Wilson, Sir Arnold, 46, 182, 183

Wilson, President Woodrow, Address to the Senate, 44; Fourteen Points of, 45; Anglo-French Declaration and, 46, 186; Colonel House acting for, 54; American attitude clarified by, 60; Faiṣal and, 65; At the Council of Ten, 69; At the Secret Conference of the Four Heads of States, 72, 75; Memorandum of the Secret Conference submitted to, 76; French Mandate and, 80; Secret Diplomacy and, 85-86; Inter-Allied Commission and, 86; Great Britain expressing view on Mandate for Syria to, 92-93; Lord Curzon and, 94n24; Syrian independence and, 144; Faiṣal's telegram to, 202; The "Old World" and, 203, 205, 206

Wingate, Sir Reginald, Arab affairs and, 5; General officier commanding the Hedjaz, 17; King Huṣain and, 21; Capture of ʻAqaba and, 23n59; The Arab Revolt and, 185; Saʻd Pasha Zaghlūl and, 189

Yale, William, 36, 88n15, 96n30, 104n16, 100, 104n16, 110n27, 197

Zaghlūl, Saʻd Pasha, 189, 196

Zaid, The Emīr, 16, 115, 119n14, 133n38, 134, 170

Zionists, 59, 88, 104n16, 122, 142